# THE TOUCHSTONE OF SINCERITY

Jeff Albert was brought up in California and studied Theatre Arts and Chemistry at the University of California at Riverside, and later Film and Television at New York University. Since becoming a Bahá'í in 1978 at the age of 22 he has taken part in the production of several documentaries on Bahá'í subjects, including the films 'Education in India' and 'Trustees of the Merciful' on rural educational development. He moved to South Africa in 1981 and is at present head of television productions at the black Medical University of South Africa, MEDUNSA. He also makes television commercials and is screenwriting a major motion picture.

CW01426331

To my beloved parents
Manny and Rita
who allowed me to ask difficult questions
and search the world to discover the answers

# THE
# TOUCHSTONE
# OF
# SINCERITY

J. D. Albert

**GR**

GEORGE RONALD

OXFORD

First published by
GEORGE RONALD, Publisher
46 High Street, Kidlington, Oxford OX5 2DN

**British Library Cataloguing in Publication Data**

Albert, J. D.
 The touchstone of sincerity: a novel.
 I. Title
 813′.54[F]          PS3551.L2/

ISBN 0–85398–223–6

Set by Sunrise Setting in Bembo 10$^{1}$/$_{2}$ on 12 point
Printed in England

The characters portrayed in this book are fictional though the circumstances surrounding the persecution of the Bahá'ís in Iran are factual and documented.

*All men will perish and die except the believers; all the believers will perish and die except those who are tested; all those who are tested will perish and die except those who are sincere; and those who are sincere will be in great danger.*

Islamic Tradition

# CHAPTER I

# The Warning Call

Saffa was teaching his little sister how to move the round pieces across the backgammon board, but when he heard his uncle subtly clear his throat he quickly folded the game and slid the set on to the center of the low table. He helped little Mitra to the edge of the sofa to sit properly. It was time to say a prayer.

Uncle Hakim uncrossed his legs and sat up in his favorite chair, ready to begin.

He pulled his old gray wool sweater down over his distended stomach, then crossed his arms over his chest and waited patiently. His wife was a good cook, he thought with a deep breath, inhaling supper's delicious aromas of mince and spices which still lingered in their large guest room.

Mitra wiggled her dangling feet above the deep red Persian carpet, waiting too, until Saffa gave her a nudge. Only then did she close her eyes tightly and fold her arms across her chest like her uncle had. In a whisper she managed to chant from memory the dozen words of a prayer she had been taught.

The room around them was well furnished. Cloth tapestries of classic Persian handiwork fell across the backs of modern imported sofas and chairs. A fine silk carpet woven with highlight colors of turquoise, cream, and blue hung on the wall beyond the dining table, its scene portraying two lovers of ancient lore nestled beneath the shade of a garden's tree. Open shelves partitioned the dining area from the lounge, half filled with books and magazines. Another wooden shelving was equipped with a stereo, a row of albums, a color TV, and a new video recorder. There was a clear vase filled with dried rose petals set beside a santour, whose musical strings had scarcely been struck, except by the rust of age. And there were pictures of family, from generations back to the newly born. And books neatly arranged, volumes of art and history, classics by oriental poets and mystics.

After a moment's reflection Hakim spoke in his commanding voice, loud enough for everyone in the room to hear him begin his usual evening lecture.

Ziya knew the purpose of these talks. She had heard her husband, the esteemed physician, Dr Hakim Rahbari, expound the evidences of his vast knowledge throughout their marriage for more than thirty years. And she knew why he made special efforts to guide their nephew whenever they came together. Hakim loved to be challenged and Saffa loved to ask questions, which always inspired Hakim to elucidate even loftier themes, which inspired them both.

'Uncle Hakim?' Saffa asked. His youthful face was lined with seriousness. 'Yes, Saffa,' he said, pausing to allow his expected deep-searching question.

'Could you change the topic of discussion?'

The room became uncomfortably silent to Saffa. He accidentally glanced towards his mother and aunt, who had suddenly stopped clearing the dining table. They were staring at him as though he had just stabbed his uncle in the back.

Then without any warning, Mitra decided to take advantage of the hush. She leaned around Saffa's arm, peering over at Uncle Hakim.

'A Mulla Nasrud-din story!' she said, requesting her favorite children's tale, then scooted back behind the protection of her brother's shoulder and hid.

Mitra was only five. Now Saffa was in deep trouble for both of them. She wasn't responsible before God for her actions yet. But he was. He was fifteen, at the age of spiritual maturity. He was going to have to explain the reason for his request. He mustered up his courage, reminding his heart it was a virtue to be honest, and a clear sign of maturity. But his voice betrayed his fearlessness with an adolescent crack. 'We're just tired of hearing stories of death and martyrdoms, Uncle Hakim.'

Saffa turned his head slowly towards his uncle's chair. Surprisingly, Uncle Hakim did not appear too upset by the incident. He was gazing at a swirling design in the carpet beneath his feet. He looked rather sedate, as though he might have been listening in his private office to one of his patients telling him of his afflictions.

After a long moment, Hakim glanced up. He tucked his double chin to the tie of his shirt and peered over the rim of his silver-framed glasses at Saffa. His gray hair glowed from the light of the side lamp.

Saffa knew that look. He was about to hear his uncle's diagnosis of the serious disease he had, which meant another hour of discussion before his father or another relative would arrive to take them home. The topic would be how spiritually immature Saffa was to make such a suggestion.

Grumbling and shaking his head, Hakim set his gaze towards the dining table. 'Are you sure these are your children, Asiyih?' he asked his plump-faced sister.

Asiyih heard his question but went on cleaning without a word. She knew he was up to his old teaching tricks again. There was no need to answer, just listen.

'Do they remember what country they are living in? What the history of Iran has been for the Bahá'ís? What's happening here today?'

Saffa too was aware of his uncle's technique, and answered, 'We know, Uncle Hakim.'

'We know, Uncle Hakim,' Mitra said, repeating Saffa's words, and bobbing her head to her mother.

'Really?' he asked, unconvinced.

Saffa felt the moment of being proven unspiritual had arrived as he watched Uncle Hakim take off his glasses and rub the dark circles under his eyes. He then lifted a small mosaic-framed photograph off the table beside his chair and showed them the old black and white picture.

'Who is this, Mitra Khanum?' he asked gently, aware that the title of respect he added would make Mitra feel a grown-up woman.

Mitra put her hands to her mouth and tugged on her upper lip, studying the elderly face in the photograph. ''Abdu'l-Bahá,' she said confidently.

'Very good, Khanum,' he said, then glared at Saffa, pointing to the picture. 'He knows! The rest of us are only students.'

Saffa had never sought an argument with his uncle. He paid attention, thinking how he could say what he really had meant when the chance availed itself, but he certainly was not going to interrupt again; that would have only incited another more serious rebuke.

Hakim returned the delicate frame to its place. 'Students study,' he said, starting another lecture. 'If I didn't study my medical journals, how could I take care of my patients? If you don't study, Saffa, how can you become a doctor? And if we don't study the Cause of God, how can we cure an ailing mankind?'

Saffa nodded, emphatically agreeing with him.

Hakim sighed, then combed his fingers through his thinning hair. He rested back into his chair, pleased to see Saffa's returned enthusiasm, and continued more at ease. 'I was a good student when I was your age, Saffa. I wanted to be a good surgeon and a good Bahá'í. Why do you think I did my schooling in Teheran, studied with the greatest of Bahá'í scholars, then came back to Kashan?'

Saffa had the answers in his thoughts, having heard this before.

'I did it for a purpose, as a preparation,' Hakim said, not giving him time to answer.

Mitra yawned, which went unnoticed by the two, yet received a compassionate look from her mother and aunt.

'What do I mean by preparation? How does one prepare for tests?'

'Prayer,' Saffa said immediately.

'Prayer,' Mitra said to agree.

'Good. My father, may God advance his soul, and the soul of my mother in all His worlds, knew the importance of prayer. As children we were up every morning before dawn to say our prayers. It was our preparation. Do you remember, Asiyih Khanum?'

Asiyih's reddened cheeks lifted with her smile. 'Yes, Hakim, I've told them this many times.'

'I've told them this so many times that hair is growing on my tongue!' Hakim shook his head and folded his arms, then looked at his wristwatch.

Saffa hoped that this was the end of the instruction, and eased back into the sofa.

'When I was a child,' Hakim said at the top of his voice, causing Saffa to sit up again, 'we longed to make the supreme sacrifice. If this is the Cause of God, what act is greater than offering ourselves to proclaim His Cause, and teach its veracity?'

The front doorbell rang, destroying the height of the lesson. It changed Hakim's mood instantly. The intense seriousness on his face reflected his thoughts. He expected no one this early after

4

supper. And if it was who he feared, he would have to move quickly to get everyone out of danger.

'Rahbari?' Ziya said calmly. She addressed Hakim by their surname when she respectfully sought to speak with him in front of others.

He glanced over to her call.

'It's only Amin. He called earlier to say he'd pick up Asiyih and the children for Jamshid on his way home.'

Saffa was relieved.

'He called before you arrived,' she added reassuringly.

Hakim held back his questions. He didn't want to pursue the matter in front of the children or Asiyih. Ziya's tone was sure. He would have to trust her calmness. He thought more lightly – Amin would be the only one to ruin his supper. And if it was who he first thought, they would not have rung the bell or knocked, they would have broken the door down, being kept so long.

'Where are the girls?'

'In our room putting your grandson to sleep.'

Hakim glanced at his watch again. He felt an uneasiness building in the room, then added, jesting, 'Make sure, Ziya Khanum, that our honorable Amin brings in the tea from the kitchen himself. I don't want him to accuse me of being a bad host.'

He succeeded in getting smiles from everyone. He relaxed his frame, but kept his ears sharp, listening to the voice of the man Ziya greeted at the door. The thought flashed through his mind how foolish he was to let Ziya go out and answer the door without his presence. She had left the room in such haste to prove it was Amin. A strong, deep laugh broke into Hakim's thoughts. It was Amin. They all heard him being forced from the courtyard in the direction of the kitchen.

The alarm was over. Hakim wanted to forget the incident. He turned his gaze towards the two on the sofa, then shook his head and sighed deeply. 'These are not Bahá'í children.'

'Yes, we are,' Mitra said, nodding her head.

Hakim opened his palms to them, playing the dramatic. 'Then why don't you and your brother show interest in the story I was relating of Varqá and Rúḥu'lláh?'

Saffa had his chance now. He spoke up with conviction, though soft. 'I just think no one cares today, Uncle Hakim. As one says, "It's a bowl hotter than the dish."'

5

Hakim clapped his hands. 'Of course people care, Saffa! And don't use clichés to explain your ideas, use analogies. Remember how 'Abdu'l-Bahá used to teach. I've told you this so many times, hair is growing on my tongue!'

Saffa apologized.

Mitra tried to look at her tongue.

'May my life be a sacrifice to Rúḥu'lláh!' Hakim declared with a powerful tremble, running chills up Saffa's spine. 'The boy was twelve years old when he was cruelly martyred with his father. And what was his crime? Were they murderers? Thieves? Assassins? No, they were the embodiments of uprightness and virtue. They were Bahá'ís. Ponder this in your heart.'

Hakim was so stirred by his own speech that Saffa couldn't help being inspired as well. Hakim could see the sincere return of Saffa's interest and went further.

'I could take you all around Kashan, the hospital, the government buildings, the bazaar, to Teheran, all through Iran, Asia, Africa, America, to friends or enemies. Everyone knows about the Bahá'í Faith – and the ill-wishers want to rob us of our faith.'

Hakim turned to the picture of 'Abdu'l-Bahá, pausing for a moment respectfully. He opened his palms as if surrendering his case. 'What did the Master say? "If a cause were of no significance, who would take the trouble to work against it!"'

Saffa pondered the quotation. It was a fact that so many lies were levied against the Faith to misinterpret its teachings. Still people would investigate its claims for themselves. He wondered what fears made some people blind themselves to seeking out the claims of the Cause for themselves. At school many people wouldn't associate with him because they knew he was a Bahá'í. He had never discussed his beliefs openly with them. It made him wonder if he was afraid of losing his small group of friends, or afraid of becoming martyred himself. It was possible.

'Uncle Hakim?' he asked seriously. 'What if they rob us? I mean, what if one recants his faith?'

Before Hakim could even consider the question, Amin entered carrying the tray of tea for Ziya.

He was a lean man with dark stringy hair. He was a good five years younger than Hakim's fifty, with facial lines as plentiful as Hakim's, but more gleefully carved.

'*Alláh'u'Abhá, Alláh'u'Abhá,*' he said, greeting everyone, followed by his usual hearty laugh. Hakim stood up respectfully and returned the greeting. Saffa followed his uncle's example, watching his father's brother, Uncle Amin, place the tray on the dining table.

Hakim gestured for Saffa to come closer and said aside to him. 'Don't let this greeting be a bowl hotter than its dish. God is Most Glorious,' he said enunciating its meaning clearly.

Saffa gave his promise in his nod.

Amin put the tray in front of Asiyih. 'I would serve this myself, Asiyih Khanum,' he said, teasing her, 'but I'm a guest in this house.'

'You're too late – we finished all the food,' Hakim said, breaking up Amin's poor attempt at a joke.

'What is your wise Uncle Hakim filling you with now, Saffa?' he asked, turning to the sofa, then acknowledged Hakim's presence with a bow. 'Please. Be seated, Doctor. This is your home.'

Before Hakim could reseat himself, Amin slipped into his chair, forcing Hakim to take a seat beside the children on the sofa.

Saffa was glad to see his Uncle Amin. There was always a good laugh when he showed up.

'Were you laughing at my question when you came in, Uncle Amin?'

'Not at your question, Saffa,' he said, taking the boy seriously. 'But at an incident you reminded me of.'

Amin leaned forward and confided. 'Up in Kurdistan there was this old Bahá'í, a very simple villager, who lived in an area where they were persecuting the Bahá'ís, forcing them to recant and return to Islam or die. Well, this old man, may my life be a ransom to the wrongs he suffered, was brought into the mosque. And before they could threaten him to give up his faith, he volunteered to recant.'

Amin roared with laughter. 'He thought he could help his fellow believers better if he pretended to be a Muslim.'

Hakim was not amused. 'What's so hysterical about that, Amin?'

'It's serious, Hakim!' he said, still chuckling, wiping his eyes with a tissue. But he couldn't contain his laughter. 'None of the Bahá'ís ever spoke to him again.'

7

Ziya, hearing this, shook her head sadly.

'What is it, Ziya Khanum?' Asiyih asked softly, while preparing the tray.

Ziya topped up the half-filled cups with steaming water, to make the tea weak. 'This is what I was talking about earlier. The simplicity of so many of the beloved friends who make innocent mistakes because they are not deepened in the Covenant of Bahá'u'lláh.' She sighed. 'It's hard to explain in words . . . I feel a special closeness to them. They have recognized the Blessed Perfection, Bahá'u'lláh, as the Promised One of all religions. But they fail to study his teachings and apply them to their daily lives. We all fail.'

Asiyih lifted the tray. 'How many remember the Messenger, but forget the Message.'

The quotation brought a smile to Ziya's eyes. 'True.'

They served the tea with sweets shaped in swirls of dough, fried and filled with honey-sweetened rose-water – Hakim's favorite.

'I still don't see how you can laugh,' Hakim persisted, taking a swirl.

'Because it doesn't make any sense. See a little humor. It aids the digestion.'

Ziya placed Hakim's teacup on the low table before him, then offered him a cube of homemade sugar to sweeten his mouth. She succeeded in diverting his interest.

'Where are the girls, dear?'

'Still in our room. Your grandson's not feeling too well.'

'I'll take a look in a moment,' he said tenderly, then turned his gaze back to Amin with a new thought. 'I suppose the demolition of the House of the Báb in Shiraz doesn't make you very serious either?'

'That's different,' Amin said earnestly. 'They desecrated that sacred House, making the site into a highway intersection.'

They all became silent. It had been over a year since that atrocity occurred, yet it still weighed heavily in everyone's heart.

Amin put his teacup down. 'You missed your calling in life, Hakim. You should have been a Mujtahid, an Islamic doctor of law, rather than a medical doctor. You could even have become an Ayatullah had you not been a Bahá'í. Who could defeat your reasoning powers in an argument, your able defense in proving the validity of the Cause of God? Who can compare with your knowledge of the Faith throughout the province when you quote from the Holy Writings? Why, everyone in Kashan knows you've learned at least ten meanings for every word!'

Was this Amin who was giving him such praise, Hakim wondered as he lowered his head, embarrassed and surprised. He muttered, dismissing the flattery, 'In this day it's deeds, not words.'

'Precisely!' Amin shouted, snapping his fingers, jolting everyone. 'It's how one uses the knowledge.'

Hakim felt the fool. It was as if Amin had slapped him across his face as a lesson in arrogance.

'If you and I, Hakim, were in Shiraz when the fanatics destroyed that holy place of pilgrimage – you would have tried to stop it with your friends in high places and I would have rendered thanks to God – '

'– for having the House torn down?' Hakim said, cutting him off. He had had enough of Amin's tongue.

'I wasn't finished, Hakim.'

'I'm not going to let you finish. Be careful how you judge other people, Amin. Bahá'u'lláh calls knowledge the greatest gift to man. We should all make efforts to acquire knowledge. And as for knowing people. One goes to the head not to the tail. If a mule's braying you don't pet its hindquarters, you close its mouth.'

The two of them had become red-faced from the discussion.

'Hakim,' Asiyih lovingly called to her brother, wishing to put an end to their quibbling. 'Is that how you treat my husband's brother?'

'That's how Jamshid treats his own brother.' Hakim sat back. 'I'll forgive you this time, Amin.'

'God-willing,' he answered back, finishing his tea to the bottom of the cup.

'Why didn't you pioneer, Amin?'

Asiyih gave up trying to talk sense to either one of them and Hakim was being particularly impossible. She repaired to the other sofa with Ziya, listening as the men entered into another debate.

'My older sister, my son,' Hakim said, going through all his fingers, 'everyone in my family has pioneered. What about your family?'

'How could we now? I have a business. And Jamshid needs me

9

to teach his son his craft.'

'Saffa's going to become a doctor, not a watch repairman. Isn't that right, Saffa?'

'Yes, Uncle Hakim.'

Asiyih was used to the two either not speaking to each other or getting themselves into an involved argument. But tonight the conversation was much more acrimonious. It was Hakim. And it wasn't like him.

Ziya kept her hands busy taking out her knitting, telling Asiyih, 'He's unusually defensive.'

'The phone calls?' she asked, guessing.

Ziya nodded. 'They've been more frequent through the week.'

'What do they say?'

'Threats mostly. Hakim won't let anyone answer the phone now except himself.'

Asiyih looked over at the arguing couple. 'Does Amin know about this?'

'No. Hakim thinks it's better to say nothing, in case fear spreads through the community to the weaker friends. I've tried to convince him to bring it up at the Assembly meeting tonight.'

Saffa glanced over at his mother. Asiyih indicated that the tea-cups should be cleared while he was doing nothing but listening to the chatter, which he did immediately. She thanked him with her smile, then turned back to Ziya. 'How's the teaching going in the villages?'

'Very wonderful. If it were not for this oppression, Asiyih Khanum, honest to God, no one would be investigating the Cause as strongly.'

'That's true. I heard that one of the clergy became a Bahá'í.'

'Yes, a mulla. He couldn't understand why there was so much slander spread against the Faith, as he had met Bahá'ís who were doctors, businessmen, teachers, people of good character who didn't fit in with the incessant lies.'

'So he became a Bahá'í?'

'Yes, but he had to leave. The other clergymen and villagers threatened to kill him and his family if he didn't go elsewhere.'

'But they respected him.'

Ziya's face broadened in a smile and she shrugged. 'They respected his title. When he lost that he went to Hakim in the hospital, all beaten and bruised.'

Asiyih clicked her mouth in disbelief and sighed. Ziya touched her thigh and leaned near. 'Hakim had an argument with the mulla about why the poor man didn't think to teach the villagers while he was being stoned.'

They burst out in laughter, quieting the men.

The phone rang. Hakim stood up quickly. 'I'll answer it.'

Amin pounced from his chair to the phone before anyone could stop him.

Hakim watched Amin's face become serious as he listened to the caller. Amin glanced over to him. He was worried. He said a few 'Yeses', then agreed, 'In fifteen minutes.' He hung up the receiver and said to everyone, seeing how concerned they all appeared, 'My wife. She's not feeling well.' A false alarm. Hakim responded to his next duty.

'Shall I come?' He offered without hesitating.

'No. Thank you, Hakim. I think it's just the change in weather.'

Two slender dark-haired girls came into the room, one holding a small child to her shoulder.

'Yes, Sholeh?' Ziya said, seeing her elder daughter carrying her little boy.

Sholeh was in her early twenties, a few years older than her younger sister, who had followed her into the room with a basket of toys and children's clothes.

Hakim took a look at his grandson, examining him with a gentle touch and a glance. 'How old are you?'

The boy held up a couple of fingers, trying for three.

'I'll give you something to give him.'

'You did already, Baba.'

'Good, good,' he said, remembering that he'd given her the medicine before supper. 'Good. Then Amin can drop you home when he takes Asiyih.'

'We're ready to go,' Asiyih said to her children.

'Shiva wants to come, too,' Sholeh said for her sister.

Hakim and Ziya prepared everyone to go out, getting Shiva a chadour to cover her western-style clothes. It was wiser for women to wear the thin robes over their clothes these days, in accordance with the stringent laws. Ziya tied flowery scarves over her daughters' hair, then sent them out with kisses on their cheeks.

11

They went into the open central courtyard. Overhead the clouds were fast becoming dense, blocking out the pale crescent moon. It was unusual to have such weather at night in spring.

Mitra sat on the tiled floor and slipped on her shoes by herself, then ran to be first at the front door.

'Uncle Hakim?' called Saffa.

'My dear,' he answered, ready for the next question looming in his nephew's mind. 'Ask.'

'Is God allowing all this suffering of the Bahá'ís?'

'That's a good question,' Amin declared, trying out his answer first before allowing Hakim to share his insight. 'It's man that causes the suffering of each other, not God. Isn't that true, Hakim?'

'In one sense,' he said, considering the question more deeply. Hakim thought for a long moment, then said, "Abdu'l-Bahá tells us that there are three great mysteries. And that only when the condition of spiritual maturity is achieved will one be able to understand their complete significance.'

Hakim went to his fingers to count. 'Why children and animals suffer, the mystery of good and evil, and . . .'

'And?' Amin said, wanting to hear the third.

Hakim searched his memory.

'You're getting old,' Amin said, teasing him.

He turned to his wife for assistance. 'Ziya Khanum?'

She repeated them to herself, then added, 'Free will.'

'I eat mule brains,' Hakim said, reprimanding his faulty memory. 'Free will. I am getting old.'

Saffa didn't appear to be satisfied. Hakim asked, 'What do you want to say?'

'Isn't there a mystery called the Mystery of Sacrifice?'

Hakim was pleased to hear this. He gave him a hard stare, then waved a finger at him. 'You've been studying, haven't you?'

Saffa stood tall, as tall as his uncles, and smiled proudly.

'There's no room for self-esteem,' Hakim said, knocking the air of egotism out of Saffa's stance. The evening ended there. 'All right. Good-night, Good-night.' He opened the door and let everyone by. 'And drive safely, Amin.'

The girls kissed their father good-night. Hakim bent down to Mitra and gave her a big kiss on her cheek, then smacked his lips. 'Mmmm. You're so sweet, mice eat you.'

She giggled and ran into her mother's dress, following her out the door.

Anyone could see how dejected Saffa had become, when he merely followed the formality of pressing each cheek against his uncle's.

'I have a book that I have to send to the Universal House of Justice. I've kept it in a very special place for many years. It's a handwritten volume of the Book of Certitude. I'm saving it for you when you finish medical school. And it was a good question you asked.'

'Good-night, Uncle Hakim,' he said with a growing smile on his face.

Hakim made sure they got to the end of the alleyway, to their car safely. He came back, locked the front door and went over by Ziya who was clearing the litter around her collection of potted plants. He couldn't help but inhale the fragrance of the jasmine blossoms which perfumed the night air.

'It was a good question. He's going to make a fine doctor one day.'

They looked up at the cloudy sky.

'It's going to rain,' she said.

Hakim knew the tone in her voice. 'Don't tell me it's an omen. I have a tough enough time with your dreams.'

The phone rang in the guest room. Hakim debated whether to answer it. For all he cared it could ring all night.

'It could be Amin's wife again,' she suggested.

Neither of them believed that. They slowly went into the room.

'Do you think they're watching the house?'

'I don't know, Ziya.'

'Maybe the Assembly shouldn't meet tonight. It's Friday. The mosque will be full.'

'Don't worry,' he said and lifted the phone. 'Yes?'

There was a long pause, no voice spoke at the other end.

Hakim nodded to Ziya. It was whom he had hoped it wasn't.

'Dr Rahbari?' the man's voice asked.

'Yes,' Hakim answered, identifying himself.

'Can you come to my house, I am sick.'

Ziya overheard the demand. She could see Hakim ready to explode, and gently put her hand on his shoulder to ease him.

13

'You are sick,' he said, feeling her touch. 'Your illness can only be cured by God, not by me.'

'If the mountain does not come to Muhammad, Muhammad will come to the mountain . . . tonight.'

The phone clicked and hummed its disconnected tone. Hakim slapped the receiver down. 'I'm going to the Revolutionary Guard headquarters and stop this once and for all.'

'Hakim,' she said with a purr. 'I wish you wouldn't.'

'Bahá'ís are to fear God, not governments!'

He bent down and pulled the phone cable out of its socket, then wrapped up the cord and stuffed the phone in a drawer of a cabinet. 'And if we had gone pioneering, there would be no one to protect the others from these accursed mongrels,' he said, anticipating her next comments, then added, 'And we won't mention Amin. It's against the law of God to backbite.'

'Yes, dear,' she said, waiting for him to get all his tension out.

Hakim stared at the floor and huffed, then said in a low voice, 'I'll apologize to him tomorrow.'

He reopened the drawer and pulled out the phone, fidgeting with the wires to reconnect it in the wall. 'I'd like to meet that soul who keeps calling and really teach him a lesson.'

Ziya straightened out the cloths and pillows on the sofas to tidy up for the Assembly meeting. 'It sounds like he wants to teach you a lesson, too. Let's pray to God that these difficulties pass quickly through Iran. I'm going to go prepare the tea.' She went over to him and brushed her hands through his hair, then rubbed his cheek. 'Don't let it bother you, beloved. They're doing this because you are a prominent Bahá'í. Chant a few prayers and rest your heart.'

She left him to himself, carrying on with her chores. He gave up on the phone wire and plopped himself in his chair. He loosened his tie, mumbling to himself. 'They are doing this because I am a prominent Bahá'í. I'd really like to show that bastard how good a surgeon I am . . . protector of Islam.'

He laughed in disgust. It was not going to harass his thoughts any more. They could bring an army tonight if they wanted to. The greatest glory to Hakim would be to be remembered as a martyr in the pathway of God. If this was the worst that could happen, then he was ready for God to send this Revolutionary Guard as a test to his steadfastness. He was ready and waiting.

# CHAPTER 2

# The Convictions of Men

Isfahani entered the prison hours before daylight in his neat khaki uniform. The prison guards had to respect his right to visit solitary confinement. He was a Revolutionary Guard. And not merely a guard, but a Commander's Assistant.

He had duties to attend to, and pacing in front of the solitary corridor's locked gate gave him time to review them. He did not allow the two corridor guards who were arguing over why it had rained the last two nights to deflect him from his purpose. He kept to himself, pacing, preparing, brushing against the steel bars.

The meeting was arranged for dawn. Ayatullah Rustami would be there. It was Isfahani's chance to prove his abilities before one who had great political influence. It was his plan that called for the Ayatullah's presence and if he had chosen the wrong prisoner, he would never achieve his career aims; but then he did have the support of his superior, Commander Rashti.

Isfahani gazed through the gate focusing his eyes on the lone pair of hands which clung to the cell bars at the end of the corridor. The prisoner's grasp had not moved since Isfahani had been there. A cold draft carried pungent odors through the hallway, reeking of moldy plaster. The prisoner must be aware of it too, he thought.

Isfahani understood his role. He was a protector of Islam. It was his sworn duty to uproot corrupt foreign influences and squelch all anti-Islamic factions against the revolution. All enemies were to be dealt with according to Islamic justice, whether it meant that the offenders had to be confined for their criminal acts, or required indefinite detention in prison, or demanded execution. Nothing was greater than justice in Isfahani's eyes; he had dedicated his life to it. This is what brought him to this prison.

In childhood he had been taught to hate one group more than any other. He considered it his highest honor to take part in erasing this group from influencing society with its ideas. These heretics required much more stringent methods of removal than mere imprisonment or simple execution. They deserved a precise and systematic eradication. And Isfahani had a plan. This one prisoner would prove that he knew how to deal with enemies of Islam.

Isfahani struck a crackling match to his cigarette and leaned his back against the bars. He inhaled deeply, sending the smoke into the shadows along the walls where the guards sat. One of the guards cleared his throat. He was in his mid-twenties or so, a few years younger than Isfahani himself, but Isfahani's thick mustache made him appear much more mature. The older guard, a sergeant by the designation on his old jacket's sleeve, leaned forward to the edge of his seat. He placed his hand across his chest and mumbled a few words of respect to their visitor.

Isfahani returned the gesture. He knew why the two had stopped their discussion: they wanted cigarettes. He pulled out his pack, thinking he'd have a few moments of entertainment before he went off to the meeting room.

'Do you smoke?' he said, offering it to the older guard.

'Only when its offered, Commander,' the sergeant replied, taking a cigarette from the pack.

'Assistant,' Isfahani said, correcting him.

The sergeant nodded knowingly, which amused Isfahani.

'And you?' he said, tilting the pack to the other guard.

'*Merci*, brother,' said the younger guard, thanking him.

Instantly Isfahani withdrew his offer, staring with rage at the guard. '*Merci*?'

The guard jumped to his feet, apologizing, 'I mean, *Moteshakeram,* brother.'

Isfahani held his hardened gaze on the guard for a few extra moments, then smiled, extended the pack, letting the guard remove his reward.

The sergeant watched the smirk across Isfahani's face. It was clear that this Assistant would not allow spoken any French of the court of the deposed Shah. The Assistant had heard the correct Persian phrase he demanded. This made the sergeant more cautious and more fascinated by the Revolutionary Guard's purpose. They were considered ignorant fanatics by many, but this one seemed to him filled with cleverness.

Before the sergeant could change his thoughts into words, his companion decided to start the conversation. 'Forgive me, brother,' he began, 'If you don't mind me intruding into your affairs, my sergeant here would like to know how come you're so interested in that one particular prisoner down the hall?'

Isfahani saw the expression of shock and embarrassment on the sergeant's face. 'Does our brother here always speak for you?'

'No, Commander – Assistant. Please forgive him,' he asked, looking at his partner. 'What he meant to say was, is, that we too were just interested in that particular prisoner's special, particular case.'

Isfahani played the fool. 'Special?'

'This row used to be under SAVAK,' the sergeant quickly explained, 'before the revolution. And unless the prisons are filling up fast, this must be a special, important prisoner for a cell on this block.'

'Do you know the prisoner?'

'Dr Hakim Rahbari,' they said together.

Isfahani changed his view: he was not talking with complete fools. He stepped back and bowed slightly. 'I am indeed impressed.'

'Do you think he's dangerous?' the younger guard asked.

'He's poison,' Isfahani said coldly.

'Granted he may be as poisonous as you say,' the sergeant went on, 'but more poisonous than the others?'

The younger dismissed his comment. 'Why else would the Revolutionary Guard send over one of their trusted Assistants in the middle of the night?'

They both turned to Isfahani for greater insight.

Isfahani wondered where these two had come from. He satisfied their inquisitiveness. 'Yes . . . This case is very special.'

'Do you mind if I ask you one more question?' the younger guard said, reseating himself.

'One more?'

'Who's going to interrogate the prisoner?'

Isfahani could have kissed him for asking that. He looked down the corridor, making sure that no ears could overhear them, then gazed into their eyes. 'Have you ever heard of the Ayatullah Rustami, or Commander Rashti?'

The sergeant clicked his mouth in amazement, then nudged his companion. 'You see, I told you this was a special case,' he said, then turned back to Isfahani. 'And how long have you been in the Islamic Sacrificers?'

Isfahani could feel his face reddening. He tried to change his embarrassment into anger. 'You two have a way of asking a question. Who said I was an Islamic Sacrificer?'

'Well you're either an Islamic Communist or an Islamic Marxist, a member of the National Party, or an Islamic Sacrificer.'

Isfahani stared at the sergeant, stroking his mustache, listening.

'If you were a Leninist or Marxist, you'd be waiting to be executed,' the sergeant said, pointing over to the cells. 'Or dead or in exile planning to overthrow our new regime. But you don't look like a communist. And I don't know what a politician looks like. So you must be an Islamic Sacrificer.'

The two of them agreed seriously.

Isfahani's head was in a spin trying to figure these two characters out. 'Where did you learn all this?'

'My sons are Revolutionary Guards!' the sergeant said proudly. 'My eldest was also a Marxist at the University of Teheran, but swears he was only an Islamic Sacrificer. He was smart like you.'

Isfahani glanced at his watch, escaping from the discussion. 'Very good. Now that I know the prisoner is protected by such erudite guardians, I can leave without fears.'

The two guards rose and correctly thanked him for the glowing praise.

'Just one more suggestion,' Isfahani said, warning them, 'Watch your tongues or you'll end up on the other side of those bars.'

The two guards turned to each other, then burst into laughter.

'Who do you think we are, the Shah's prison guards?' the younger guard asked.

'The prison guards were replaced by us during the revolution,' the sergeant explained. 'We were released from there.'

Isfahani did not see the humor and walked away. 'I'll send for the prisoner in a few hours.'

Once out of their view, he waited in the shadows to hear what else the guards might know which would be useful to hear.

The sergeant resumed his seat and peered down the hallway to the prisoner's hands.

'Well?' said the younger guard, offering him one of his own smokes, waiting to hear his companion's conclusions.

'Definitely not a political prisoner.'

'Why not?'

'They'd have sent him to Evin prison in Teheran.'

'But our Assistant said he was a special case.'

'True,' he said, pondering the point.

'He's a criminal.'

'If he's been convicted of a crime at his trial already, why do they still bother with him? It's something else. And our ambitious Assistant wants to ascend up the ladder of politics with this poor soul.'

The younger guard studied the prisoner's position. 'I wonder what he's thinking?'

'So does the Assistant.'

'I wouldn't be surprised if they chose the weakest criminal in the place for their plans.'

'Dr Rahbari? No,' the sergeant said solemnly. 'He's not the weakest, he's just a Bahá'í.'

The younger guard snapped his fingers. 'Bahá'í? . . . Well, that's why!'

The sergeant nodded his head, confirming his reasoning.

The younger guard scratched his stubble, then turned back to his partner. 'If being Bahá'í is so terrible, then why are so many big people Bahá'í?'

Isfahani had heard enough of their babbling. He would deal with them later. It proved to him that these fools were misguided by the heretics and that what he was preparing to do to this prisoner was indeed justice. He moved quickly through the corridors towards the meeting room. His heels clicked hard against the tiled floors of the passage he searched for. Ahead he spied a group of distinguished-looking clergymen, attired in their turbans and robes, going into the room with Commander Rashti.

He ran his well-worked thoughts over again. Ayatullah Rustami . . . this one prisoner . . . career – Ayatullah Rustami. This was it.

Two Revolutionary Guards dressed similarly to Isfahani flanked the door's entrance. Their hand weapons were visible, holstered in their waistbelts over their shirts. Each also carried a rifle slung over his shoulder. It was a good show which Isfahani hoped impressed his Commander and the guests.

'Is that everyone?' he asked, coming up to them.

'Yes, brother,' they said.

Isfahani nodded.

They stiffened and opened the door for him. Isfahani went in. Scores of documents were being spread across the sole table for review by the seated men. Above the table on the rear wall hung a framed picture of the Revolutionary Leader. On the other walls posters were displayed which extolled the revolution.

Isfahani felt someone was watching him and looked to the end of the table. It was an older mulla, maybe in his sixties, of slender build and deep olive complexion. His green turban told of his lineage to the house of Muhammad. Isfahani knew who it had to be, the renowned Mulla Ahmad, a Mujtahid, admired for his piety and knowledge. It was a rare privilege to meet him and Isfahani promised himself that he would make every attempt to talk with him when the moment availed itself.

Isfahani felt unable to deeply gaze into Mulla Ahmad's eyes; his vision was piercing. He feared that his lesser qualities would be instantly revealed if he allowed the Mulla to penetrate his soul. Isfahani bowed respectfully, and received the same gesture of courtesy from Mulla Ahmad.

Isfahani turned at his Commander's chuckle. He saw the hefty bearded clergyman beside him – it was the Ayatullah. They had met before.

The Ayatullah looked up, adjusting his black turban over his thick gray brow. 'And who's this?'

'The one who I spoke about,' the Commander said. 'He was with us Friday night at your inspiring sermon.'

Isfahani wondered how much credit the Commander had taken for himself.

The Ayatullah yielded no sign of recognition. The Commander explained further. 'The one who did all the preliminary work for this case. The one you approved of as my Assistant.'

A smile of understanding crept across his deep-lined face. 'Ah, yes. What is your name, brother?'

As Isfahani introduced himself, the Ayatullah beckoned him closer to the table, causing the other mullas to take notice and look back at him. The Ayatullah's stare was penetrating as well, to

Isfahani, but not in the way Mulla Ahmad's had been. These eyes were not to be trusted, but had a commanding power Isfahani desired.

'Have you done your job well, brother?'

Isfahani returned a strong gaze. 'I have done my job well, Ayatullah.'

'Very good. Very good,' he said, giving the Commander an approving expression, then turned back to Isfahani. 'You have great courage. Allah is pleased with those who use their abilities to defend the Cause of Islam.'

'*Moteshakeram*,' Isfahani said, thanking him.

'Very good,' muttered the Ayatullah, stroking his very well-groomed beard, then returned to the papers before him.

The Commander introduced his assistant to the other mullas. With each introduction Isfahani placed his hand over his breast and mouthed the traditional '*Qurbani-shoma*', understanding full well that the words meant 'May my life be a sacrifice to you', and hoping that each mulla recognized the sincerity of his words. It was a privilege to be introduced to the distinguished clergymen around the Ayatullah, but he knew how much more important the Ayatullah would be to his career. He had heard about him ever since his first years in high school, where he learned he had been imprisoned for his political activities. The Ayatullah had stood against the Shah's increasing western alliances. And after fifteen years of struggle he accomplished his goal with the revolution, becoming a staunch exponent of expelling imperialistic influences from the Islamic Republic.

'Tea?' the Ayatullah asked the Commander.

Isfahani instantly went to his Revolutionary Guards at the door.

'Instruct the Warden to bring his personal samovar for the Ayatullah's pleasure,' the Commander ordered.

The Ayatullah waited for Isfahani to pass along the instructions. He blew into his hands to warm his knotted fingers. Isfahani shut the door and came back to the table. The Ayatullah folded his hands over his papers. All eyes turned in his direction.

'As we have released most of the political prisoners from this region, who were imprisoned under the tyranny of the Shah and SAVAK,' he said proudly. 'And having re-introduced these souls to God's Straight Path, we are now faced with a prison filled with

men and women: infidels, traitors, enemies of Islam, some who
would try to overthrow this holy and God-guided revolution.'

The Ayatullah took a deep breath. He slammed his fist
repeatedly on one of the files before him. 'Others are just risks to
our national or local security and must be dealt with according to
Islamic justice.'

In unison with the others around the table, Isfahani nodded in
agreement. While enraptured by the Ayatullah's words,
Isfahani's eyes drifted to the end of the table towards Mulla
Ahmad, who apparently was unmoved by the grand speech. The
Mulla seemed more preoccupied with his own files before him,
studying them with great care. It confused Isfahani; why was he
not as entranced as the others? His thoughts offered the excuse
that the Mulla must have been familiar with the Ayatullah's
speeches already.

Mulla Ahmad looked up from his work at Isfahani. He nodded
to him. Isfahani broke his stare and glanced at the Revolutionary
Leader's picture. He should not have been caught daydreaming.
He cautiously glanced back towards the Mulla's seat, seeing him
engrossed again in his reports. He trusted these eyes. Justice was
stamped upon the Mulla's brow. And justice was what they were
there for.

The Ayatullah's voice roared through the room. 'And Justice is
what we are here for! Isn't it?'

Shocked by the phrase, Isfahani whipped his gaze back to the
Ayatullah, who glanced at everyone, finally staring up at Isfahani.

'Isn't that so, brother?'

Isfahani nervously nodded. The Ayatullah nodded to
everyone, then turned to the Commander and took gently hold of
his arm.

'You have Bahá'ís here,' he said with a slight questioning in his
voice.

The Commander smiled with a nod.

'Good. We will see how well your Assistant has done his
homework.'

The Commander looked in his briefcase and pulled out a file for
the Ayatullah to peruse. 'We have isolated one of the men.' He
winked at Isfahani, showing him his confidence, then reached
over and pointed to the appropriate document. 'We believe this
one will fit our plans nicely.'

The Ayatullah looked away from the Commander and up at Isfahani with a sneer. 'Nicely?' He turned back, ready to spit. 'Nicely? I don't want nicely-fitting heretics.'

His whole character seemed to turn sour as he spoke with disgust. 'Do you know how dangerous these poisonous, godless vipers are?'

'Yes, Ayatullah, we know,' Isfahani let blurt out.

The silence seemed like hours.

'Yes?' the Ayatullah questioned, expecting Isfahani to carry on.

Commander Rashti tried to intervene. 'I think that – '

'Let the Assistant speak for himself, Commander.'

The Commander's obedience was immediate. The Ayatullah continued. 'You were about to tell us, Assistant, about these misguided followers of darkness.'

Any knowledge Isfahani had on the subject, he knew the Ayatullah could better. Even the subtle phrase 'followers of darkness' indicated the Ayatullah's knowledge that 'Bahá' meant light, splendor, glory. But there was one aspect that Isfahani could impress everyone with – his knowledge of the history, which he had gleaned from his investigations and arguments when he was at university.

'It is known by all sincere students of Islam,' he began confidently, 'that in the year AH 1260, a fictitious personage named 'Alí-Muḥammad of Shiraz declared himself as the Báb, the Gate, as the promised Qá'im of Islam. This man was no doubt, as suggested by many learned mujtahids, a creation of the Russian and British Governments designed to cause unrest and anarchy in Iran during the middle of the last century. Thousands of the followers of the Báb met their deaths; however, amongst them arose one who became known as Bahá'u'lláh, the Glory of God, who after the public execution of the Báb declared himself while in exile to be the promised Husayn. Ultimately, he was banished further and finally incarcerated in the prison-city of Akka, Palestine.'

The lengthy talk did not impress the Ayatullah. 'Where are the Báb's remains?'

'In Haifa, Pales – ' he began, then was cut off.

'He died being eaten by dogs!'

All the heads around the table nodded in agreement as far as Isfahani could see. It was not his place to argue, nor could he prove his knowledge merely on what he had heard or studied.

'What else did they teach you in school?' the Ayatullah asked. 'Did they tell you the rewards in the next realm of removing such instruments of Satan?'

'We were told – '

'And how they corrupt the Holy Qur'án and Hadiths. Or that the Shah's personal physician was a Bahá'í, as well as top officials in SAVAK? I knew this personally! That's why I was called in – to show you how to deal with these enemies of God.'

Mulla Ahmad stood up, brushing off his cream-colored robes. 'Ayatullah Rustami.'

'Yes, Mulla Ahmad,' he said, adjusting his turban and collar. He cooled himself off with the wave of his hand across his face.

'Even Bahá'ís can surrender their ignorance and return. Allah is merciful to those who repent.'

'I hope this Pasdar', the Ayatullah said, deliberately demoting Isfahani's rank to that of a common soldier in the Revolutionary Guards, 'has already proposed this to the prisoners.'

'Yes, Ayatullah,' Isfahani affirmed.

'And as I have dealt with Bahá'ís before, I expect they no doubt all refused. Am I not correct?'

The Commander stepped into the conversation, defending Isfahani. 'I am sure that my Assistant was more than firm in his duties.'

'Let us pray so,' the Ayatullah said, muttering, then resumed his search through the files, stroking his beard.

Isfahani watched Mulla Ahmad return to his seat. He wondered if the Mulla's timing in curbing the Ayatullah's wrath had been quite accidental. This time when he looked at Mulla Ahmad he was able to gaze into his eyes. His thoughts were confirmed and he felt his confidence restored.

The Ayatullah had more to say to Isfahani. 'Did you use persuasive measures, brother?' he asked.

'I informed them of their fate.'

'Mere words of threat do not frighten this sort.'

'My words were strong enough to allow me to determine the strengths and weaknesses of all the individuals,' Isfahani answered back boldly, forgetting whom he was addressing. He had had enough of being put on trial.

The Ayatullah waved the file at him. 'What makes you think

that this one will fit "nicely" into our plans?'

'His wife is the woman in detention.'

'Is she strong?'

'The strongest.'

'That's why you chose this prisoner?' he shouted, glancing at the others to make certain they had heard this Assistant's absurd reasoning. He threw the file into the hands of the Commander. 'Not good enough. This one, Assistant, will be the most difficult.'

Isfahani listened to the passing comments agreeing with the Ayatullah. He stepped forward. 'I have staked my career on this one prisoner, Ayatullah Rustami.'

The Ayatullah stared back at him, amazed at his audacity, but gesturing for the file to be placed back in his grasp. He didn't look down at it, just stared at Isfahani, then gave it back to the Commander. 'All right . . . '

He rose and paced behind the table, thinking the prospect over. 'Who else is in his family?'

'One son, two daughters,' Isfahani said, as if quoting from memory.

'Arrested?'

'No. His son is abroad, an engineer, working in Africa, where most of his relatives live.

'The daughters are here.'

'Yes.'

'How old are they?'

'The eldest is twenty-two, married, one child. Her husband was on their Local Spiritual Assembly. The sister is nineteen.'

Isfahani leaned across the table to show the Commander and the Ayatullah the rest of the information in the file. 'The sisters have both come to the prison in the past few days to see their father, with the doctor's sister and brother-in-law.'

Isfahani stood back up, waiting for the Ayatullah's decision. The Ayatullah took his time. He turned back to the Revolutionary Leader's portrait, thinking aloud. 'I don't like Bahá'ís. Unclean. Especially ones who marry beyond the Islamic Laws of God. No Bahá'í marriage is recognized by the Islamic Court or our Constitution. They are all adulterers.'

Mulla Ahmad stood up, but said nothing as yet, allowing the Ayatullah to continue his speech.

'These illegitimate children carry the seed of their adulterous parents. Rest assured that their fate in the eyes of God is everlasting torment. They will all be eliminated – and this one prisoner will be made an example of. As the Glorious Qur'án says – '

'He has the right to recant,' Mulla Ahmad spoke out, interrupting.

The Ayatullah's mouth was still open as he spun towards the Mulla, who continued, 'And every means should be ensured to achieve this end. Make him an example this way, Ayatullah Rustami. This would be pleasing to the sight of God.'

The Ayatullah wet his lips. He didn't say what his mind was desiring to spit, but instead thanked him with a nod.

'Please. Be seated, Mulla Ahmad.'

'Forgive me, Ayatullah.'

Everyone turned to Isfahani. The Commander put his face into his hand and massaged his brow in disbelief that his Assistant dared to speak again.

'I don't think executing this one will serve our purposes,' he said, fearless of the Ayatullah's hardened stare. 'Nor is this why I chose him.'

He knew that he had diverted the confrontation between the Ayatullah and Mulla Ahmad, but owed the favor to the Mulla, and deserved the opportunity to make his plan known.

'Now you are an Ayatullah, or maybe a judge in the Revolutionary Court, Pasdar?'

'No, Ayatullah,' he said quietly.

'Well then, what divine inspiration allows your boldness?'

Mulla Ahmad encouraged him with his nod. Isfahani turned to the table. 'It is well known that every time a Bahá'í is removed, five more seem to arise in his place. If we want to make an example of this one, we must force him to recant. Any man can kill another, but to get a prominent Bahá'í to recant, that is a greater victory.'

The Commander stared hard at his Assistant. 'And tell us how we should do this, Pasdar.'

'All we have to do is make him a hero throughout Kashan, throughout Iran.'

The other clergymen nodded in agreement.

'Wait, wait, wait,' the Ayatullah said, going to the side of the table quickly. The robes flapped back and forth with his long steps. 'Yes, yes . . . What was the name of – Khurasani!'

A cruel smile swept across his face. 'Send for Khurasani, Commander Rashti. And have him bring some of his virile men.' He put his arms in his cloak, beaming. 'What we do is sanctioned before God, Assistant. I will grant this convicted heretic a last chance to recant.'

The Ayatullah pushed up his sleeve to read the time on his gold-plated watch. 'Come. Let us proceed to the mosque for dawn prayers.' Then he said to the Commander beside him, 'Ten-thirty this morning. And I hope that the tea is prepared by then.' The papers were reshuffled into briefcases, clearing the table. Isfahani went to the door and opened it for them. The Ayatullah glanced at him as he passed by. 'A recanting hero. Excellent. I'd even make you a Commander, Assistant. Ha.'

'Your career is on the line, Pasdar,' the Commander added sternly, shaking him out of his thoughts.

Isfahani was left standing alone. He hadn't even seen Mulla Ahmad go by. The Revolutionary Leader's picture seemed to stare at him.

He shook his head and with a deep breath said, 'This one prisoner . . . '

# CHAPTER 3

# Trials of Certitude

Hakim reminded himself of 'Abdu'l-Bahá's words:

*Freedom is not a matter of place, but of condition. I was happy in that prison, for those days were passed in the path of service. To me prison was freedom. Troubles are a rest to me. Death is life. To be despised is honor. Therefore was I full of happiness all through that prison time. When one is released from the prison of self, that is indeed freedom! For self is the greatest prison.*

Hakim sighed. The corridor light spilled through the cell bars across his face. He considered the words of 'Abdu'l-Bahá, then his own set of conditions. Hadn't he already attained his freedom from prison, as his fellow Assembly members had too? The court had signed all their death sentences. So why wasn't he 'full of happiness'?

Hakim gripped the cold steel bars tighter in his fists. He wondered if the court hoped the Bahá'ís would have tried to bribe them to obtain their freedom, as others accused of different charges had tried, or did they imagine that any of them would recant their faith for the reward of staying in this mortal existence for the price of gold?

'Never,' he said, loud enough for the world to hear, certain in his own heart that none of them would be tempted by promises or intimidated by threats.

'Let them challenge this servant with any test from God to prove his staunchness,' he said defiantly. His voice echoed into the emptiness. Who could hear him in his isolation but God, he thought.

He inhaled deeply and dropped his forehead against the coolness of the bars. His hands had become painfully numb. He unpeeled his fingers, making his joints snap like dry twigs, then massaged them, walking into the darkness of his cell. It must be well past sunrise by now. When would the guards be sent to escort him out? Were they trying to unnerve his last bit of patience?

28

'O God,' he said, 'it's not easy to be a Bahá'í.'

He thought about what was soon to come, and how others had spent their blood in the path of God. 'Seven hundred and fifty bullets found their mark on the Blessed Personage of His Holiness the Báb, the day he was martyred. Twenty thousand believers followed. Now what will be the fate of this sole servant?'

The cell seemed hotter now. His thoughts drifted towards his wife's welfare: he wondered if they would release her soon. She was not on the Assembly, she had just been there to host. They would have to let her go.

He sat on the cold cement floor, on his knees, and opened his palms upwards. Perspiration dripped from his forehead. 'O Lord of the Worlds! I do not fear for my own worthless soul, I only pray that Thou wilt enable my wife to look after our loved ones when I return to Thee.'

The corridor gate unlocked. The hour had struck. Hakim closed his eyes and chanted a prayer of the Báb's:

*I adjure Thee by Thy might, O my God! Let no harm beset me in times of tests, and in moments of heedlessness guide my steps aright through Thine inspiration. Thou art God, potent art Thou to do what Thou desirest. No one can withstand Thy Will or thwart Thy purpose.*

Shadows moved across the floor before his cell. He heard the key enter into his door. He wiped his face dry. Whatever God had destined for him now, he prayed again only for steadfastness. And if Ziya wasn't released, then he prayed that they would be able to face martyrdom together.

The younger prison guard's command echoed through the cell and corridor. 'Come out!'

This was it, Hakim thought. Now he had to stand up for what he had prepared himself his whole life for. All his other worldly concerns would have to be forgotten.

'I said come out!'

Hakim stood. There was one thing he should not forget: what his mother had told him as a small boy . . . 'When you walk, walk with dignity. You are Bahá'í.'


'Why him?'
'What did he do?'
The questions whispered from lip to lip, cell to cell, amongst the imprisoned men as Hakim was escorted by the two guards

29

through the main section. And the answer that was always given – 'Bahá'í.'

Hakim had clasped his hands behind his back and looked as though he was being given a tour or taken on a stroll. With every step he silently invoked the refrain to himself, *'Alláh'u'Abhá.'*

The taunts and jeers he had been expecting the prisoners to spit at him turned his concentration. He wasn't prepared for the words they chose to hurl.

'Look. Guard. Take me instead of the doctor,' said one. 'My crime deserves death compared with his.'

'Why take the Bahá'í?' shouted another, 'If you want to kill someone kill me!'

'Shut up,' the sergeant hollered, threatening them all.

They went past the cell Hakim had originally been detained in. None of his friends remained, other men filled their place now. Hakim stopped: he imagined their fate must have been the same.

'Please, Doctor,' the sergeant pleaded, indicating that they had to move on.

'He's poison, not a mulla,' said the younger guard.

'And you shut up too. You have the brain of a mule. Even poison should be respected.'

The sergeant turned back to Hakim. 'Please, Doctor. They are not there. They were removed – to another prison.'

The tone in his voice explained which prison they had been sent to. There was only one. Evin. There was no way of knowing their fate now. Hakim remembered how many stories surrounded the horrors of the Teheran prison – Evin. There was no reason to believe that because SAVAK was no longer, its instruments of cruelty had been destroyed too. The thought wrenched Hakim's stomach. His daughter's husband was amongst them, and his friends.

Within the walls of the meeting room, the Warden directed two of the prison guards to carefully set down his enormous samovar on a small table in a front corner. The samovar landed with a thump, spilling some of its steamy contents on the covered table-top. Isfahani, the Commander and another man, who was dressed in khaki slacks and a black turtle-neck jersey, turned to the incident.

'Out, you cursed sons of a – .' The Warden remembered the others were present. He pulled out his handkerchief and wiped the brass spout dry, swearing as he watched his men hastily leave.

Isfahani took a long drag of his cigarette, anxious for the prisoner to arrive. He stood at the back beside the narrow window and looked over his left shoulder out of the open slats to the empty prison courtyard. He glanced at his watch, wondering when the prisoner would arrive, thinking he should have never trusted those two corridor guards to bring him there alone.

'Ahem.'

They all heard the abrupt sound from the doorway. There was the sergeant, alone, with his hat over his breast.

'Should I bring the prisoner in, Commander Rashti?' he asked.

'Yes, sergeant. Bring him in.'

Hakim was led into the center of the room by the younger guard, who announced, 'Hakim.'

'Doctor,' Isfahani said, cutting him off, and flicked his cigarette stub out the window.

'Yes, Doctor – Excuse me. *Merci*. I mean *Moteshakeram*.'

'*Moteshakeram*,' said the sergeant, a moment too late.

'Get lost!' Isfahani commanded.

In an instant they vanished, slamming the door shut behind them. The Ayatullah was not due for another quarter of an hour. Isfahani wondered why the Commander had asked him to send for the prisoner before they arrived. There was nothing he could do but wait to see what his Commander had devised.

'Asses,' noted the Commander, without looking up at the doctor before him. Then he glanced to Isfahani. 'I am surrounded by outspoken fools today.'

Hakim stood motionless. He wasn't worried that he was being ignored. They would make him the center of attention soon enough.

'Khurasani?' the Commander called to the other man, 'Please find our distinguished doctor a seat. To my right, beneath our Revolutionary Leader's picture. Ayatullah Rustami can sit here at my left when he arrives.'

Khurasani motioned for Hakim to come around the table, pulling out the chair designated for him.

Hakim didn't know what part this 'Khurasani' was to play. The others were obvious. Isfahani was the chess player looking for checkmate, the Commander was the organizer of the game, and the Warden was there to serve the refreshments. That left the broad-nosed, bald-headed wrestler to move the pieces. Khurasani had the appearance of a mindless hulk, committed to uprooting trees – by hand. He was a physical brute.

Hakim appeared at ease in their midst, though Isfahani was certain that the doctor's inner stance was not as confident as his stuffy posture. Even the Commander commented to Isfahani as the doctor took his seat.

'Our guest commands great respect. I too shall commend you if Ayatullah Rustami's plans, with the help of our friend, Khurasani, become effective in achieving our goals.'

Hakim glanced back to Khurasani, who was busy accepting the Commander's flattery, covering his breast and pleading self-effacement. There was something dangerous about this man. His perfume of spirituality was fouler than his cheap cologne. Hakim perceived an alcoholic glaze over the man's eyes. He glanced away before their eyes met. It was certain that his analysis of Khurasani's role was correct, and wondered when the order would be given for Khurasani's hands to squeeze the life out of his windpipe. Even closing his eyes, the man's face was not easy to erase.

'I think', the Commander began, reading over a paper before leaving it in front of Hakim, 'that you will readily sign this document without the slightest hesitation, Doctor Rahbari.'

Instinctively, Hakim reached for his shirt pocket. He'd forgotten that they had taken his spectacles from him when he was brought to prison. From a briefcase the Commander removed Hakim's reading glasses and offered them to him. It was perfect timing.

Hakim thanked the Commander, his conscience telling him it would have been better not to have been granted the opportunity of reading the paper. There was no doubt that it was filled with promises to him if he'd denounce his association with the Bahá'í Faith.

He took the page in his hands, after all he wanted to know what it said. He'd always wanted to enter the next world after a good argument for the Cause of God.

'When you've finished reading, Doctor, please sign next to the seal at the bottom.'

This is why the doctor was there early, Isfahani thought to himself. It was the Ayatullah who was supposed to be the one to present the plan. It was obvious that the Commander had no intention of waiting for him, he wanted all the credit for himself. Isfahani had been made the pawn and there was no action he could take. How he hoped that the Ayatullah would arrive before the doctor signed and see what was happening.

Hakim skimmed down the page. It was a standard letter, he thought. A confession of being an agent for the Universal House of Justice in Israel, therefore a Zionist; being a member of the Bahá'í administration; and other charges that repeated the same basic accusations in more political tones. It was the same fundamental propaganda, lies that had been levied against the Faith for the past decades.

The Commander signed a second sheet and placed it over the one Hakim was still looking at. 'You have my signature on that.'

Hakim removed the sheet and placed it down on the table. He wanted to read the last paragraph of the first document. He shook his head. There was a demand to confess that Muhammad was the 'Seal of the Prophets', too. Every Manifestation of God asserts His firstness and lastness, Hakim thought. To deny one Manifestation was to deny all of them. He shuddered at the thought of ever having to have laid eyes on such a contrived piece of rubbish.

The Commander spoke smoothly. 'You are a surgeon. We don't want you to waste your talents. If you sign the first page, I'll see that all your needs are fulfilled as I have signed in the second. Your house restored, a new job, everything.'

'Surrender my Faith?'

The Commander coolly smiled. 'Yes, Doctor. If you are prepared to be "obedient to your government".'

The Commander knew this Bahá'í principle. Bahá'ís were charged with following the Universal House of Justice, the supreme institution of the Bahá'í Faith. The government considered it political, not religious obedience. This allowed them to condemn the Bahá'ís as 'Spies'.

'Bahá'ís are obedient to the laws of the country they are in, Commander. To the extent of not denying their belief in their Faith.'

The Commander was about to speak again, but Hakim shook his head firmly at him and at Isfahani beyond. He took off his glasses. 'Is it not true in the Cause of Islam that it is against the law of Muhammad to accept bribes for your faith, or to deny any of the Prophets?'

The Commander's face reddened. 'I'm not a mulla, Doctor. We are talking about obedience to your government.'

Isfahani couldn't stay out of it. 'We are not interested in your perverted interpretations of the Holy Qur'án, Doctor. And you are not a mulla either.'

It was a fruitless argument for Hakim to continue. 'No doubt you have prepared a firing squad for my execution, as I have already refused in court to sign any such declaration.'

The Commander whipped away the papers into his briefcase. 'It's not that easy, Doctor. Maybe I should have Khurasani deal with you the way he desires.'

Khurasani slipped something from beneath his jacket. Hakim heard the click of metal. It would soon be over, he told himself.

The Commander rustled through his papers. 'Maybe it would help you to change your mind if I showed you the letter which your wife signed, recanting.'

Hakim's heart pounded loud within his breast.

Isfahani had not learned of this before. The Commander had been quite clever to have hidden this information from him.

If she had signed, Hakim could never face her again. But he prayed it was not true. He looked at the handwriting. It was similar to Ziya's. 'When did she sign?' he asked, emotionless.

'Two days ago!'

Hakim saw the rage in the Commander's eyes. He glanced at the table. 'When you allowed my daughters to visit my wife, the prison guards conveyed my wife's message saying that she was on fire with the love of God.'

Infuriated, the Commander crumpled the page, then took the gun from Khurasani's hand and pressed the barrel against Hakim's temple.

The cold steel was finally in place. Hakim thanked God for having attained steadfastness and closed his eyes.

Isfahani moved up to the table. If the Commander killed him, all his plans were ruined. 'Commander? I should think that Ayatullah Rustami would prefer that we implement his plan. We don't want to offend his preparations, Commander?'

The Warden pulled out his handkerchief and began to scrub the samovar again. He had seen enough and preferred to avoid seeing

34

any more.

Hakim opened his eyes. He turned towards the gun barrel until it came to the center of his forehead. His eyes met the Commander's. He did not challenge him with his stare. He wanted to feel no hate for the one who would act as the instrument for winning him his crown of martyrdom. He closed his eyes.

The Commander's arm shook. He couldn't do it, and bent his elbow away, then extended the weapon to Khurasani. 'Put it away.'

He shredded the second document, and moved behind Isfahani, throwing the bits out of the window to the wind, then turned back. 'My Assistant told us that few Bahá'ís fear their own deaths. So it seems. You are the bravest misguided asses I've ever known.' He came back up to the table. 'Your country could use your skills, Doctor, don't throw away all those years of practice on a false cause.'

Hakim did not feel cheated. There was more shouting and yelling at him from the Commander. He caught sight of the Warden opening the door to look down the hall, and heard the announcement of the man who was coming their way, but already his thoughts were far away, pondering the significance of the words Bahá'u'lláh had revealed in a prayer.

*Armed with the power of Thy name nothing can ever hurt me, and with Thy love in my heart all the world's afflictions can in no wise alarm me.*

The Commander leaned over to him. 'My ways would have been merciful, Doctor. We will see more proficient means of persuasion now. You will sign.'

Hakim understood. It meant that the Ayatullah was an inveterate enemy who hated the Bahá'í Faith. He would have to face the same tests of certitude all over again.

Isfahani was pleased with the strength of the doctor; fascinated. It seemed strange to him that the Bahá'ís never united to attack the mobs that stoned them, razed their property, cursed their being.

The hand of the Commander turned Isfahani towards him, cutting off his thoughts.

'I thought you said this one was weaker than the others? Are you trying to make me a fool before the Ayatullah?'

'Commander,' he said, quietly, not letting Khurasani overhear them, 'He is the weakest. I've dealt with these types before. All one has to do is find his weaknesses, his attachments, then he'll leave his ideals.'

'They all refused to recant!'

'The Ayatullah will show us other ways.'

Mulla Ahmad burst into the room past the Warden. 'I know full well what you are planning.'

His robes spun with his turn back to the door as the Ayatullah and the other mullas followed behind him.

'It is against everything we are here to represent.' The anger in Mulla Ahmad's voice was not rehearsed. He was enraged with the Ayatullah.

Ready to do battle, the Ayatullah began, 'Let us not forget the tradition which says – I have no desire before this crowd to make sport of the holy utterances for your satanic devices.'

The Arabic quotations flew back and forth between them. Few words were understood in the eloquent tongue, yet everyone seemed captivated by the flurried phrases and passages sent back and forth.

Hakim could have told them, from the little Arabic he had studied, the flaws in their quotations, recognizing many. But as Isfahani had pointed out, he was not to be a mulla.

'I've heard enough,' finally spat the Ayatullah, stopping the argument.

'Not enough,' Mulla Ahmad said strongly. 'I've been exposed to your type all my life – you and your kind seek only the Kingdom of Self. You're worse than the Bahá'ís. They're misguided, but you're darkness upon darkness.'

Everyone waited for the Ayatullah to respond. He adjusted his turban, then straightened his robes, showing everyone how unaffected he was by the parry of mere words.

'And you can forget the dramatic pauses,' Mulla Ahmad added. 'Save your breath for answering to God and Qumm. God knows, I will in truth return to them both before this week's end.'

Then Mulla Ahmad turned to Isfahani, again piercing him with his brilliant gaze. 'Don't be so stunned by my outspokenness. We were here to serve God foremost. You'll walk away too one day, the way I am, if God allows you to distinguish between the smell of manure and the fragrance of divine Justice.'

From the door, Mulla Ahmad glanced back to the prisoner. 'May the Almighty have mercy on your soul and teach you to fear none save Him.' Then he whisked around the doorway and disappeared up the hall.

The Ayatullah demanded that the door be closed, then paced up and down in front of the table. Hakim had the feeling that he was about to become the sacrificial lamb. There was no other scapegoat to protect him from the ire of the Ayatullah now that he had lost one of his ranks in front of them all.

The Ayatullah stopped and glared at Hakim. 'Khurasani!' he shouted meanly, getting Khurasani to wipe the grin off his face. Then he pointed at Hakim, and asked the Commander, already knowing what had gone on, 'Did you get this man to sign the document, Commander Rashti?'

'Not yet, Ayatullah,' he said innocently.

Hakim felt Khurasani's short hard breath against the back of his head. The man was nervous for some reason.

'How could you?' the Ayatullah said, lashing out at the Commander. 'This is why I am here – to see that this godless heretic receives the Justice of God, the God of Islam!' He turned to Khurasani. 'When this trial is finished, see that Mulla Ahmad is granted his heart's desire to be with God in Qumm . . . Now go bring your assistants with our other guests.' Khurasani moved quickly to leave, only to be stopped by the Ayatullah's quiet call.

'Khurasani?'

Khurasani went over to him reverently, his eyes directed at the ground. 'Yes, Ayatullah.'

The Ayatullah waited for him to lift his head, turning away so the others couldn't overhear his words. ' . . . Yes, my dear Khurasani . . . I just wanted to compliment you on your efficiency in bringing our guests here at such short notice this morning.'

'My pleasure,' he said, darting his eyes.

'I know!'

Khurasani covered his heart with both hands. 'I had nothing to do with – '

The Ayatullah grabbed his forearms, shutting him up. They spoke quietly.

Hakim was glad he couldn't overhear what they were discussing. Did they think that by breaking an individual they would destroy the validity or establish the falsehood of God's Cause, he wondered. He would find out soon enough. He looked over to the Warden busying himself with cleaning his samovar, obviously waiting for a favorable comment from the Ayatullah.

The other clergymen gathered by the Ayatullah, conversing with him. Khurasani went out and bellowed a command for someone to 'come'.

The Ayatullah kept calm as he turned, looking back at Hakim, assessing him with his glance. 'I suggest that before your eyes behold this sight, you quickly sign the offered statement.'

Hakim made no effort even to acknowledge the warning, but watched the Ayatullah again confer with his fellow-clergymen. Their robes acted like a stage curtain, not allowing Hakim to see the doorway. His heart began to pound. His thoughts began to torture him more than any bastinado or hot irons could do. The world around him was not of science and enlightenment, nor of love.

'Not him!' Khurasani shouted.

Hakim envisioned who 'he' might be. Whoever it was, he had to prepare himself. His heart beat faster in anticipation. He tried to think what 'Abdu'l-Bahá would have done in his place.

He could hear something moving closer, dragging, sliding along the floor up the hallway, and the murmur of muffled voices. They must have tortured one of the friends, he told himself. He was a doctor. He'd seen worse before.

Khurasani came in alone and took his position behind the doctor. Hakim saw the top of two heads of black curly hair, men, coming in with something, or pulling someone. He couldn't see through the clergymen.

The door shut and Ayatullah went to the side of the room. The mullas parted their curtain, revealing two women draped in black chadours, crouched on the floor, released by the men. He tried to stand, not sure who they were, but knew, as he rose, that they were meant to be someone special to him. But Khurasani put his hands firmly on his shoulders, arresting him, forcing him back into his chair.

The women's stifled whimpers filled the room. Isfahani studied them, trying too, to determine who the Ayatullah had had Khurasani's men bring there. He looked at the doctor's face. They must be his family.

The Ayatullah gestured for the Commander and the mullas to take their seats. The chairs in front of the prisoner remained

38

unoccupied, the better for him to see.

The Commander once again set the first document before Hakim. Isfahani stood along the side wall glancing from the doctor to the men towering over the women, then across at the Ayatullah in front of the samovar, pacing across the other side of the room.

Like a dream, rather as if a nightmare were unfolding itself, Hakim fought off realizing who it might be on the floor. It didn't have to be them. Yet his heart screamed – a father knows his children's cries!

The Ayatullah reached past Hakim and lifted the document, reading it clearly for all to hear, approving of its fairness, restating his authority to uphold his divine obligations, then placed the page back on the table he had taken it from. His honey-suckled words rolled over his tongue, 'And all you have to do is sign this declaration.'

The Commander put his pen on the table.

Hakim ignored them. He stared at his daughters. He was Bahá'í. They were Bahá'í. They all knew their fate for standing up as such.

Commander Rashti withdrew his pen and shook his head to the Ayatullah, and everyone. 'We should just exterminate them all.'

'Shall we see, Doctor Rahbari,' the Ayatullah said, challenging him, 'whose God is stronger?'

'My God and your God are one,' Hakim said slowly. 'It is your strengths and mine that are being tested. Not His.'

The Ayatullah didn't have the satisfaction of looking Hakim in his eyes. The doctor kept his gaze on the figures in black.

'Would you suggest that a false god and the God of Islam are the same? Are Satan and Allah the same?' He chuckled.

Isfahani was beginning to see Mulla Ahmad's point, but he had too much to learn from the esteemed Ayatullah, who must know what he was doing. How would he have earned the station of Ayatullah if he wasn't worthy of the title? Isfahani convinced himself, dismissing his own questioning.

The Ayatullah stepped away from the table. 'Show the father his daughters.'

Now Hakim turned his head, staring directly into the eyes of the Ayatullah, without hatred, and without fear.

'Take a good look at your illegitimate offspring.'

39

Khurasani's men ripped away the scarves from the girls. Their hair fell over their bowed faces.

Hakim still stared at the Ayatullah, which made the latter uncomfortable.

'I said "Look at your daughters!"'

Hakim still fixed his gaze.

'Make him look at his daughters!'

Khurasani grabbed Hakim violently by his thinning hair, turning his head away from the Ayatullah. Hakim's glasses flew across the table to the ground.

'O Lord of the Worlds!' he cried within his breast. Tears welled in his eyes. His once pounding heart froze still. The faces of his daughters were revealed, drawn upwards by their thick hair. Hakim's tears couldn't cloud the bruises he saw inflicted on their faces, nor could his daughters raised arms hide them from their father's view. Shiva's lip quivered as she whispered above her breath her shame. 'Oh, Baba.'

Hakim's thoughts filled with human hatred, battling his frailties as a father, searching for his qualities as a Bahá'í. They were his daughters, his children, his loved ones. That was how they wanted him to react. They wanted him to fight, he thought. It was the only way they could achieve their dastardly scheme.

'All praise be to God!' he said with a sigh, then relaxed his tensed frame.

Isfahani was awed by the doctor, and began to wonder if he hadn't chosen the wrong prisoner after all. Unless the Ayatullah was willing to spend months on this one man, Isfahani could no longer see any way to win their goal.

Khurasani released Hakim's head from his grip, wiping off the loose hairs between his fingers. Hakim looked at his Shiva. He couldn't protect her in his arms. God would have to do that. All he could do was inspire her to go on. They all needed to remember their purpose. '*When the swords flash, go forward! When the shafts fly, press onward!*' he said, softly reciting.

'Since you have all violated the laws of the constitution –' the Ayatullah said loudly.

Hakim lost the end of his words, seeing the Ayatullah waving his hands to the men behind his daughters. The nightmare was entering its midmost darkness. There was no way to escape. It was too unbearable to be reality, and yet was.

Out of nowhere, Shiva fell flat on her side, arching, as if kneed in her back by the man who loomed over her. Sholeh cried out in pain, vainly struggling to pull her head free of the hands that still grasped her, only to be twisted violently to the floor.

'Sign!' hollered the Commander.

Hakim spotted a streak of blood where Shiva had slid. She was fighting to sit up, but was rolled to her side as the man pulled on her chadour ripping it open. His eyes saw how muddied her jeans underneath had become. She had obviously been dragged, then given a clean chadour.

'You are a traitor and you will be shot if you don't recant!' warned the Commander.

There was blood on her knee, drops of blood. Hakim wanted to know what vile act had made his daughter bleed. He fought against his anger, then snapped, 'You bastards.' His body shook, trying not to explode further. He began to stand.

Khurasani pressed his weight down on the doctor's shoulders, but Hakim kept rising.

Shiva's chadour was grabbed again. This time the man used it to pull her towards him, which flipped her onto her stomach, ripping her chadour to the height of her jersey.

'Sign. Spy! Recant!' the voices shouted at him continuously.

Where was God's Justice? Hakim could no longer endure this.

Shiva rolled onto her back, trying to untangle herself from the material. Hakim's eyes fell to her pelvis, to the blood-stain on her jeans. Everyone could see. The sight burned into his soul.

'No!'

Khurasani locked Hakim's neck in his arms, yet Hakim stood straight up and turned to the Ayatullah, fuming with anger. '*Kar íst kih shodih!*'

The Ayatullah heard what he said. He looked away from the doctor, then to the girls. He turned away, reluctantly commanding, 'Get the animals off each other.'

'Guards!' called out Isfahani, getting the armed Pasdars at the door to rush in.

The Warden suddenly assumed his authority, pointing at the two men still struggling with the women. 'Now! Remove them.'

The Pasdars kicked Khurasani's men and were attacked by them with punches. The Warden summoned four prison guards to assist.

41

'Put those two in a cell. They'll stand trial,' the Ayatullah made it clear to the Warden, though he glanced at Khurasani.

Khurasani released Hakim from his hold, as the guards rushed his men out. Hakim sank slowly to the floor beside his chair, exhausted.

The Commander glanced over to Isfahani and shook his head. It summed up the whole effort.

Isfahani looked at the weeping girls. He had seen everything. The doctor was right, it was something which 'couldn't be undone', *Kar ist kih shodih*. The Ayatullah had lost the moment, as far as Isfahani was concerned. The girls' innocence had already been destroyed before the show. Khurasani's men would only receive a fine. Isfahani wasn't about to give up his plan. He could still get the doctor to recant; he knew the doctor was still vulnerable – they still had his wife.

Hakim crawled beneath the table to his girls. He gently lifted Shiva, having to reassure her over and over again that it was her father's arms that held her. He wiped the tears and grit off her swollen cheeks. Her mascara blackened her eyes and streaked down her face. She cried over again, '*Kar ist kih shodih*,' as he rocked her gently in his arms. He turned his face to Sholeh, who sat herself up.

She stared into his eyes. 'Oh, Baba. Did you think this display was the first time we suffered this crime at their hands this morning?'

He struggled to find the strength to answer her, then shook his head. 'No, Sholeh dear. I know.'

The command from a firing squad was heard from the courtyard. The blast from the guns rang through the room.

Khurasani spoke aside with the Ayatullah. 'I can go get his wife.'

'Just take the women out! . . . I have to think.'

The Ayatullah pulled his robes forward and went over between Isfahani and the Commander, asking them both. 'Any further suggestions before he's sent to the firing squad? You, Assistant?'

Isfahani spoke out strongly. 'Their innocence would have caused him to recant. He was at the end of his endurance.'

'Their death, too, will be a *kar ist kih shodih*,' the Ayatullah said, ignoring Isfahani's insight. 'And I am at the end of my endurance.'

Khurasani interrupted. 'Should I take the boy out, too, Ayatullah Rustami?'

'Just do what I asked you to do. Take the girls out. OUT!'

Khurasani backed away from the Ayatullah and called for two prison guards to quickly carry out the orders. The girls were removed from Hakim's side. He was able to do nothing, not even find the strength to hold them with his words.

'Be resigned to the will of God, Baba,' Sholeh said, as the guards lifted her to stand. 'He knows your difficulties and ours in His path. *Yá Bahá'u'l-Abhá!*'

His arm reached out to touch them one last time, but they were too far. The sweat poured down his face, burning into his eyes, as they were taken away. It was the last time he would see them, he knew. Sholeh raised her voice, chanting down the hallway,

*O Son of Man! Write all that We have revealed unto thee with the ink of light upon the tablet of thy spirit. Should this not be in thy power, then make thine ink of the essence of thy heart. If this thou canst not do, then write with that crimson ink that hath been shed in My path. Sweeter indeed is this to Me than all else, that its light may endure forever.*

Khurasani moved Hakim back to his chair. The chanting disappeared. His thoughts turned sour, wishing revenge on those who had committed these atrocities. Then his head sunk to his chest . . . He had never thought he was capable of seeking revenge for tests which were to prove his faith. He was far away from the court of God, he thought sadly.

The Ayatullah was engrossed by the Warden with his samovar, studying the ornate piece. He left Isfahani and the Commander to themselves, going over to the small table. He smiled, as if meeting the Warden for the first time. 'Is the tea ready, Warden?'

'Of course, Ayatullah Rustami,' he said proudly, reaching for a small tea pot to transfer the liquid into a serving vessel. 'This samovar has been in my family – '

The Ayatullah stopped him from pouring just yet. 'Is it still hot?'

'Like pure steam!'

'Very beautiful,' he said, smiling even more broadly. 'And may I ask a favor of you?' He beckoned the Warden closer.

The Warden drew reluctantly near, fearing the request would mean the loss of his samovar to the Ayatullah's possession. He listened carefully to the Ayatullah's whisperings, then sighed, with an expression of relief, 'Of course, Ayatullah. I thought it was about the samovar.' He excused himself from the room.

The Ayatullah glanced back to Isfahani. There was no more anger in his demeanor. There was a scheme in his eyes.

'Innocence,' he said, repeating Isfahani's word, nodding his head. Then he turned to the doctor. 'Can I offer you a cup of tea, Doctor?'

Hakim raised his eyes. Through the doorway the Warden re-entered leading a little three-year-old boy by the hand. His cheeks were still red from crying. The dirt streaked canals down his face. 'Baba,' the boy kept whimpering.

Numbed, Hakim stared at his grandson.

'Shut the door, Warden,' the Ayatullah instructed, then told everyone, 'You know, this dear child hasn't eaten all morning.'

He put out his arms. 'Come here, son,' he said gently, going over to him and taking his trusting hand.

Isfahani wondered what the Ayatullah planned now, even seeing how confused everyone else appeared. No one could imagine what was about to happen.

'Tea?' he asked the boy, then glanced to Isfahani. 'Please. Help the boy get some tea.'

Isfahani moved quickly to the samovar, passing the Ayatullah.

'No, no. Take the boy!'

Impatient the Ayatullah called Khurasani. 'Take the boy.'

Isfahani stepped out of their way. His feet stepped further back until his shoes hit the rear wall, as he watched Khurasani stand the boy beneath the spout of the samovar and hand the boy an empty cup to hold. Then Khurasani waited for the Ayatullah's instructions.

The boy looked into the cup, then over to his grandfather.

Hakim closed his eyes, silently imploring, 'O God! He's only a child. I am the Bahá'í. It's not fair. O God, please, please. It's not fair!'

'Now sign the declaration, doctor,' the Ayatullah said coldly. 'Give the doctor your pen, Commander.'

The pen point clicked out, as the Commander placed it on the table again. Hakim sat motionless, keeping his eyes closed, sweating profusely.

'. . . Khurasani? . . . Give the boy some tea.'

The boy's hand couldn't hold the cup. It fell, shattering on the

44

floor. No one made a move. Khurasani looked over to the Ayatullah.

'I said, "Give the boy his tea!"'

Khurasani got the boy's attention, then pointed to his own mouth, showing the boy how to open his.

'Doctor?' the Ayatullah asked once more, turning away from the samovar. 'This is your last chance. Recant.'

There was utter silence. A torturing scream echoed through Hakim's inmost being, melting his heart. He was a Bahá'í. He was a doctor. He had to stop the pain.

He reached for the pen, scribbled his name across the declaration, then dropped it on the table, burying his face in his hands.

The document was whisked away.

Isfahani had faced the wall, unable to watch the act. Figures rushed into the room. A photographer's flash went off in the doctor's face. Isfahani turned to see Khurasani lift the small limp body from the floor with another guard's help and disappear with it out of the room. His Commander was proudly showing the mullas and the Ayatullah the signed document. They had achieved their goal. The means mattered little compared to their important purpose, he reminded himself.

He crossed behind the table, lighting a cigarette. He looked out the window he had opened for a snap of fresh air, only to catch a glimpse of Khurasani, and the boy being carried out of the courtyard. He closed the slats.

The Ayatullah spoke strongly to the beaming Commander. 'And whatever you promised the doctor for his reward, you will carry out.'

The Commander nodded his assurance, then turned to Isfahani, making sure he had heard the order as well. Then he pulled his briefcase towards him and closed it, ready to leave when the Ayatullah was ready.

The Ayatullah nodded to Isfahani. 'Very good, Assistant. I will be interested to learn how well your work progresses in your duties to our government. Release the doctor. Give him back his possessions.' He turned to the Commander. 'If you are as clever as your assistant, bring me the wife's declaration with your career on the line.'

'Of course, Ayatullah. Of course.'

As the room emptied, a volley from the firing squad again

echoed, jarring Hakim from his stupor. His eyes wandered aimlessly, meeting Isfahani's face. What had they done? . . . What had he done?

Isfahani darted his eyes away. He had to forget the individuals who had to face justice. It was the whole. Whatever had been achieved was for the good of Iran – Islam. They were Bahá'ís. Traitors. Bahá'ís. He couldn't hold his thoughts inside. 'It could have been far worse, Doctor! You didn't spit on your Faith. You're alive! Fortunate. Get out! Go home. We'll call you when we're ready. Now, get out! Guards!'

Prison guards rushed to Isfahani's call.

'Put him outside the confines!'

They removed Hakim from his chair, dragging him out of the room.

Isfahani stood alone. From the hallway he heard the doctor shout out hoarsely, 'Kill me! Kill me! . . . Kill me . . .'

The picture of the Revolutionary Leader seemed to stare down at him. It didn't inspire him at the moment. There was more work to be done. 'Damn heretics!'

# CHAPTER 4

# The Veils of Mind

The summons to dawn prayer echoed through the old section of Kashan as the star-filled sky became tinted by the magenta horizon. The sun rose, casting its first beams of light across the flat row of roof tops, where a few children awoke and ran from house to house playing.

Through a wooden doorway in the alley a little girl danced out into the street singing merrily. She pressed a sweet lemon she held in her hand along the endless storey-high walls and skipped away from home. Her airy dark blue chadour flapped behind her, and her scarf fell to her neck, letting her dark brown hair bounce free.

Hakim's tired figure rested against the same wall. He had been there all night, unable to walk any further. He never considered that anyone would bother him, until the child stood beside him. He looked over at the girl. Her eyes were lovely, almond-shaped, with dark irises like chocolate. Her nose was small and delicate, her cheeks high, her jaw long and smooth. She was a pretty one. It made him wonder how anyone could hate Muslims, seeing such a creation as this. He didn't have the energy to tell her to go play somewhere else. He just hoped she would go away and leave him be.

Up the two steps, out of the doorway came an older woman robed in a black scarf and chadour searching for the girl. When she saw her granddaughter before the strange man, she held her scarf at her chin and scurried up to the scene. It was only after a few steps out that she realized who the man was, and gasped. 'O Lord of Creation!' she said, not daring to go any closer, then tried to get the attention of her granddaughter by hissing.

Hakim heard the woman treating him like some poor leper.

A man's voice called out from inside the opened doorway. 'What's wrong, mother? Who are you yelling at this early?'

'Your daughter,' she called back.

'Ssst! Let her play,' he said tiredly.

47

Hakim stared into the girl's unflinching eyes. She certainly wasn't going to move: he was supposed to do that, by the look of her frozen stare of warning. There was no love in her eyes for Hakim to see. She appeared ready to spit on him if he didn't move instantly. Hakim lost his respect for this progeny of Islam. She wasn't so sweet anymore, so he growled, 'Muhammad eats you!'

The girl dropped her lemon and ran back to her grandmother, who immediately scolded her and towed her away to the house.

The girl's father came out and saw them. Beyond, he spied the strange man against their outer wall. 'Who's that?'

'Dr Rahbari,' his mother answered, rushing inside past him.

'Dr Rahbari?' he asked with a question on his face.

'Call your father.'

The son left that for his mother to do. He buttoned up his shirt and headed for the doctor. He kept his eyes on the other doorways and the alley behind him, making sure no one was watching his movements.

After a moment the father came out and shouted to his son, 'Leave him be!'

The man stopped beside Hakim, ignoring his father's command.

Hakim couldn't have run even if he wanted to. The first vulture to pick at his remains had arrived, he thought, certain of the man's intent.

The man saw his father coming up the street after him. He turned to Hakim, speaking sharply. 'Go home, Doctor. We don't want any trouble with devils like you.'

'You've burnt my house down,' he said frankly.

'We had nothing to do with that.'

'I told you to come!' the father said, halting halfway to them and pointing to the ground.

'I'm coming!'

'Now!'

Other neighbors began to come out to see what the ruckus was all about. The son said to Hakim with a snarl, 'Then go to your relatives' house. Do you understand me, Doctor? Get lost!'

Another door opened across from them. A middle-aged man dressed in his work clothes came out. 'What's all the shouting?' he asked, coming over to them. He stopped beside the standing man, shocked to see it was Doctor Rahbari in such a disheveled state.

The way his neighbor's son wouldn't look at him or at least offer an explanation made him suspicious. He called out for his wife. 'Khanum!' A petite red-headed woman peered out from the entrance towards his call. 'Run and ask Asiyih Khanum to come for her brother.'

The woman slipped on a scarf and hurried up the alley.

'Don't send your wife to bring those people on our street,' the father snapped at his neighbor. 'They're all Bahá'ís. Do you want to place our lives in danger?' He cleared his throat and spat on the ground in the doctor's direction.

The neighbor lashed back. 'If your wife ever needs a surgeon again', he said, loud enough for the man's wife to hear from the doorway she was hiding in, 'make sure she's not admitted to the hospital – take her to the cemetery. The doctors are all Bahá'ís!'

The old woman followed her husband's example and spat out into the street.

The neighbor's wife searched up another alley, hoping that the door she knocked on was the correct one. Asiyih opened her door and greeted the woman as a dear friend.

'Please, Asiyih Khanum,' the woman said, forgetting the courtesies. 'Come quickly.'

'What's the trouble?'

'It's your brother, Dr Rahbari.'

Asiyih shouted to her husband, 'Jamshid, come!' then rushed out in her dress, forgetting the chadour.

Jamshid came to the courtyard trying desperately to finish knotting his tie. The front door was wide open. Where was his wife, he thought fearfully, and dashed into the alley. He caught sight of the two women hurrying up the street. It had to be one of the family.

The cruel whispers of gossip that encircled Hakim made him long for death. He hoped that someone would douse him with petrol and end his misery with the strike of a match. It wouldn't be long before the Revolutionary Guards or some vigilante group came to disperse the crowd and drag him away, he thought.

When the crowd parted, he heard someone call his name, but didn't recognize the face. It was the touch he knew.

'Hakim,' she said with a sigh, lovingly. Her hand reached out

49

for his shoulder, soothing him.

Jamshid burst through the bystanders, out of breath. 'What's happened? Asiyih . . . Hakim?' His body slumped, shocked at Hakim's condition.

The thoughtful neighbor came over to Jamshid and addressed him gently, 'Mr. Danesh. We found the distinguished doctor in this condition. He hasn't moved.' Jamshid nodded his thanks, then slowly walked in front of Hakim and faced him. He put his arms on his shoulders. 'Hakim?'

Asiyih looked back at the neighbor and his wife. 'Thank God he is safe. May my life be a sacrifice to you – you have been very kind.'

Jamshid slipped Hakim's arm over his shoulder and pulled him away from the wall. Before their first steps towards the crowd the father and son came forward and blocked their way.

'I want you to know', the father said stoutly, 'that neither my son, nor I, nor any of my family had anything to do with the doctor's house being burned down – or with any of his belongings being swiped.'

Jamshid wasn't interested in the man's confession. 'No one has ever suggested it, sir.'

'Or with any of their arrests!'

'I am neither a court of law nor God. Save your confessions for them.'

Jamshid turned away from the discussion, knowing it would have only led to a fight.

'I don't need to confess anything to anyone!' he swore.

'Leave them be, brother,' the neighbor said, stepping in.

'You are becoming a lover of Satan!' the father said accusingly.

Asiyih placed her brother's other arm on her shoulder and they walked him away between them.

The neighbor saw their move. He smiled; his mind became full of thoughts. 'You know, my dear neighbor, he began purpose-fully, 'the Pasdars wanted to know if there were any other Bahá'í meetings in the area. Now I may be wrong, but as I remember overhearing in the bazaar, your home was mentioned as a site of activity.'

'Who said that! Who said such a lie?' he shouted above the crowd's whispering.

Jamshid and Asiyih had slipped beyond the other side of the

crowd, when they heard the jeers beginning. The testy young man was trying to pick a fight with another neighbor to defend his family honor. The kind neighbors had also found a way out and were disappearing behind the safety of their front door.

Without delay, Jamshid headed home. He kept the conversation light, telling Hakim about trivial occurrences, about his business, how well Saffa was doing in his studies, what they would enjoy for lunch that afternoon.

When they arrived home, Jamshid helped Hakim into their bedroom. Saffa had just come home from school and rushed to help them.

Asiyih pulled the bed's quilt back, then placed the pillows against the headboard. 'Saffa, bring some juice for your uncle!'

Hakim sat on the edge of the bed. Jamshid tried to help him to lean back against the pillow, but he leaned forward, preferring to rest his elbows on his knees and his head in his hands.

Asiyih couldn't relax, seeing her brother like this. She didn't know what to offer him. 'Please. Lie back, Hakim.'

He shook his head. Saffa came in with a sweet mint drink and held it out to his uncle, who only shook his head. Asiyih tried to give it to him, but had to resign herself to leaving it on the table beside the bed. With every offer of food or drink she made she could only get Hakim to shake his head. Finally she gave up, looking at her husband, hoping he could do something.

Mitra entered struggling to take off her chadour over her blouse, and came to stand silently beside her brother. Saffa couldn't imagine what horrors his uncle had actually undergone while in prison. He only saw that his uncle, the pillar of faith, had crumbled. It meant the defeat of the whole community to him. Who would the friends turn to now in difficulty, he wondered.

Jamshid glanced at the faces of his family, all in shock. It was his place to unravel what had happened. There were still seven more believers in jail, whose fate was unknown. He had to find out everything.

He crouched on his knees at the bedside before Hakim and spoke slowly, softly. 'Are you hurt anywhere, Doctor?'

Hakim finally shook his head.

A sigh of relief fell over Asiyih's lips, and gratitude. '*Yá Bahá'u'l-Abhá.*'

Jamshid took a deep breath. 'Do you want to talk about it?'

Hakim couldn't gather his thoughts. He felt as though his mind was robbed of them, of its direction.

Jamshid pursued with ease. 'The others?'

Hakim's head was throbbing within. He didn't know where to begin. Where were all his friends? he thought in desperation. Then he breathed, remembering, 'No . . . '

'No?' Jamshid listened, hoping Hakim would say more.

'. . . no . . . '

Asiyih covered her mouth, and closed her eyes, moaning.

Hakim looked over at Jamshid for the first time. The agony in his eyes was intolerable to Jamshid. He took Hakim's hand, holding it tightly. Their tears flowed long before the words.

Hakim had to tell them, however painful. It was his duty. He looked at Asiyih to speak, sniffling between his words. 'They, ah, were sent to Evin prison – I don't know.' He looked down, unable to tell them anything else. After a while he looked into Jamshid's eyes. 'Where is Ziya?'

'She's doing fine. She's doing fine. Right now it's more important – '

'Don't treat me like a geriatric case, Jamshid,' he roared hoarsely through a cough.

The room became uncomfortably still. They too had knowledge they were not revealing to him. It showed in Jamshid's and Asiyih's faces. 'Where have they taken her?' he asked them.

Jamshid stood up, unable to answer him. Asiyih was at a loss for words. It meant Ziya was still imprisoned – they hadn't yet let her go. He had to go back.

'Sit down, Hakim,' Jamshid said, seeing him rise.

'Ziya needs me.'

'Don't be ridiculous,' Asiyih said. 'They won't let you in to see her. Do something, Jamshid!'

Jamshid showed Asiyih his empty hands. 'What can I do? If it were you, I would do the same.'

When they had visited Hakim in prison the barred aisle between them and the guards that paced it had never allowed them to speak freely. 'We weren't able to tell you what happened to your house after everyone was arrested.' She didn't know what else to say.

'I saw last night,' Hakim said, then headed out towards the front door.

Jamshid was first to follow, stopping Hakim in the courtyard. 'I'll come too.'

'I'm going alone.'

'Must you always try to do things alone?' he demanded, losing his temper with him. 'Rely on us – your family, your loved ones, your friends. Even the strong souls need companions.'

Hakim turned away. 'You don't understand.'

'You don't have to be a martyr to prove your courage!' he shouted after him, then ran out, leaving Asiyih with the children. 'Hakim!' He finally got ahead of Hakim halfway up the alley; his anger left him. 'There's more,' he revealed. 'One of the friends woke us before we found you this morning . . . the Revolutionary Guards came for your daughters yesterday morning. They just went to collect a few things from Sholeh's house . . . We searched everywhere. They deny having taken them.'

He expected Hakim to fall to the ground, shattered, over-whelmed by the news, but instead it was he who was shocked by his coldness.

'If you believe in prayers, Jamshid, then pray for my forgiveness,' he said, walking away alone. 'God has ceased to hear my prayers.'

He left Jamshid standing there. He didn't have time to be pampered by his sister's family. He had to get to Ziya. She was the only one he could turn to who would understand. She was his companion; she knew his shortcomings and his greatness. She would understand why he had done what he had to do. He was still a Bahá'í, he told himself.

His shoes pounded the pavement to the tall tan brick wall of the prison. He headed along its side towards the main gate, unaware of the morning traffic of cars and people who passed him by. Then without any warning, he slammed his fist into the wall beside him, screaming within. Where was the justice of God? How could He leave this pitiful, worthless servant alone at the time of his greatest longing? How could God suffer His chosen ones to be inflicted again with the same cruelties and humiliations which the Dawnbreakers had endured, the same vile acts which had been perpetrated against the followers of the Báb and Bahá'u'lláh only a century ago. What good was it? What did it win? Where was

God's protection when one needed it?

He rocked himself, holding his throbbing hand. Weren't twenty thousand lives of defenseless men, women and children already enough to water the tree of existence, he thought.

Three women arguing amongst themselves passed Hakim by. They lined up in front of the gate behind the other people waiting to get into the prison. All he could see were the tens of black chadours solemnly standing, as if waiting to attend a funeral. He joined them, giving up his futile war within, suggesting to himself that maybe the world had plunged a little deeper into the darkness of persecution and ignorance, even more than in the early days. He shouldn't lose hope. Behind everything there was a wisdom.

'Who do you want to see?' the prison guard asked when he finally reached the gate.

Others were impatiently waiting to enter behind him. Hakim saw the center prison block ahead across the outer yard. 'My name is Dr Rahbari. I've come to see my wife.'

Another guard in the security post heard his name and made a quick call, telling his comrade to make the doctor step aside.

Hakim did as he was instructed, watching where the 'passed' visitors were queued up again at the center block, seeking further admission to the visiting rooms. He didn't want to see his wife in a cage and be unable to touch her, to be separated by the walk of guards and bars as he had been when Jamshid and Asiyih had visited him. He needed to be near her, alone with her.

Two Pasdars appeared at the post, directed by the gate guards to the doctor. Hakim followed them to the visitors' area.

He recognized the hall they turned down. There was the worn red tiled floor he had passed through on the day before. As they went by the now closed door of the room he had been tortured in, he kept his chin to his tie, watching the steps of his feet. This was not the way to the visiting area. He was ushered into a room at the end of the hall and left alone. It was the same kind of room: one table, a few chairs, a frosted window at the rear to the courtyard, and propaganda plastered on the walls. Had God answered his request, he wondered, or was this another stage of a trap he had walked into?

The moments passed. No one had come. His thoughts ran over

a thousand questions; was she coming, were they listening, was she not coming, was there more for him to endure . . .

The door knob twisted open and he spun around, catching a glimpse of a passing clergyman's robe going up the hall. Into the room, striding majestically, came Ziya. Her issued black scarf and chadour could not dampen the radiance of her spirit. Her eyes sparkled, her whole being seemed to resonate serenity. It was hard for Hakim to realize this was the same simple village girl he had married so long ago. His legs had frozen, unable to step towards her.

She saw his condition and said, to cheer him, 'Are you happy, my beloved?'

He couldn't even shake his head to answer, so overwhelmed was he by her presence.

She placed her hands between her breasts. 'I am. My heart is on fire and my soul is burning with joy.'

His head fell forward. 'Ziya?'

She stood where she was, paces from him. The door was still open behind them. She closed her welling eyes, letting her tears splash to her cheeks. 'I'm here, my beloved.'

'. . . Where are you going?'

Her smile illuminated her face. Her words trembled with courage. 'Unto God, the All-Possessing, the Help in Peril, the Self-Subsisting.'

'You can't go. I need you. I –'

He choked on his words. He covered his face, pouring his anguished heart into his hands.

Ziya came close. She stroked her fingers through his hair. 'Oh, Hakim . . . Don't be sad. The greatest bounty we can obtain is to die to this transient world of dust, sacrificed for the glory of His Cause. Oh, Hakim dear, what has happened to your longing after God?'

She seemed cold, distant to him. 'I don't long for God, I long for you.' He turned away.

She tried to reach out, but restrained her hand from touching him again. 'I know what trials you have faced and the Blessed Beauty knows. These trials I must now face, too.' Receiving no response from him, she said painfully, but with faith, 'If you long for true reunion, with God, then you will find me.'

'Ziya, don't you understand? I am dead, alone without you.'

She came close and took his rough face in her hands. 'We are only dead if we allow our suffering to become a veil which separates us from God. Tests and trials do not happen to us by chance, they are sent to us for our own perfecting. Isn't this the reality of this transitory realm?'

He turned his head from her hands. 'I'm not perfect. Oh, Ziya. Let's go home. I'll take care of everything. Everything will be all right.'

'What has so unnerved your constancy?' she said, trying to snap him back to the reality around them.

'You don't know what I've suffered!'

'God knows what we all have suffered. He is the All-Knowing, the All-Wise!'

'Don't speak to me with mere words.'

He stared into her eyes. She seemed so distant to him. It wasn't that she didn't understand what he was bemoaning, it was that he was far away from understanding himself.

They all stood outside, listening. The Ayatullah looked back at Commander Rashti in the hallway beside the door. 'So much for your promise. Her faith is like a mountain. And as for your hero.' He shook his head, disappointed, then motioned for everyone to enter behind him.

'It's an honor to see you again, brother,' the Commander said, greeting the doctor, although Hakim ignored them. 'Your husband is a great man, a son of Islam. You should follow his example, Khanum.'

Ziya kept her gaze on her husband, not answering them, hoping that Hakim would look into her eyes to see her love for him.

Isfahani stood beside the other clergymen, deliberately keeping himself in the background. The Ayatullah crossed his arms over his chest. 'Have you nothing more to say to your honey-tongued wife, Dr Rahbari?'

Hakim wiped his face dry. 'My wife, Ayatullah?' He stared into her eyes and felt her support, then turned back to the assemblage. 'My wife is not here in this nether world like us.'

The Ayatullah walked around to see Ziya's face. 'And your husband, Khanum?'

Ziya took her stare from her husband's frame. Her eyes became sharp as they glared at the Ayatullah fearlessly, 'This morning you showed me a picture of my daughters and grandchild. Did you not also show me a picture of my dead husband?'

'We most certainly did not! Your husband is alive.'

'My husband is dead,' she re-affirmed. 'Only God grants life. Not clergymen, nor nations, nor those who join partners with God.'

'Take her out! I've had enough of heretics!' the Ayatullah spat, then swung around, calling in the guards. 'Out! I'm weary of this foul-odored poetess!'

She did know everything, Hakim thought, as the guards came, taking her past him. He saw the gentle glance, the silent love she still had for him as they took her away.

Hakim stepped forward towards the door. His arms reached out, appearing to Isfahani as though he was going to strangle the still complaining Ayatullah now in front of the doorway. Isfahani couldn't pull out his gun quick enough, and instead lunged forward in front of the Ayatullah and stopped Hakim. The sudden movements caused the Ayatullah to raise his hands in defense and howl for help. Seeing that Isfahani had his attacker, he hollered, 'You call this a hero! Did you see what he just attempted? Commander?'

Hakim gazed aimlessly beyond the doorway. 'No,' he gently whispered.

The Ayatullah was being calmed by the other clergymen and the Commander. Isfahani came to realize there never had been any fight in the doctor's action; it was a mistake. He released his grasp and just watched the doctor.

Like his daughter, Ziya too was chanting as she was taken away.

*Cause me, O my Lord, to be reckoned among them who have been so stirred up by the sweet savors that have been wafted in Thy days that they have laid down their lives for Thee and hastened to the scene of their death in their longing to gaze on Thy beauty and in their yearning to attain Thy presence.*

Hakim followed the direction of her voice until he faced the back wall of the room, towards the inner courtyard.

*And were any one to say unto them on their way, 'Whither go ye?' They would say, 'Unto God, the All-Possessing, the Help in Peril, the Self-Subsisting!'*

The peel of gunfire rang beneath the firing command. And the chanting ceased.

Isfahani stared at his ex-prisoner.

'. . . And I want that man made an example of!' bellowed the Ayatullah, continuing. 'Assistant? Are you listening? Make him a public hero. Then bury him somewhere far from here. Poison is poison!'

The mullas and Commander followed him out.

Hakim's mouth dropped open, 'What have I done? What have I done?'

Isfahani paced, then stopped abruptly and looked at him. 'You could have saved her life!'

'There was no choice,' he answered back.

'Don't give me that philosophical trash. YOU chose to live!'

'She chose too.' Then he said, more softly, 'To love God.'

'Words. Stupid words separated you!' Isfahani left in a rage.

Hakim closed his reddened eyes. 'Not words. Not words. Worlds, worlds . . .' He drew his hand to his mouth and bit the ring on his finger. 'I'm not dead,' he said, alone. 'Damn! Where are You when I need You!' He beat his bruised fist against his leg. 'Why, why, dear God, have you abandoned me unto my own self?' he moaned, his voice hoarsening. Violently, he ripped his ring off his finger and flung it across the room, then fell on the floor exhausted, sobbing.

Isfahani came back with two Pasdars. 'Take him out!' As they removed him, Isfahani shouted up the hallway, 'Render thanks to God that you're still alive, Doctor.' Isfahani was breathing hard. His thoughts whipped inside like a sandstorm. What did they gain, a recanting? Justice? A puppet hero for the restless masses to admire?

'Career!' he said, reminding himself. 'Duty.'

His eyes caught the glint of a golden object on the floor of the room. He went over and picked up the ring, then polished it off and studied the engraved design of unusual calligraphy.

'There's a tradition,' a Pasdar began, standing in the doorway watching Isfahani.

Isfahani stared over at the man, seeing who was spying on him.

'. . . that there are three thousand names of God,' the Pasdar continued. 'One thousand are known by the Angels; another thousand by the Prophets and chosen ones. Three hundred are recorded in the Torah, three hundred in David's Psalms, three hundred in the Gospels, and in the Holy Qur'án ninety-nine names are recorded. Yet there is one remaining Name, the Most Great Name, which will be revealed when the Promised One arises. It is said that that is the symbol.'

The Pasdar clearly pointed to the ring Isfahani held.

'You talk too much. Move on.'

The Pasdar shrugged, saluted and obeyed.

Isfahani studied the design more closely, then dropped the ring into his buttoned shirt pocket. 'This is my rightful reward.'

# CHAPTER 5

# Fallen Idols

Jamshid slipped off his shoes inside his front door and rubbed his burning soles. He wasn't so used as he had thought to so much walking, and there were more places to search before the day wore through. The shallow courtyard pool looked soothing enough to dip his toes into, or a tub of water would have been more inviting, but he'd only come home to see that everyone was all right. He heard Mitra's voice coming from Saffa's room, then Asiyih answering her. He headed slowly towards them. 'Asiyih Khanum?'

'Yes,' she called out. 'In here.'

Jamshid was surprised to see Saffa sitting on the bed with them. He wasn't supposed to be home this early from school.

Asiyih wrung out a small cloth over a bowl of water, then handed it to Saffa, who pressed it against his left cheek before turning to his father.

'Anything?' Asiyih asked him.

Mitra bounced off her bed and ran into her father's arms.

Jamshid bent down. 'Kiss?'

She planted a smack on his cheek, then ran back to the unattended book she was flipping through.

Jamshid took his time, there was no hurry to see Saffa's hidden bruise. He came over to the bed and sat between his children, slowly. There were other parts of him that weren't as fit as he had imagined.

'How are you, Saffa?' he asked casually.

Saffa nodded, not looking over at him.

'School!' Mitra said proudly.

Saffa glanced past his father to show Mitra how much he appreciated her assistance. He was going to have to teach her when to speak her views and when not to. He caught his father's stare.

'Were you fighting, Saffa?'

'Defending, Baba,' he answered.

'Yourself?'

'No, Baba. I was defending the Cause of God.'

Jamshid raised his eyebrows, then shook his head with a sigh. 'A Bahá'í must not fight.'

'I didn't fight, I defended,' he said, cooling his bruise with his cloth, then, reconsidering his statement, 'I should have attacked.'

'Saffa dear,' Asiyih said, reprimanding him.

'I didn't,' he said, swinging around to her.

'Why did you fight?' Jamshid asked, getting Saffa to face him again.

'Because the teacher spoke out in class against the Faith. And I spoke out against his accusation.'

His parents waited for him to explain. Saffa sighed. 'He said that the Bahá'ís were against Muhammad, and I told him Bahá'ís were the followers of all God's Messengers. So then he accused Bahá'ís of being against Islam. So I said, "Bahá'ís are to consort in fellowship with the followers of all God's faiths." He said I was against the government, and I quoted the words of Bahá'u'lláh about being the well-wishers of every government and how we consider loyalty to our government as a virtue before God.'

Asiyih felt very pleased by her son's bravery. She perceived the same pride on Jamshid's face.

Saffa looked at the floor, throwing his cloth down beside him. His bruise was visibly deep purple, following his cheek bone under his entire eye. He was more than upset.

Jamshid glanced to Asiyih. She knew that he wanted to be alone with Saffa for a few moments. 'Let's get some fresh water. Come, Mitra.'

She fetched the cloth and picked up the bowl of dirty water. Mitra grabbed up her oversized book and followed her mother out.

Jamshid tried to sit more comfortably. He slipped his feet out of his slippers and rubbed one foot with the other. He spoke without rushing Saffa. 'Anything else?'

'No.'

That answered Jamshid's question. Saffa was covering up for someone else – only one person. 'What did your teacher say about Uncle Hakim?'

'. . . That he was loyal to the government, not I.'

61

'And?'

Saffa glanced directly into his father's eyes. 'I told him that no true Bahá'í would surrender his Faith even if persecuted. At that, the student next to me smacked me with his book. When I raised my hands to stop him from hitting me, another boy grabbed me. I kicked the one in front of me to stop him from hitting me with the book. The teacher had me thrown out of class for starting the fight.'

Saffa's eyes welled. 'I used to look up to Uncle Hakim, Baba.'

Jamshid lowered his head. 'I know, Saffa. Maybe one day we'll all be able to look up to him again.'

Saffa wiped his face, before anyone else might enter.

'Why'd he do it?'

'I don't know.'

'I'm glad I kicked that – '. He held his words back, seeing his mother and sister coming back in. She handed him a fresh damp cloth.

'They suspended me because I am a Bahá'í.'

'You must just keep studying if you want to become a doctor one day,' she said positively. 'This will all pass and you'll be back in school before long.'

Saffa turned to his father. 'I'm proud of what I did. I felt like a king and all the people were gathered around cheering and applauding as I walked home past the bazaar.'

Mitra giggled. 'There was no one in the street!'

Jamshid tickled her, then grabbed her close in his arms. 'He knows that.' He whispered in her ear, 'Maybe angels were applauding.'

Her face lit up, imagining the possibility. 'Ah,' she sighed, understanding.

Asiyih changed the mood to one more basic. 'Have you eaten, dear?'

'Not now,' Jamshid said, standing up beside Mitra. 'Saffa and I will have to keep looking for Hakim.'

'Let the boy rest.'

'I want to go,' Saffa said energetically, and dropped the cloth back into the bowl still in his mother's hand.

'Good,' Jamshid said, stretching his arms and legs as best he could. 'Go by the prison, then to the bazaar. And I'll take a bus or a taxi for the rest of the afternoon.'

'Yes, Baba,' he said and dashed out before his mother could stop him.

She called after him, 'Stay out of trouble. Please, Saffa!'

Saffa jumped over a small potted plant in the courtyard, nearly falling into the shallow pool, and landed clumsily on his feet, which jarred his cheek painfully. It was then he decided the rest of the journey was better at a walk.

He made a detour of the prison to go and see his uncle's home. It hadn't been safe to visit before this, but he determined now was his best chance. He had heard the rumors that floated through his school halls, but wanted to see for himself what had actually happened.

What he found, pushing open the splintered wooden door, was only the fragmented skeleton of a home. Graffiti, red and black, were painted and sprayed all over the once white walls. The rooms were charred from burnt furnishings that couldn't be stolen so easily. His aunt's vegetable garden was dug up, her potted plants spilled out. There was nothing left. He picked up a dead plant off the now broken tiled floor and walked into his uncle's bedroom. Saffa found burnt pages of old books. He guessed what they were. Uncle Hakim's Bahá'í books that he kept hidden in his room. Some were irreplaceable.

He put the plant down on the ashes. Uncle Amin had related how the same type of scene had happened with much more intensity in the city of Shiraz. One marvelous story was about an old woman who had lost everything. When the friends found her still in her home, she wanted to stay, and showed them the orange tree in her garden. For sixteen years it had never borne a single fruit; now it had unexpectedly become laden with oranges, which she saw thankfully as a sign from God . . .

Saffa said a prayer quietly, then picked himself up and went out without being seen.

He followed his father's instructions from there, and planted himself across the street from the prison gate, watching the traffic pass by and the visitors come and go. Some other boys were kicking a soccer ball up the pavement, which made Saffa itch to play. Another youth whistled from across the street near the prison entrance. The ball sailed over the traffic to him. Saffa admired the way this youth handled the ball, bouncing it on both knees to his shoulder and head, then slamming it off the wall back to the other boys. Now Saffa really wanted to show off his skills.

The talented youth cut across the street near Saffa. He was about to speak to him when he noticed a bus exchanging passengers in front of the gate. Saffa wouldn't forget the youth – there was a scarf of unusual color dangling out of his back pocket. He could catch up with him as soon as he checked the bus out.

The traffic caught him in the middle of the street. As he waited to go, his thoughts drifted to Uncle Hakim, who had given Aunt Ziya the most beautiful silk scarf for New Year, Naw-Ruz, last month. He remembered how the vibrant colors stood out, and how much his aunt loved the simple gift.

The traffic cleared. Saffa stopped half-way through his step. Then he asked himself, what was a guy his age doing, walking around with a silk scarf hanging out of his trouser pocket? He turned back and saw the youth in the distance up the main street. 'Aunt Ziya's scarf! Hey you! Wait a moment!'

Saffa ran at full speed up the middle of the street calling to him. The youth must have thought he was wanted on some charge, and wasted no time in running away.

'Wait!' Saffa shouted after him.

The youth dodged through the traffic and disappeared up an alleyway. Saffa picked up his legs and dashed after him. A car swerved, nearly hitting him. He leaped to the other side and accidently plowed into a woman with groceries. He helped the lady up, filling her bags with the fallen goods, apologizing.

Two Pasdars heard the woman shouting, saw Saffa pick her up, then rush away. They went after him.

Saffa had lost him. He searched up and down the next main street with a quick glance, then decided to go up a further alleyway, trying to out-guess the one he chased. He went up the alleyway with the least people and the most rubbish bins. Out of nowhere the youth jumped out in front of him, wielding his pocket knife.

'I should cut your guts out,' he said, ready to fight. 'Why are you following me?'

'I thought I had lost you,' was all Saffa could say, relieved to find him but scared of the weapon.

'I wish you had,' he said, pointing the knife beyond Saffa to an approaching Pasdar who now spotted them. From the opposite direction a second Pasdar closed in.

Saffa looked at the youth. 'Put away your knife or we'll both be thrown in jail.' He closed his knife into his hand, holding it in his pocket as the two came up and cornered them.

'Which one knocked the sister down?' asked the grizzly-faced one.

'Not me,' said the youth, gesturing with his head to blame Saffa.

The Pasdars turned to Saffa. The youth tried to make a run for it, only to be grabbed and slammed into a trash can by the second Pasdar. The knife fell to the ground. The Pasdar stepped on it, then picked it up, holding the youth at arms length.

The grizzly-faced Pasdar grabbed Saffa's arm to hold him, looking at his struggling comrade. 'He wouldn't have tried that if he didn't have something to do with it as well.' He shook Saffa. 'What were you doing back there?'

Saffa trembled, searching for an answer. He didn't want to lie, he only wanted to get out of the situation. So he told a half-truth. 'Then you saw me help the woman up?'

'I thought – '

'And then run after this one, after helping her up?' he said quickly. 'Check his pocket. He's got my Aunt's scarf. In his right back pocket, brother.'

The second Pasdar pulled the youth closer to him and removed the scarf from where Saffa said it would be. A crowd of bystanders started to gather around them.

'He's a liar!' the youth swore, as the scarf went across to the first Pasdar's hand. 'That scarf was given to me by my sister.'

'So where's your sister?' the second Pasdar asked.

'In prison,' he said. 'Some older woman gave it to her as a gift before they executed her. Now give it back.'

It definitely was his aunt's scarf. And the youth's story went through Saffa as if the pocket knife had cut out his heart.

'How do you know she was executed?' the first Pasdar wanted to know.

'May my ears be cut off if I am lying!'

The second Pasdar pulled the youth up by one of his ears. 'Great story, little brother. I should cut this off!' He swung him around and sent him to the dirt, letting him go.

The first Pasdar tucked the scarf in Saffa's shirt pocket, then kicked him in his rear into the crowd. Someone caught him from falling, but Saffa rubbed his sore cheek, which was stinging horribly, against his well-wisher's arm.

'If I catch you fighting again you'll get a lot worse!' the Pasdar warned him.

The other Pasdar opened his acquired knife. 'And I'll cut both your ears off!'

The first Pasdar jumped towards Saffa to frighten him, and he fell back into the crowd and hurried away, till an arm reached out at the alley corner and pulled him around the block. He tried to cry out.

'Saffa!'

There was his father, sternly looking at him, holding him in his strong grasp. Jamshid walked him away. 'What happened back there?'

Saffa reached in his shirt pocket and gave his father the scarf, explaining simply how he had got himself into so much difficulty. Jamshid kissed the cloth and placed it in his own pocket. They would talk about Saffa's conduct when Jamshid got home later; in the meantime he pointed Saffa in that direction.

Saffa watched his father go off to continue to look for Uncle Hakim. He went to the intersection and checked the street light, waiting for the green. On the other side of the street he saw a hand waving towards him and heard his mother call his name. He quickly looked the other way, to go in the other direction, but the lights changed. He had nowhere to hide.

'Saffa dear, didn't you hear me calling you?' she asked, coming across to him.

'Yes,' he said, then changed the subject, asking himself what his mother would want to hear from him. 'Any news?'

They both shook their heads.

'Where are you going now, Saffa?'

'Home.'

'Have you seen your father?'

'No – Yes.'

'No, yes, what? Saffa,' she said, knowing she'd have to pry it out of him.

'Yes. He met me and told me to go home. We thought you were there, too. Where's Mitra?'

'Uncle Amin's. And why aren't you wearing a jacket or a sweater? It's not warm enough yet to run around in only a shirt.'

He became apologetic, happy though that her concerns were turned away from what he hoped his father would be the one to disclose to her. 'I'll go by Uncle Amin's and get Mitra.' The light changed and he ran across the street. 'He's in your father's shop. And stay by the phone,' she shouted after him. She couldn't understand why he was in such a hurry until she spied a group of Saffa's rougher classmates heading up the street in her direction. It was better he had left so suddenly.

By dusk as many of the friends as could come safely to Jamshid's house had assembled. It was dangerous for the Bahá'ís to gather in one place, considering how high the tension still was in the city around them.

Saffa had hoped that his mother would be back before they began the simple memorial. His father chanted the prayer for the dead. Saffa sat beside Mitra on the carpet, looking straight ahead at the framed picture they had of Aunt Ziya and at her scarf sitting on the table. The photograph had captured his aunt in a candid moment, when Uncle Hakim had wanted to take her picture while she was watching television. She was looking at the camera disapprovingly, but with a smile of amusement. That was Aunt Ziya, now a martyr.

The cries and moans simmered as Jamshid concluded the Tablet. It took him a long time before he could open his eyes. When he did he saw that Asiyih had arrived and was standing by the door of the room, still immersed in deep prayer.

Jamshid waited until most of the friends looked up. 'Although this is a very difficult time for us all, we must be very happy for our beloved Ziya Khanum. She has attained what we all sincerely long for. We can be happy at the greatness of her station. She has joined the ranks of the Concourse on High and attained to the presence of her Lord.'

Asiyih took a deep breath.

'Let us hope that the fate of the others is as glorious,' one of the friends said.

'Or at least they are returned safely to our care,' one of the wives said.

Someone asked Jamshid, 'The girls?'

67

'We have to believe that they suffered the same fate as their mother.'

'And the Doctor?' another asked.

None of the friends knew. Jamshid just shook his head.

'Remember all our family and friends in your prayers. We all need the prayers.' said an older man.

Jamshid rose. 'Beloved friends. I think it best that we retire to our own homes before it gets too late, and the fanatic elements consider this meeting too a reason to cause havoc. If there is a need to meet, if there is any trouble or news, it's safest to have the youth be our telephones until the atmosphere calms down.'

The friends agreed, then began to go out. Asiyih comforted those who needed the support, and was comforted herself. They shared the names of those to remember specifically that night in their prayers. Saffa met some of the older youth who were organizing the business of getting everyone out of the house safely. He took care of the nearest neighbors, leading them up the old cement stairway to the roof. They crossed safely to their adjoining houses without causing suspicion, as many friends habitually came and went this way to each other's homes.

When the last friends had left, Jamshid locked up. He brought Asiyih into their room and shut the door. They sat together, his hand in her lap, holding her near. She saw how tired he was, beaten by his long days of search. 'He is dead too, isn't he?' she asked, expecting the worst still to come. 'We have to find him.'

'Is he alive? Jamshid?'

He shook his head no, then yes, then no. So she hadn't seen the evening newspaper yet. He couldn't find the strength to show her what he had thrown away in the trash. 'He's . . . he's. Oh, Asiyih. He has recanted.'

'That's impossible! He was released.' She covered her mouth, realizing. 'He was released.'

She bowed her head. 'I'm too tired for this news,' she said, getting up. She went through her dresser and removed a knitted wrap, which she threw over her shoulders. 'My eyes are burnt dry.'

'Asiyih,' he said, trying to discourage her from attempting to go out.

'He's lost everything, Jamshid. He's not going to come to us.'

'Asiyih, sit down. Please. You haven't had a cup of tea yet to

68

even warm you. And the children haven't eaten. We all need to be together for a while.'

'Do the friends know?'

'They know,' he sighed. 'They don't believe it, nor do they want to talk about it.'

Jamshid's gaze went to the picture of 'Abdu'l-Bahá they kept beside their bed. 'Hakim was more than a surgeon of bodies; he was to many of us our spiritual physician as well.' He dropped his spinning head. 'You don't expect the strong ones to waver, let alone fall.' He got to his feet and went to her, drawing her into his arms. 'I'll search everywhere I know. Again.'

She pressed her cheek against his. It had all happened so quickly. There had to be an explanation, a misunderstanding; but then, anything was possible. Her brother could have recanted. She had to consider that possibility. 'We musn't judge him too harshly,' she began. 'You know how sensitive he's always been. That's what made him a good doctor. That was his faith. And Ziya was his inspiration.'

'I know,' he said. 'I'll call every hour, wherever I can find a phone.'

'Yes.'

# CHAPTER 6

# O Son of Dust!

Saffa chose to be alone the next evening. He wandered down the alleyway to the corner of the main road and stood beneath the night shadows of the towering eucalyptus trees that lined the avenue. The street lights overhead were encircled with insects and moths, fascinating him. He watched the cars run up and down the street. The smell of freshly baked bread from a nearby home filtered through the fumes of motor exhaust. Across the street a gang of boys from his school played with a soccer ball. It was wiser to remain hidden from their view unless he was looking for another fight. When the worn-out brakes of a taxi squealed to a stop alongside the curb, Saffa moved to the deeper shadows of the closest tree. The street light silhouetted the passenger inside the taxi, paying the driver. The windows were rolled down, letting Saffa overhear their argument.

'You should be thankful I picked you up,' the driver shouted.

'You should be thankful I'm even paying you,' the passenger snapped back.

Saffa kept a cautious eye on the gang; so far they weren't interested in what was happening beside him.

'Is this where you live?' the driver asked, inquisitively.

'This is where you're letting me out, unless you think you can squeeze this piece of rubbish down the alley.'

The passenger got out with his suitcase. The driver stuck his arm out his window expectantly, waiting for his tip. 'You're finished, brother. Go.'

The driver began to heap him with abuse.

Now the gang stopped to listen. Saffa was sure that they would come across any second. At least the passenger had enough sense not to stand around and had already moved up the alleyway. Saffa wasn't going to wait around either, and followed the man, wondering who he might be.

'Kashanis are all pigeon-lovers!' the driver yelled.

70

Saffa glanced back. The gang moved on that insult and were heading towards the taxi. The driver was quick to start the engine and drove off as objects were being hurled.

The stranger turned back at the noise. Saffa was certain he couldn't be seen as he was still in the shadows. But the light shone on the man's face, which sent a chill down Saffa's spine. He knew that face.

'Payam?'

The man turned to the shadows, squinting to see who called him, and saw a lone figure come out into the middle of the alley. 'Saffa?'

'Payam!'

Saffa ran into his cousin's arms, knocking him off balance. The two danced in a circle, rough-housing each other. Saffa couldn't keep his mouth shut, asking a thousand questions. He took his cousin's suitcase for him directly to their front door, then knocked and ran into the shadows, leaving Payam by himself.

'Please, Saffa. This isn't the time to play around. Saffa!'

From behind the door Asiyih asked who it was. 'Yes?'

Payam straightened himself up. It was a few years since he'd been home to Kashan, to Iran. He wondered if being twenty-five and traveled would make him any different to his aunt or to any of his family. He felt at home, introducing himself at a door he had known since he was a small child. 'Can I take Saffa to the cinema, Aunt Asiyih?'

The door opened until she could see his face. If Hakim was a young man again, there was the only person who would look exactly like him. 'Payam?!'

'*Alláh'u'Abhá*,' he said, greeting her.

She returned the greeting, drawing him into her arms, kissing him on both cheeks and weeping uncontrollably. Saffa followed them in, taking Payam's bag for him into his room. It was the only way to see if the heavy bag had any gifts within, while his cousin was occupied.

Payam found a box of tissues for her, letting her regain her composure, then asked, 'Where's Mitty?'

'Asleep,' she said, ending her sniffles. She looked up at him again. The tears rolled from her eyes. She lost control, saying, 'She'll be so thrilled to see you.'

Payam put his arm around her, handed her tissue after tissue until she calmed down again, then asked, 'And Uncle Jamshid?'

'He went out for a while. Come.'

She took him into the kitchen and reheated some left-over food which she had cooked earlier. He was already full, but there was nothing like a good Persian meal. She whipped up the fried green vegetables with eggs, scooped out the thick soup, and scraped the bottom of the rice pot to fill his plate. He finished everything, recounting his adventures, telling her how he had got there by bus from Teheran and the trouble he had had getting down to Kashan. Afterwards, he helped her clean up, even though she kept telling him to go away from her work. 'You must be tired,' she said. 'Go sleep in Saffa's room.'

'How much rest do you think I would get there?' he said, knowing Saffa would keep him up all night. He spoke frankly. 'I came home for a purpose, not to rest. Your telegram said they were imprisoned.'

Asiyih avoided the subject, wiping off the pots, then stacking them away. 'How are you going to get out of Iran?'

'I have a ticket. If that doesn't work, then I'll walk over the mountains to Turkey.'

'That was not the brains of a mule you just feasted on to speak so foolishly.'

He stopped her from putting the last pot away, taking it. 'I didn't want to tell Saffa that I'd already been to our house before I came.'

She sighed deeply, putting her towel down.

'Auntie. Where is my father?'

'We don't know, only God knows.'

'Is he in prison?'

'No. He was released. We just don't know where he's gone to.'

'And my mother? Shiva?'

'Payam, please,' she said, unable to take the barrage of his questioning. 'Wait until your uncle returns.'

He went out to the courtyard.

'Where are you going?'

'For a walk.'

'You're tired,' she told him. 'You've just arrived. Wait for your uncle.'

Saffa came out carrying the pieces of a soapstone chess set and a rolled African mohair carpet. 'Which gift is mine?'

They both stared at him. Saffa's smile faded. 'I was just putting away your clothes in my drawers,' he explained.

'The chess set,' Payam said, then turned to Asiyih. 'I won't be long.'

Before Saffa could volunteer Payam made it clear he was going out alone.

'You better practice your backgammon too. In both games I'm going to kill you.'

Payam realized he was more tired than he had thought; the hospital was a long distance to walk. The fresh air and vigorous pace were good for him. It shook his over-extended stomach and brought the circulation back to his legs. He wondered if all his old school friends still lived in the same houses he was passing – who was married, how much they had changed, what the revolution had done to their lives. He would find out some other time. First he would find his father. He knew where he would be, especially if he did not want to be found. He could find the way to his father's consulting rooms blind. His father only did operations in the hospital, and rented a series of rooms in a nearby office building. Not that every doctor did this, but his father liked the western approach. Kashan wasn't exactly a cosmopolitan city, it had only a few modern multi-storey buildings. The prestigious office was the only place his father would disappear to when he wanted to be alone: his refuge.

Payam climbed the steps to the glass door of the building. Inside a night watchman sat behind the reception counter reading the evening paper. Payam rattled the door, getting the guard's attention, then mouthed, 'Is this building open?'

The watchman put down his paper. 'What do you want?' he shouted.

'Is Dr Rahbari's office still here?'

'We're closed, brother. See the doctor with your problem in the morning.'

'I know you're closed!' he shouted, motioning for the watchman to come to the door.

'The office will be open in the morning. You're the second one to ask. And he's not here,' he said, without budging. 'Go across the street to the hospital.'

73

Payam determined that his Uncle Jamshid must have been the one to have tried earlier. 'Did you let the other man in?'

'Did I what?'

'O God. This is absurd,' he said under his breath, then hollered again. 'Can I come in and see if he's here, please?'

'Who in the name of God do you think you are?'

'In the name of God, his son! Open the door!'

Payam unzipped his jacket and brought out his passport, pressing it against the glass for the watchman to see. He didn't believe this guard had ever seen a passport, but hoped as he came over to look at it that he'd take it for an 'official pass' and be impressed by it.

And he looked. '. . . I can't let you in . . . we're closed.'

Payam saw the bright smile on the watchman's face. He was back in Iran. And bribery still opened doors.

He reached into his slacks and pulled out some bills of tumans and wedged the money through the narrow gap between the doors, knowing it was more than enough. The watchman took it and slipped it away, unlocked the door, letting Payam in, then locked it again behind him.

'Did you let the other seeker in?' he asked again.

'No. Just don't be long,' the watchman warned him.

Payam went up the stairway to the first floor. He walked along the carpeted hallway, reading the names and office titles of the doors he passed, till he came to his father's office.

He tried the door. Locked. 'Damn,' he swore, then moved down the hall to the next door. It was unmarked. Payam remembered it was his father's private entrance. It was locked too.

'This is the only place he'd go,' he said to himself, thinking what to do next.

Payam looked down at his shoes. There was a light illuminating the tip of the black leather from under the door.

'Baba, are you in there?' he said with a knock.

The hallway echoed his question, then silence.

'It's me, Payam . . .'

He leaned his ear against the door, listening for the slightest sound.

'. . . Go away,' came the slow reply.

Payam didn't recognize the voice, but it had to be his father. Who else would be in there, he thought. There was something awfully wrong. He didn't like the situation. It was his father in there. 'Baba? It's your son.'

'. . . Payam?'

'Yes, Payam. Please, open the door!'

He couldn't just stand there waiting for his father to let him in and began to pace nervously, wondering what could have happened to have so shaken his father's once proud voice. It frightened him.

The door was unlocked. 'Thank God,' Payam sighed.

Hakim turned away as his son entered. He went to the side of his lamplit desk and stared out of the window, gazing at the lights of the hospital across the street, beyond the trees.

Payam went behind the desk. He put his hands on his father's old chair and stared at his father's reflection in the window. His father's face looked beaten. 'What happened?' he asked softly.

'I didn't pioneer.'

'I know you didn't pioneer,' Payam said, a bit too impatiently. He took a deep breath. This was so hard for him too. 'I'm sorry. I haven't slept much these past days. I just want you to tell me what happened to everyone. Mama, Sholeh, Shiva.'

'. . . I killed them,' he said emotionlessly.

'What?' He rubbed his brow. The tension was too much. 'Baba, look at me . . . Please?'

Hakim remained unmoved.

Payam glanced down at the desk. He noticed an unfinished letter his father was writing, which was partially hidden beneath the evening paper. 'What's this?'

Hakim turned around. At last Payam could see his face clearly: he hadn't shaved for a few days, nor, judging by the bags and dark circles under his eyes, had he slept either.

'It's my will,' he admitted, not looking up at him.

'For the love of God. Tell me what is going on here! I'm not a mind reader. What's happened to my father?!' He pounded his fist on the desk. The newspaper unfolded, revealing the top of the front page, the picture of his father, his name, and the deed he had performed.

Hakim turned away. There was nothing he could say to his son; everything was self-evident. 'Go back to your post in Africa, or you'll meet the same fate.'

Payam tried to speak. What he read wasn't possible. Yet everything pointed to its horrible reality. He couldn't bear to stand there any longer. In desperation he grabbed up the newspaper and hurled it across the room, hitting his father's image in the window, then ran out slamming the door behind him.

As he reached the glass doors, the watchman slowly got up.

'Did you find your father?'

Payam unlocked the bolt for himself. 'Yes,' he shouted, then ran into the darkness. 'He's dead!'

The watchman didn't find the joke amusing. He locked up, then debated whether to check up on the doctor's office. He'd have a lot of answering to do if he'd let in an assassin. He went up to the doctor's office and knocked quietly, then tried the handle. He unlocked the door and went inside the reception area. There was no one there. From room to room he checked, turning each light on and off.

Finally he came to the doctor's private office door and knocked. There was no answer, but a light was definitely on inside. The knob twisted easily in his hand. As he peeked in, he saw Dr Rahbari moving from his desk chair. 'Forgive me for intruding, Doctor,' he said, watching the doctor more carefully. The doctor was not rising. He slid along the side of his desk out of his chair, then fell unconscious to the floor.

The watchman rushed to his side. 'O my God. The doctor's been assassinated!'

Hakim vaguely heard the call for help being phoned by the watchman, the medics' voices, and all the movement hustling him across to the hospital. They forced him to vomit repeatedly. He remembered the dizziness, a fellow doctor trying to revive him, then he saw black . . . He thought he'd finally escaped. He imagined the scene that must have taken place when Jamshid, Asiyih and Payam arrived, waiting for the results. Although he couldn't control what was being said, he felt more than obliged to be there. He wanted to hear his fate as well.

'He should be awake by mid-morning, maybe early afternoon,' the doctor said solemnly. 'We'll see how he progresses. You can all go home and get some rest until then.'

'At least tell us what happened,' Asiyih pleaded. 'Was he shot, injured?'

'Your brother has been under a great deal of stress, Khanum.'

He spoke as a friend. 'And that's an understatement. In all the years I've known him I've never seen a man of his character in such a depressed state – and I've seen a lot of depression these days. It's not like the esteemed doctor at all.'

Asiyih still wanted to hear the answer to her question. The doctor reluctantly lead up to it.

'He wasn't shot, Asiyih Khanum. The injury was self-inflicted. Overdose.'

Payam turned away. 'It's my fault.'

'Are you his son?' the doctor asked. 'Payam, isn't it?' He put his hand on Payam's shoulder and looked at him with great compassion. 'Your father loves you very, very much. I want you to know that. But it would be very painful for him to face you now. All of you,' he said, glancing back to Asiyih and Jamshid. 'He needs time. A long time before he can face you all again, especially you, Payam, without being overwhelmed by the shame he feels inside . . . Do you understand?'

'How long?' Payam asked.

'At least a few weeks, maybe a few months. It's hard to say.'

'I don't have a few weeks. I have responsibilities that I have to return to.'

'Good.'

'His work is in Africa,' Jamshid explained.

'I see. Then I suggest, Payam, that you wait until your father writes to you and invites you home.'

Asiyih didn't see the wisdom of the doctor's suggestion. 'Why?'

'Because he feels that he's failed his son and his family. He can't be the example to his son that he's desired to be. That seems to be the central reason why he attempted this act.'

'How do you know he tried to kill himself?' Jamshid questioned.

'We spoke for a few minutes before he was sedated. He really wanted to die.'

'He is dead!' Payam burst out of the room.

'Payam! Payam!' Asiyih called out after him.

The doctor held her from running. 'Don't worry. It's a shock to us all.'

Jamshid took hold of Asiyih. 'Please call us when he's ready.'

'We know he's in the best of hands,' she said confidently.

Their relative calmness perturbed the doctor. He couldn't understand how well they both were taking all this. 'Forgive me for asking, but I think it's important to Hakim's recovery. Why do you think he did this? I know from my years of association with him that Bahá'ís also frown upon one who takes his own life.'

'The Bahá'í Faith frowns upon any soul who would try to cut off his arm or leg before leaving this worldly womb,' Jamshid explained.

But the doctor wasn't in the mood for a glossed analogy.

'We're not talking about any soul – we're talking about your brother-in-law, who is a Bahá'í.'

Asiyih corrected him, shocking her husband with her frankness. 'My brother is not a Bahá'í.' She took Jamshid's arm for support. 'He is a human being, and he is my brother. Please call us when he's ready to see us.'

Hakim thought that all he could hear were the words that were spoken, but came to realize that Asiyih's thoughts were also there. He wasn't dead to her, he was lost. And in the pit of his stomach he knew she was right. The blackness that enveloped him was not the tunnel leading to the realm of the next world. He was still painfully alive and it seemed that God intended him to suffer longer in this nether world. Hakim's design had failed miserably. Even the Qur'án reminded him of it:

'Man schemes. God schemes. And God schemes best.'

To the two nurses who were engaged in tucking him in his corner bed he appeared still unconscious. One of them kept shaking her head. 'And to think that I used to respect Dr Rahbari.'

'It is peculiar that a man of his repute would attempt such a vile act,' the second nurse said.

The first nurse propped up the bed's pillows. 'Not so peculiar when you know the motive.'

'The motive?' the second nurse said sarcastically, closing the curtain around his bed. She did not expect to hear the unadulterated truth from her gossipy colleague.

They walked to the foot of the bed. The first nurse whispered confidentially, 'Someone was telling me that the Pasdars found out that the doctor was holding Bahá'í meetings.'

'So . . .'

'So. A few days ago his beautiful home was burnt to the ground, and he was charged with spying as a Zionist. So!'

The second nurse rolled up the old sheets and tossed them into the 'used' bin. 'I don't believe a word.'

'By my life, it's the truth! Think: Why would Doctor Rahbari try to take his own life? That night watchman should have thrown away the empty bottle and let him die.'

'How can you talk about him like that? It's all slander. Rather we should render thanks to God for having saved his life,' the second nurse argued, pointing an accusing finger at the first. 'Maybe the doctor was poisoned to make it appear like a suicide. How about that!'

'Ladies,' moaned Hakim from behind the curtain. 'Could you have your stimulating conversation somewhere else?'

They both scurried to his side, letting the curtains fly open. The first nurse took his pulse, while the second kept him awake, talking. 'How are you feeling, Doctor?'

'Dry.'

The first nurse looked at the second, asking him, 'How long have you been awake?'

Hakim closed his straining eyes, trying to remain conscious. 'Long enough to know who's spying on whom, nurse.'

She dropped his arm to his side and said coldly, 'Your heart is beating much stronger now, Doctor.'

Hakim attempted to sit up. He coughed sorely, then leaned over the side of his bed as his stomach cramped. The second nurse sat beside him holding his shoulders back.

'Get me a glass of water,' he ordered.

'Get him a glass of water,' the second nurse shouted.

'The doctor's orders were to do nothing until he came.'

'I'm a doctor,' Hakim croaked.

The second nurse dashed around the curtain herself and filled a cup, then helped Hakim to drink it slowly. The first nurse walked away. 'I'll call for the doctor,' she said arrogantly. Hakim coughed as he sipped, then gave the nurse his cup after a few swallows and rested back against his pillows.

'Looks like you've been through some nightmare,' she said.

'Iranians don't discuss their dreams, nurse. Especially when they're nightmares.'

Hakim opened his eyes and looked over at her. The bitterness was uncalled for. 'I'm sorry, nurse.'

'Quite all right. Maybe that's why no one discusses their nightmares. The reality's too painful. I mean. Well, you understand.'

His physician came back with the first nurse. 'How are you feeling, Hakim?' he asked sincerely, pressing a cold stethoscope against his chest.

Hakim kept silent, waiting for the prognosis.

The doctor lifted his instrument. 'Much better. Blood pressure, nurse?'

'140 over 80,' answered the first.

'Better. That will be all for now,' he said, dismissing them.

He dropped his stethoscope into his lab coat and pulled the bed sheets over Hakim's chest, then spoke lightly. 'I saw your sister and brother-in-law earlier, but I haven't as yet seen your charming wife.'

Hakim covered his eyes with his arm. 'What time is it?'

The doctor understood that his prying was still a delicate matter, though he wanted to test Hakim's resilience. He glanced at his watch. 'Nine in the morning. I'm supposed to call your sister when you're ready to see them.'

'Did anyone else come?'

'There was another man.'

'My son.'

'Yes. He came too. But I'm referring to another man. I sent your son away for the time being. In your delirium you made it more than clear that it would be too painful for you to see him for a while.'

Hakim let his arm drop from his face. He saw the doctor's expression of sincere concern, but Hakim didn't want his sympathy. 'Who came?'

'A Commander's assistant from the Revolutionary Guard,' he said, repeating the grand title, then adding, 'Someone from Isfahan originally, as I recall.'

Hakim turned his head away, growing tired of being trapped, of being bound to his bed.

'Hakim. I tore up the letter the watchman found on your desk.'

Hakim nodded, then said, 'I need to rest, my friend.'

He hoped that would give him the chance of being left alone. It did. Then he felt the unexpected needle enter his arm and the induced sleep slowly bring him back to the calm of darkness. His mind slipped to the action his co-worker had taken as an 'act of mercy', destroying his last will. He would have preferred it read at his unattended funeral; he deserved at least that act of mercy. His spirit was dead, and his body should have met the same fate.

The sun still warmed the room, lighting Hakim's drawn curtain, when he finally came around. But the time of the day was a mystery to him. He relaxed his stare on the drapes, watching them breathe gently in and out.

The metal curtain railing rattled open, letting someone in at the side of his bed. He would have assumed it was the nurse with some form of nourishment, but a waft of a familiar men's cologne passed over him. Hakim didn't turn. He watched the ripple in the curtain circle around him, knowing full well who had entered. He was too weary to hate the man. When he was feeling stronger, he thought, he would hate him better.

Isfahani scratched his mustache, looking the doctor over.

'It was very difficult for me to see you alone, Doctor,' he began rather casually. 'Your physician didn't want me to see you at all after he had a look at last night's paper in his office.'

Isfahani chuckled to himself.

Hakim rolled his head round, looking straight into his eyes. And now he saw the one he hated. He really wasn't interested.

Isfahani lost his grin. He sensed the hate for the first time, strongly. 'I came to tell you that I've arranged for your transfer, as I have been instructed. I can imagine that you will want a new place to start your new life. Our Commander chose the place. I'm here to fulfill his command.'

Hakim had had enough of seeing him. He couldn't wait to see what they had concocted, he thought sarcastically.

'Whether you believe me or not, Doctor, I can tell you that I fully understand why you tried to take your life.'

It looked to Hakim as though Isfahani was here to stay, ready to reveal his life story, by the way the man seemed to be searching his thoughts, gazing up.

'I had a dream last night, Doctor, about a white bird, a nightingale.'

Interpreting spiritual significance was the last thing Hakim wanted to do. Even if it would give him an insight into this

81

narrow-minded fanatic he didn't want to hear it. But what could he do to stop it?

'I remember it was a nightingale because it was the first of spring, and this bird perched itself on the top-most bough of this tree, high above a verdant valley.'

The attempt at descriptive poetry was not at all intoxicating to Hakim's ear. But Isfahani was really getting into his story.

'When it warbled, all the branches of the tree shook the ripened fruit to the ground. A mulla then came and gathered up all the fruit and placed it in his casket, crushing it in the container. He opened the hole in the bottom and withdrew a glass of pure nectar, with which he fed many Muslim children from the nearby village. When the juice was gone and everyone had had their fill, the old mulla threw away the mash for the animals of the field to finish.'

If Hakim really told him what he thought of that dream, he might still succeed in getting to the next world. 'Your interpretation?' he asked drily.

Isfahani smiled broadly. 'We have thrown away your mash, Doctor. We will leave you to the animals to finish off.

Hakim laughed, which surprised Isfahani. 'Do you disagree with my interpretation?' he asked the doctor seriously.

'Sometimes we have dreams because of an upset stomach,' Hakim said straight to his face.

Isfahani laughed heartily, pulling a roll of paper from inside his jacket. 'One day you will see that this dream will bear fruit, but enough of this. I have made a special request on your behalf, that your name be changed. It has been agreed – Dr Irani. You will enjoy the front lines of the gulf port of Abedan. It's pleasant this time of spring.'

Isfahani put the papers on the bed. 'The army truck is waiting outside. In another hour you will be officially healthy – without interference.'

He backed away from Hakim's side, placing his hands across his chest. '*Khoda Hafez*,' he said, wishing him good-bye, 'Dr Irani.'

# CHAPTER 7

# To the Ends of the Earth

'That's the fourth time!'

The military driver was in a rage as the steam poured from the carrier's bonnet, completely obscuring his view. He had to pull to the dusty roadside; the tar was too hot at mid-day to stop on. With a screeching skid the truck came to a halt, engulfed in dust. The driver jumped out, slammed his door and went over to look under the bonnet.

Two army men hustled out of the passenger door to join their comrade, leaving their non-uniformed passenger to himself on the front seat, still dressed in his loosened tie, shirt and trousers.

It was the first time that Hakim wasn't smelling their sweat since they had left Kashan. God knew how far they had traveled, and how much farther they had to go. Hakim didn't care if the war went on without them for one more day. He hoped that the engine would boil over another hundred times.

As the bonnet was propped up over the windscreen, and the driver began to curse, Hakim slid out along the seat to get away from the noise.

'That's the fourth time in two days!' the driver howled. 'You miserable machine. Imperialist parts stink.'

Hakim made his way along the side embankment, stumbling over the stones and gravel in his hard shoes, which became covered with the fine tan silt. It was hot and dry out there. The scorching sun blinded his view of the rocky desert surrounding them. The suit jacket under his arm would have been better torn in strips and worn around his head, like some bedouin. No shepherd would have grazed his animals in the desolate mountain landscape around them. Even the crows and gazelles had enough sense to hide under shrubs and cliffs at this hour.

Hakim turned, hearing the rear tail-gate slam down against the back of the carrier. The new recruits piled out in their unsoiled uniforms, jumping down from the canvas carrier section to stretch their legs. Then came the voluntary recruits, the Pasdars in their spotless attire, loaded with weaponry from pistols in their belts to automatic rifles on their shoulders. The children of Iran were going to play war. A continuous rally over the radio, on TV, in the mosques, called for the young men of Iran to arise and defend their country against their advancing enemy from the west – Iraq. Such a noble station in the realms above was promised to them all. Hakim wondered if they really believed they would be so lucky as to attain such a bounty. No one was that lucky. How many would be wounded in battles, by an enemy they could scarcely see, crippled, disfigured. Then they would have to return to the lives they had left behind. These were the fruits of war.

Far behind them was raised the dust of another vehicle speeding along the same road, heading swiftly towards them. One of the would-be soldiers called it to the attention of the driver, who glanced with his men at the billowing cloud in the distance.

One of the soldiers said, without too much concern, to stir up the new men, 'If he doesn't stop, just shoot out his tires!'

Immediately, and obviously anxious about their first 'threatening encounter with the enemy', the recruits crossed the road and prepared their handguns and rifle for the major battle.

The questions soared. 'Are we near the border? How will we know if it's the enemy?'

'Ask them,' the driver suggested, pulling off his shirt to cautiously remove the radiator cap. 'Maybe they'll take this traitor of a mechanical nuisance to Iraq with them.'

Hakim moved down near the rear of the truck, seeking what little shade the shadow from the canopy offered. At least there he could duck down behind the rear tires and hope that he would be in the safest place if the trigger-ready combatants fired.

The driver poured the remaining contents of their water canister into the radiator. 'Pray that the jeep has more,' he said to his companions.

'How do you know that it's a jeep?' one beside him asked.

'The sound of the engine.'

'And what if it doesn't stop?' asked the other.

They listened to the jeep's increasing whine. It didn't sound as though it was going to stop, nor did it appear that way. Through the flaming waves of heat, they saw the jeep's lights flash on and off, timed with the warning blare of its horn.

'Now what?' said one.

The driver went into the cab and pulled out his issued rifle from beneath his seat, then positioned himself in the middle of the road. The recruits watched him.

'In ten seconds, soldier,' a Pasdar said, warning him, 'that vehicle will be wiping your remains from its windscreen.'

The jeep kept coming, its speed unslackened.

'Don't worry, brother,' said another Pasdar. 'He's army. He's expendable.' The comment won a good laugh from his friends.

The driver stared hard at the joking man, till the Pasdar's laughter died. The driver took his sights down the road and raised his rifle. The jeep came, winding at full throttle, now close enough for them to see its characteristic shape. The driver waited until it was only a few hundred feet from them, then pulled the trigger, blasting off one round. The rifle slammed against his shoulder with the blast. The brakes of the jeep screeched, the vehicle skidded as it tried to hold to the middle of the road, finally coming to a halt only fifty feet from the rear of the truck.

Hakim was crouched behind the back wheel, listening to the recruits howling their Islamic victory cheers as they ran to descend on their fresh kill. Hakim dusted himself off and stood up.

The helmeted jeep driver climbed out and looked across his hood at the spider web of shattered glass blown out of the passenger's side window.

'Missed,' the carrier driver said, with a shrug. They had conquered a medical supply truck, by the looks of the insignia, complete with a medic. The driver tossed his gun to one of his companions, telling them both, 'It must have water canisters. Take a look.'

The agile medic jumped back behind his wheel, threw the jeep in gear and plowed haphazardly through the approaching recruits, scattering them. He braked beside the truck before pulling off his helmet and heading towards the three army soldiers. His short slender figure didn't appear tough, but his voice boomed, putting them in their place.

'All right, who's the jerk with the rifle?'

He looked accusingly at all the uniformed men encircling him. 'You've got a lot of explaining to do!'

The two soldiers went around the other side of the jeep and

searched the covered back. They found two water canisters amidst the supplies and removed them.

'Hey, you! What do you think you're doing? Those are sterilized!' the medic shouted.

Hakim moved into the crowd. Things were obviously going to get difficult for the medic. He was putting himself in danger, but he was thinking about the importance of the supplies. History could at least remember him as a defender of medicine. The first medical martyr in the struggle of sterilized water against radiator maintenance.

A Pasdar jumped in and pushed the medic aside. 'Sterilized? It's water, isn't it?'

'Leave the man be,' Hakim said, peering into the jeep. The supplies he carried actually were very valuable.

'Who do you think you are?' said the Pasdar, coming over to him.

'He's a doctor,' the carrier driver said, stepping in between Hakim and the Pasdar. 'Don't be his first patient, brother.'

'If you want water, take the drums in the back,' the medic pleaded. 'But put the sterilized containers back.'

'All right. Do what the medic says!' the driver shouted. 'So we can get out of this oven.'

The Pasdar backed away, taking a few of his companions with him to do the work. The medic grabbed his canisters and covered them back under their tarpaulin. The carrier driver was handed the water drums and emptied them full into the radiator, letting the excess bubble onto the steaming tar. He twisted the cap back on and threw the empty drum, bouncing, to the side, then dropped the bonnet shut.

'Good. Let's go,' he said, taking the second drum back into the rear to keep for safety. The recruits began to load up.

The medic looked over at Hakim, studying his older face. 'You look like you've been in the war from the beginning. Where's your motley crew heading?'

'Let's go, Doctor,' the driver shouted, locking the tail-gate up.

'Dr Irani?' the medic asked, hearing whom he was speaking to.

Hakim was going to have to get used to that name, or he'd have to explain to everyone who he really was and what had got him out there. 'Yes, I'm Dr Irani.'

'I didn't take this road in the middle of the day just to deliver some supplies.' He popped open his shirt pocket and handed Hakim a telex. 'You're to come with me the rest of the way, Doctor.'

The carrier driver shouted from the door. 'Doctor, please.'

'He's to come with me,' the medic shouted, and gave him the orders.

'Good,' the driver said, then gave a half-hearted salute and kicked the engine over. 'Follow us.'

The truck spun forward, sending a whirl of dust in their direction. They shielded their faces until the cloud settled.

The medic extended his arm to Hakim. 'Mostaqim. Firuz Mostaqim.'

Hakim shook his hand. 'Dr Hakim Rah-Irani.'

'*Qurbani shoma*. Please get in, Doctor.'

Firuz tossed his helmet in the rear as Hakim climbed in, then ran back to the side of the road to collect the discarded drum and reattached it to the jeep. 'Where's your bag?' he asked Hakim, checking through the supplies.

'I don't have one,' Hakim answered, watching him remove a roll of tape and scissors.

'Lost in the war?' Firuz asked, amused by his little jest.

He jumped into his seat and leaned over to Hakim's side, taping up the webbed screen securely.

Hakim didn't acknowledge the humor. He had heard enough jokes. There were too many Uncle Amins in the world.

'Do you smoke?'

'No.'

'You will. And that grip in front of you is to hold onto.'

Hakim looked out his open side. He would have been better off in the carrier than with a wise-mouthed man half his age. The medic clutched the jeep into first gear and sped off. Hakim held on tightly to the handle in front of him. They came quickly up to the carrier, then swerved to the dirt, throwing up the dust, to the angry cries of the driver.

'That ought to clog up their engine,' said Firuz, glancing back into his rear view mirror at the now weaving truck. 'It'll take them another week to reach Kirmanshah.'

'They're headed south, for Abedan,' Hakim said, correcting him.

'No, Doctor. Kirmanshah, too. We should be there in a few

87

hours.'

The medic was obviously not listening to what Hakim was telling him. 'I'm being sent south, to Abedan.'

'Kirmanshah. Tonight we head west, Doctor. It was in your orders. This is certainly not the road to Abedan.'

'I know that,' Hakim said defensively.

'So do I. It would be marvelous to be in Abedan though. Shatt-al-Arab waterway, the Gulf. It's much better than this desert.'

Hakim turned to watch the passing terrain. He had been tricked, he thought bitterly. Then again, what had he expected – a holiday resort? No one was interested in his life anymore. Dr Irani was all that remained, and that, he supposed, was to vanish too.

'Are you married?'

Firuz got no response. 'Children? Parents? Cats? goats? pigeons? chickens?'

Hakim glanced at the bothersome medic. And Firuz glared back at the tight-lipped doctor.

'Are you sure you are a doctor?'

Hakim ignored the sarcasm.

Firuz put his gaze over the wheel, driving ahead toward the next mountain rise, then mumbled, 'Probably a village proctologist with a severe case of piles.'

At dusk they entered a suburb of Kirmanshah, stopping beside the front gate of a large wall-surrounded home. Hakim looked at the trees and greenery which rose over the wall. He turned to Firuz, breaking the long silence. 'What's this?'

'Dr Khamsi's home, an ex-military physician. He's your host for the evening.' Firuz put any argument Hakim might have to rest. 'Orders, Doctor. Orders . . . And you don't have any money, or relatives here, now do you?'

Hakim had to get out. The medic was right, he had no money. And if he did contact the friends, any Bahá'ís, he couldn't convince them he was a Bahá'í, nor did he want to. The medic had won his case. Hakim stood at the side of the jeep, then thanked him. 'Maybe some other time we'll meet again.'

Firuz shook his head. 'I'll request rather that someone else takes you to your camp. I hope we don't meet so soon, not profession-ally. I wouldn't want to learn from you. The way you operate – your silence and solemnity – would kill any patient trying to hear some last word of comfort. Good-night, Doctor.'

The jeep lurched forward and spun a circle in the street, zipping around the corner from which it had come.

A middle-aged man watched the sight from inside the house gate, then leaned out to see the lone man standing with his suit jacket still under his arm. Hakim was still facing in the direction of the jeep, now gone. It wasn't his fault if he wasn't idly sociable, he told himself.

'Dr Irani?'

Hakim turned. 'Yes,' he said, getting used to his bland name. 'Dr Khamsi?'

The two shook hands, re-introducing themselves, and went inside the house together.

'That was Firuz, wasn't it,' Dr Khamsi said. 'It had to be. He drives too fast and talks too much if you give him the chance. But he's the best medic in the whole damn army. I worked beside his father years ago . . .'

Hakim was given a change of clothes, as the two doctors were nearly the same size. It gave Hakim a chance to refresh himself and an opportunity to wash his foul-smelling clothes.

He was introduced to a couple who joined them for supper, which allowed him a rest from being the constant center of attention.

After the meal the three men rose from the table, complimenting Dr Khamsi's wife on her divine culinary achievements, and went over to the easy chairs and sofa to talk amongst themselves.

'I received a communiqué saying that our distinguished surgeon would be arriving from Teheran,' Dr Khamsi began, taking out his pipe. His hefty friend pulled out his pack of cigarettes, offering them first to Hakim, who refused. It looked as though he was in the center view now.

'Yes. I suppose you could say that I was from Teheran, if you considered that my degrees were taken there – when I was a younger man.'

His eyes followed the billowing smoke rising around him.

'Being a civil engineer', the guest said, puffing away, seeing Hakim's reaction, 'you learn to smoke more than your share these days.'

89

'Even doctors, Ali,' Dr Khamsi added. 'I imagine you too, Doctor, will begin to smoke once you're up to the fighting.'

Dr Khamsi rose, seeing his wife coming with a bowl of fruit and a tray of teacups. He helped her put everything on the table between them.

'Thank you, Khanum . . . There are only three cups?'

'We are still cleaning up everything Ali and you managed to eat,' she said, returning to her chores.

'She said nothing of you, Doctor, because you ate moderately. You know the story of the woman from Isfahan who got pregnant and waited twenty-five years till she thought that something was wrong because she hadn't delivered yet. When the obstetrician put his stethoscope on her stomach he heard the voices of two twenty-five-year-old men saying to each other, "No, no, after you – No, no, please, after you . . ."'

The three laughed, especially Dr Khamsi. Then Hakim made Ali take his tea first. There were too many 'no, no, after you' comments, which brought the joke to life, and more laughter. Hakim was not used to seeing anyone put milk in his tea.

'Don't worry,' Dr Khamsi said, noticing Hakim's surprise. 'Ali is from Abedan.'

'I'm part British,' Ali said with a wink, showing in his manners that he was aware of the influence of his city's custom.

'I thought I was going there,' Hakim slipped out.

'Well, it's a shame they didn't station you there,' Ali began. 'I would have liked to have shown you our beloved city. The Shah's strength! I mean – well. No Iraqi troop would dare attack the center of the Imperial Navy. It's still the Imperial Navy.'

Dr Khamsi was apologetic for his friend, explaining, 'It's rare for us to have visitors here. Everyone's afraid of the nearing war –'

'Revolutionaries!' Ali interjected. 'Abedan was a glorious city, till those bastards blew up the movie theater during the early days of the Islamic Revolution.'

'Ali. The report said it was SAVAK.'

'Garbage, Muhammad Khamsi. Hundreds were burnt in a flaming inferno. Now they're sending every mother's son into a 'Holy War'. Our boys shoot from the front lines and the Pasdars stand in the back, letting the others take all the bullets and shells!'

'No one knows how many were killed, or who committed the act. Let's change the subject.'

'A hundred thousand inhabitants,' Ali said in disbelief, putting out his cigarette. 'Today, there aren't more than ten thousand in the city. Murderers.'

Dr Khamsi offered Ali some dates to quiet him, which were instantly accepted and popped into his mouth. Hakim was satisfied with his cup of tea and the home-made sugar. He put the sugar on his tongue and sipped the tea past it.

'What made you come?' Dr Khamsi asked.

'I suppose I needed a change.'

Ali read into that statement, and smiled. 'It must have been some woman.'

Dr Khamsi studied Hakim. 'No, Ali. I don't think it was a woman. Doctor? May I see your hand?'

'I thought you were a medical doctor, not a palmist,' he said with a nervous laugh. It was too late to play games. 'No, I'm afraid that I don't put much credence in all that fortune telling.'

'Aren't you at least interested?' Ali said, gently pushing. 'I should think one doctor would trust another.'

He was curious, but afraid they would talk of lines of fate and other such nonsense. This was the age of science, not superstition and genii. He wasn't interested.

'I can tell you I've already had a good enough look at Dr Irani's palm at the dinner table, but it wasn't easy. Your hands, Doctor, when not spooning your fair portion of rice, were always tightly clenched.'

'What did you see?' Ali asked, intrigued by these findings.

'A man who has been in great difficulties.'

'I can see that on his face!' Ali said, not learning anything new.

Dr Khamsi taunted his friend. 'Now you claim to be a reader of faces?'

Hakim leaned back, leaving the two to amuse each other. His time wasn't made for such slothful chattering. There were more important topics. The tongue was for the mention of God, the hearing for being attracted to the divine Call, the eyes . . . Who was he judging? Had he forgotten why he was there at all?

'Had you been more observant about more important lines than on the forehead, my dear friend, you would have seen the cross in the center of the doctor's hand, encircled by an island!'

This shut Ali up. 'So, learned Shaykh, what does it mean?'

'I don't know,' confessed Dr Khamsi.

Ali raised his hands with a shrug. 'Some palm reader.'

'But it has something to do with his fate, heart and life lines. Ah, it's very confusing.'

Ali rolled with laughter.

Dr Khamsi turned to Hakim. 'My only advice is: Don't be too brave out in the field, Doctor. Let the other poor soldiers and zealots come back to you in pieces to be sewn up.'

'Thank you, Shaykh Muhammad.' Ali roared, then prostrated himself on the carpet, facing Dr Khamsi. 'Qurbani shoma. Great Master.'

Dr Khamsi saw how tired Hakim had become. It was enough for one evening. Ali too saw the tiredness on both their faces. He sat up, reaching over to the fruit bowl. 'I think it's time I rescued my wife from yours, and retired,' he said, popping a few more dates into his mouth all at once and chewing them like a horse.

'You'd better stop eating those', Dr Khamsi warned, 'or you'll be excusing yourself from whoever's company you happen to be in.'

Hakim was able to say good-night without too many apologies after the last light joke, then followed his host's directions to the guest bedroom they had prepared for him. Dr Khamsi had even laid out a pair of pyjamas for him to sleep in.

Alone, Hakim turned off the light, letting the moon cast its pale blue beams through the window, across his bed. He lay on top of the sheet listening to the clatter of the night insects. He turned to the center of the room. To his surprise, his suit was hanging in the open closet, already ironed. He reached for his glasses on the bedside table and put them on, then held his hand open, until his palm reflected the moon.

'It looks like a double cross,' he said to himself, examining carefully the mark Dr Khamsi had seen. He put his glasses back on the table. It was just superstition. But if you believe in something, is it a superstition or not, he wondered, gazing up through the window at the array of stars . . . God could be a superstition. People make up their own gods and pray to their imaginations. Wasn't the same true of his God?

Hakim rolled onto his side, disrupting the current of his thoughts.

'The front lines of war,' he whispered. 'I'm not a seamstress,

I'm just a city surgeon. It's such a foolish war to die for. If you're going to die, you might as well enlist in a cause that will unite the world, not destroy it – like the Cause of God.'

His heart burned. 'Damn. Why'd I say that.'

He stretched his arm across the bed and touched the cold plaster wall beneath the window sill. It was not his habit to just go to sleep; he used to read, read the Writings. But now his heart was not inspired. He had no One to pray to, no one to pray for – he didn't know how, now. He couldn't understand where he had gone wrong. He had said his obligatory prayers each day, persevered in his profession, taught fearlessly, served on committees, given generously to the Fund, the Right of God, had been elected year after year to his local Assembly. 'I did so much.'

He sat up. 'I?' His chest heaved with his deep breath. Every act circled around his selfish pride. No, that wasn't true – it had been for his loved ones: his parents, his family, peers, friends and children, too. 'Did I fail because I couldn't bear to watch my family suffer? Is that my crime? Doesn't God know my limits? Doesn't He hear the crying of His children – I am His child.' His fists flew up in the air. 'Damn all those years of just accepting all as Truth – how does a parrot know what truth is?'

He jumped to his feet and paced up and down like a caged animal until his anger subsided. He came up to the window and pressed his forehead against its cool pane, looking out into the dark garden. 'I have been robbed of all that I have held dear. Everything that I have ever loved. And yet now I feel so empty of ever having loved. Do these thoughts make any sense? . . . Does anyone care? . . . You could have stayed. Ziya? Do I start again?'

He lay back on the bed. 'I can't. Who would hear my prayer? It's just words – if God wants me to believe in Him, I will not go through the motions . . . No more prayers . . . No more hollow faith . . .'

Hakim tucked his arm under his pillow and rested on his side. His hand, which hung out beyond the bed, slowly opened, allowing the light to fall across his palm. He sighed, falling to sleep, '. . . O God . . . My God . . .'

The Khamsis fed him well for breakfast; fried eggs, toasted rolls, delicious salted cheese and home-made jams. The army carrier arrived early to take him, giving him scarcely enough time to thank his generous hosts properly, as the driver was in a hurry. Dr Khamsi explained that the truck was filled with perishable supplies that had to get to the military base immediately.

Hakim threw his jacket up and climbed up into the carrier's cab. He was about to greet the driver when he recognized Firuz behind the wheel.

Neither spoke a word. Hakim passed the time looking at the scenery, or rather the remnants of it. The mountain range slowly disappeared. It meant they were traveling south, but well before Abedan they veered south-west toward the flat lands of the war zone, where date tree groves once had flourished. Now all that remained were sawn-off or uprooted trunks. Tanks had woven through the plantations leaving treadmarks across everything in their path.

The road became busy with military vehicles, more carriers with fresh recruits heading in the same direction. Firuz's tactic was not to follow behind a long convoy. He would pass any vehicle at the first opportunity, risking an occasional near miss with the trucks headed in the opposite direction. The only time he would not pass was when he recognized a medical truck coming towards them, as though he innately knew they carried the seriously wounded out to other facilities. It made Hakim want to know more about where exactly he was headed and what he was going to be doing, but he was at a loss how to begin to speak to Firuz.

As they neared the military area, Hakim heard the occasional burst of explosions from the invisible war front, and the high whining speed of the low-flying jet fighters streaking overhead.

Firuz tried to pass the slow vehicle they were approaching, but swerved to stay behind it. He had recognized another medical carrier coming at them. He shook his head, looking back in his rear-side mirror. 'They're at it again,' he sighed, breaking the silence.

Hakim took the chance to speak. 'How long have you been out here?'

'A few months – it interrupted my studies, but I had no choice.'

'I'm sorry we didn't talk yesterday.'

'I talked!'

'I know. I didn't.'

They glanced at each other, managed smiles, and went back to a more friendly silence.

The tar road ended and they traveled over a dusty track for kilometres. Hakim asked, 'How many surgeons do you have?'

'At our camp? Three. Four, including yourself. They'll need you. This area's becoming heavily fought over lately. You've seen the carriers – both ways. Our 'beloved' republic is calling for every available fanatic to grab his weapon and defend our Islamic nation. You were with some of the zealots yesterday.'

Firuz reached the camp area and drove through. Soldiers were all around, pitching tents, loading equipment, arms, shells, water, food.

'As soon as I get these medical supplies unloaded, I'll take you to see the captain. He'll brief you then.'

An awful feeling put Hakim in a cold sweat. This was not a game. The war was real. The one he had so often heard described as 'corpses bestrew the ground, and severed heads are fallen on the dust of the battlefield' was all around him.

'Hey!'

Hakim stared over at Firuz.

'If you're here to save these guys, Doctor Irani, you had better forget what's bothering you and just think about sewing up. They don't need depressives, they need surgeons.'

Firuz slammed his foot on the brake and hit the horn. He shoved his door open, then glanced back to Hakim. 'Good luck, Doctor . . . And welcome to hell.'

# CHAPTER 8

# Illumination Across the Sands

It was one of those rare instances when the medical staff on duty had the incoming casualties under control. Hakim habitually chose to work overtime, taking on others' responsibilities. It kept his mind occupied and his hands busy. On this occasion, however, he had been relieved of all duties and ordered by the commanding officer to rest. The orders forced him back to the doctors' tent – there was nowhere else to go. Television, buses to local bazaars and cinemas weren't yet features of camp life.

So there he was, sitting on his cot without a thing to do. The other medics and doctors were out on duty, busy. It was just beginning to get hot, early morning, summer hot. He took out a pad of paper and pulled out his pen, then scribbled down his thoughts:

'One of the other doctors says that he passes the time writing in a diary. It's supposed to cleanse your mind.'

This wasn't as ridiculous as Hakim had first thought. He carried on.

'Five fast months. What a war. Most of the time our supply truck doesn't arrive when we need it the most. Too often we've been forced to administer inadequate anesthetics to sew up wounds, repair breaks or dislocated joints. Maybe the others are more desensitized to the cries of pain – but then it has helped me to forget my own, though.'

It was the end of summer. He never thought about how long he had been away from home. It seemed ages ago . . . He forced himself back to his line of writing.

'The long hours of understaffed surgery and our constant shifting of camp to keep us far enough away from the shelling seem to be all that describes my days. All one can live out here for is to keep alive that one mother's son on the table before you – to keep your own sanity. Physically recovered, some return to the lines, ready to fight until death; others need to be sewn up emotionally; and some are just confused, frightened, beaten out to exhaustion . . . And they are so young. One boy was literally blown to pieces. There was nothing I could do, nothing any of us could do. Firuz brought him in. There was an Iraqi minefield. The troop commander called for a volunteer. The boy was only fifteen. They tied explosives to his body and he ran with his warrior scream through the field, until the troop was able to advance once again . . . for Islam, for Iran, for a place in paradise.'

Hakim turned the page, continuing his history.

'Firuz's job has changed. Some slandering snake of an officer, wounded in action, told me that because Firuz was a Jew they could "lose" him better in the front lines, rather than a Muslim youth. It was my desire, while the officer was on the table, to remove another festering shrapnel piece without anesthetics.

'Each day Firuz's truck spirals in from the war, covered with dirt and smoke, carrying the wounded. He just keeps driving. How he goes on without becoming insane day after day – he must be writing a diary too.'

Hakim had to write one story about what had happened.

'Last week, he miraculously returned unharmed after his truck was shelled. Those who witnessed the inferno said they saw Firuz pulling out every one of the injured he could, without a thought for his own safety. I saw him crying that evening . . . Bravery and humility are a rare combination in any soul.'

'He is good,' Hakim said, then wrote:

'He's sent out in the jeep on special, emergency runs. Several times he has refused to take me, always finding one of the other doctors instead. His excuses are phenomenal.'

Outside Hakim's tent a soldier yelled, 'Casualties are on their way!'

'Firuz!' shouted a commanding voice.

Hakim stuffed his writing pad under his pillow and went outside, then went back in again and pulled out his book, shredded the pages he had just written, then threw the whole mess in a bin. 'Cleansed,' he said, going out to find Firuz.

'Mostaqim?' yelled the voice once again through the area.

At the side of the jeep, resting in the shade, Firuz woke up and scurried to the command. The lieutenant handed him a sheet of paper. 'We have a report. Take Doctor Irani with you. If you radio it's safe, I'll send the carrier in afterwards. Get in and get out.

We don't know the circumstances.'

Hakim couldn't hear what they were discussing, but guessed it was another one of Firuz's runs. This time Hakim was determined not to be turned away and deliberately walked towards them.

Firuz crumpled up the paper. 'What about sending another doctor?'

'He's going.'

'He's not ready. You know how dangerous it is!'

'You read your orders. "DOCTOR IRANI FRONT LINES."'

'I can read,' he said under his breath, seeing Hakim coming towards them. 'Somebody back there doesn't like the doctor too much.'

'Move it, medic! We've lost contact with that troop for six hours. Now move!'

The officer turned to Hakim. 'Get your kit, Doctor. Go with Firuz.'

Before Hakim could say anything, Firuz dashed away. It took him a moment to realize what had happened. He only knew he had to get his bag as quick as he could or Firuz would make another excuse to leave without him.

He assembled what he needed in record time. Firuz was already revving the engine to go and slammed it forward into gear as Hakim jumped in.

Hakim threw the stick into neutral against his hand. 'Slow down!'

The command infuriated Firuz. 'Don't you tell me what to do!'

The stares between the two were intense.

'Slow . . . down,' Hakim repeated firmly. 'There's no use in a good medic getting himself killed.'

'Don't patronize me,' Firuz said, looking away. 'And put your helmet on.'

Hakim released the gear stick to Firuz and did as he was instructed, taking a spare helmet from the rear.

Firuz slipped the jeep into first and drove off. 'Hold on to the grip in front of you,' he said protectively.

Hakim nodded, taking hold of the bar.

They drove deep into the low, hilly terrain, searching through traces of war for signs of life, witnessing only the carcass remains of burnt-out tanks, carriers and other fighting machines. It made Hakim wonder why his burning desire had been to get in a jeep and bounce through the devastated area just to get fired on by some hidden sniper whom he had nothing against.

The jeep's overworked engine howled.

'They've been fighting nearby,' Firuz yelled above the noise.

'How can you tell?' Hakim hollered back.

'Burnt oil,' he said, pointing to his nose, shrugging, 'I don't know, just intuition.'

The jeep slowed at the top of an exploded ridge. Firuz stood up and drove, seeing better over the dirty windscreen than through it.

'What's wrong?' Hakim asked.

Firuz looked to the left and right. 'I think we took a wrong track.'

Hakim held tightly to the bar and stood up too. He didn't want to hear that. He looked too. 'What's that?' he said, seeing a black shape. He pointed it out to Firuz, to their left.

Firuz sharpened his focus on the spot. 'It looks like another turned-over carrier. It doesn't smell right. Let's go back. We've come too far west . . . I think.'

'I smell oil. We should investigate. There may be wounded.'

Firuz noted his points, but turned the jeep around, away from the smell. 'I'm not putting you in danger.'

'Thank you. I'm not here for personal safety.'

'Nor am I!'

They sat back into their seats and sulked.

Firuz mumbled, then headed the jeep towards the carrier.

'All right. But we'll just drive by and get out. There are too many low mounds to be targets from.'

He drove cautiously, glancing in every direction. The carrier they neared was definitely theirs.

'Look!'

Hakim pointed to a soldier apparently wedged under the truck. Firuz forgot personal safety and accelerated to the carrier's side. Hakim jumped out and ran with his bag to the half-buried soldier and checked the man's pulse. He was still alive, yet crushed from the hips down.

The area had been bombed by mortar fire, by the looks of the multiple holes. Firuz became interested in reconstructing the action. 'One hit in front of the truck.'

'See if there are any others, Firuz.'

The back of the carrier was empty, which didn't make too much sense to Firuz. He went around to the under side. About fifty meters from where he stood another jeep smoldered its last drops of burning oil into the atmosphere. The charred remains of its occupants were still seated in their ghastly funeral pyre.

'Firuz!' Hakim called out for him.

'I found our oil well,' Firuz said solemnly, coming around to Hakim, still certain that there was something suspicious about no one else being around.

'He'll be coming around soon,' Hakim said, scrubbing a spot on the soldier's arm clean for the injection. He put his glasses on, reading the amount of c.c.s in the hypodermic needle.

Firuz wasn't paying attention to Hakim. 'It must have happened last night.'

Hakim injected the man, then threw the needle away. 'Let's get a few planks and tilt the truck enough to slide him out.' He stood up, dusting the dirt from his legs. 'I'm not amputating here if I don't have to.'

Firuz followed Hakim down to the other jeep, searching for any scraps to use, totally ignoring the dead soldiers.

'There's nothing here,' Hakim said, then suggested as he walked to the next hill, 'Let's search over here.'

Firuz was still trying to figure it out. There was no sign of a radio, no other injured, a completely empty truck, and a demolished jeep. He spotted some shapes along another incline. 'What's that?'

'Where?'

'There, against that hill.'

Hakim lifted his glasses to his forehead, squinting towards the fallen object on the ground. It looked like a pole or another body. They were too far away. So Hakim stepped in that direction.

Firuz grabbed his arm, thinking quickly, 'It could be a trap.'

'It's not a trap. Those could be the poles we need.'

'You know!' he said, tired of Hakim's lack of caution. 'Why do you want to get yourself killed?'

'Young man. I am a doctor. And if I don't get myself killed this trip, I can get myself killed the next.'

Hakim freed himself and went alone through the rocky sand, reluctantly followed by Firuz, who watched all around them just in case. They stopped beside the body of a uniformed Iranian soldier, and there was more than one.

'The missing men,' Firuz said, summing up his investigation.

Hakim walked silently to the feet of the bodies, lying in a row face down.

'Three men, three new uniforms,' Firuz said.

Hakim bent down and turned over one of the stiffened corpses.

'Couldn't be more than nineteen,' Hakim said quietly, then looked over to Firuz, who still kept a careful eye around them. 'They're not your lost troop. They've been dead too many days.'

'This doesn't smell right.'

It didn't to Hakim either. They'd all been shot in the back.

Firuz noticed that as well. 'Probably all running from their attackers,' he said, envisioning their demise. 'We're finished here. Let's go.' He took his own advice and began to walk away. After a few steps, he walked backwards, then finally stopped. 'We're going!'

Hakim opened the stuffed shirt pocket of the soldier he had overturned, and removed a folded letter from an unsealed envelope he found.

'Before the Iraqi troops return and shoot us in our backs, please. Doctor?'

Hakim sank to the ground. 'O my God.'

His face went pale, his free hand gripped his shirt over his breast as he glanced over the page.

Firuz ran to him. 'Doctor, what is it?'

Hakim handed the letter to him. Firuz took it in his hand, letting the envelope fall to the ground.

'It's a prayer,' Hakim said.

'A what?' Firuz said, then saw what the doctor meant, though he was not interested in reading it. 'So?'

Hakim was visibly shaken by what they had discovered. He had to tell Firuz what they had stumbled across. 'It's a Bahá'í prayer.'

'Are you saying they're all Bahá'ís?'

'I don't know, yes – all. In the back.' It was God's way of punishing him, he thought. He felt to blame for every one of their deaths. 'Let's bury them.'

'Are you insane? What are you saying?'

'I'm saying', he repeated more strongly, 'I think we should bury these poor souls.'

'You didn't want to bury the bodies back at the jeep over there! Forget these. And what about the soldier back there?'

The crack of a rifle peeled from the direction of the carrier. Firuz dropped the letter and ran towards the sound.

'No, Firuz!' Hakim yelled; and ran after him. He picked up the letter, stuffing it with his glasses in his shirt pocket.

One after the other they hurried along the twisting bottoms of the bomb-created mounds. A second shot was fired, this one just missing Firuz, who instantly dived to the ground, crashing against the hard ground and clutching his helmet over his head dearly. Hakim caught up with him and landed beside him.

Another shot exploded into the embankment over their heads. Hakim was breathing hard as he rolled up against the hill. He yelled out in Arabic, 'We're not soldiers, we're Iranian medics!'

'Where'd you learn Arabic?' Firuz asked in a whisper.

From over the hill a voice called out in Arabic, ordering them to get up. Hakim started to his feet, forcing Firuz up with him. 'Yes, all right! . . . stand up slowly. And keep your hands high.'

As instructed, the two stood up at the top of the incline. They could see half a dozen or so Iraqi soldiers moving out from behind their position at the overturned carrier.

'Well, Doctor, now neither of us will have to wait for the next trip to be killed,' Firuz said, aside.

The Iraqi soldiers encircled them and directed them with their rifles pointed back to the far side of the carrier, and to their commanding officer.

As Hakim and Firuz passed the half-crushed soldier under the carrier, they noticed the single bullet hole through his head and realized the aim of the first shot they had heard.

'Doctor?' the burly officer asked.

Hakim nodded and pointed to Firuz and himself.

The officer had them immediately spot-searched, stripping them first of their helmets to the heat of the sun. Their arms were tied behind their backs. Then he ordered his men to pull out. The jeep had been stripped of all the vital supplies they could carry.

There weren't that many of them. Hakim reckoned that it was the scouting party of a larger force.

The officer gave Hakim's medical bag to one of his soldiers, the jeep radio to two other men to carry between them. They were in a hurry to get away. The two prisoners of war were blindfolded.

Hakim couldn't help but think that the 'mercy-killing' shot was a mistake, military-wise. The Iraqi officer must think so too. That explained why they were being rushed at a quick march. It didn't explain why they were back-tracking on foot for such a long time.

It was an hour before the officer let everyone stop to rest. He summoned one of his men to go ahead. The soldier went out only a short distance, stopped, and looked up at the sun, shielding his eyes from its brilliant glare, then pulled out a small pocket mirror and angled its glass to the distance ahead. After a few minutes another mirror reflected its flashes back to their position.

Their blindfolds were temporarily removed when they walked into an Iraqi encampment troop of a hundred men or so. They had jeeps, artillery launchers and a couple of carriers. And the missing Iranian soldiers, seated on the ground, denuded of their weapons, belts, helmets; tied and blindfolded. Captured, too. There were a few wounded amongst them, which Hakim wanted to attend to. If he could.

Firuz had the same idea, and walked immediately over to the soldier with Hakim's bag. 'We need this bag.'

Hakim was too late to stop him.

Two Iraqi soldiers grabbed Firuz by his arms and dragged him away. 'Your prisoners are injured! It's not as though this heat were exactly helpful in their condition!'

Hakim turned to the burly officer and asked in broken Arabic for his medical supplies to treat his fellow-prisoners of war. The officer had the bag emptied on the ground, dumped. Bandages, stethoscope, knives, needles, drugs, everything.

Hakim's hands were untied. He was allowed to clean up the mess, but his knives were taken. Firuz was cut free too. They were both escorted to the prisoners.

'They took your scalpels.'

'*Khafih-sho,*' said the soldier in clear Persian, telling Firuz to shut up, which he did.

They were allowed to see to each prisoner's condition, watched closely by their accompanying guards. Up rows of paired prisoners they steadily worked. Firuz pulled out some anti-bacterial gel and gauze to bandage a wounded forearm, looking around to count the number of captured. 'These are the missing troop,' he told Hakim, aside. The soldier warned him again, '*Khafih-sho!*' And Firuz shut up once more.

103

Hakim spotted where the reconnaissance officer was, standing with his superiors. The order came from them to move forward. The prisoners were stood, flanked by most of the foot soldiers. The armoured vehicles would lead the way save one, the machine-gun-loaded jeep, which was kept back to cover the rear. Hakim and Firuz were lined up. They didn't resist their blindfolds or hands being tied up again.

Hakim was certain that the troop was moving due east, into Iranian territory. It meant either the war had forced back their adversaries well into Iran, or they were heading in the wrong direction. His glasses jabbed him in his breast with each step, reminding him that the soldier's initial search had not been thorough. The letter was still there, crumpled in his shirt pocket behind his glasses. He was anxious to read its entire contents, but knew his captors would confiscate it if they found it on him.

Beneath the sounds of the grinding machines, Firuz slipped out, 'They're lost.'

'We'll see,' Hakim said simply.

Near the front an Iranian soldier fell to the ground, which tripped up the rows behind him. Extra soldiers were hustled to clear the mess. The soldiers diverted the captives around the wounded prisoner, forcing them ahead. Hakim and Firuz were unbound and brought to the man for attention.

They lifted him to standing. Firuz carried most of his weight, one arm around the man's waist and the other over his shoulder. Hakim snapped an ammonia salt beneath his nose, reviving him. The soldiers forced them to start walking at pace. Hakim went ahead, keeping pace sideways and sometimes backwards to tend to the wounds.

Firuz wiped off the man's bloodied face. 'He's got a few broken teeth and a few more missing.'

'Broken?' Firuz asked.

Hakim nodded. 'Looks fractured.'

The reconnaissance officer saw the uncolumned clump. He left his command position and headed towards them.

Hakim stuffed cotton in his patient's mouth, antiseptic over his minor wounds, anything he could to comfort him.

The reconnaissance officer seemed to come from nowhere and kicked Hakim to the ground with his bag. He made it clear by his raving gestures that there would be two in a row, in step, or else.

Firuz bent down to help Hakim up with his supplies. Another prisoner defiantly defended his friend's need for attention. The officer raised his rifle to strike him down, and Firuz, in a burst of insight, now knowing how the soldier had gotten his jaw broken, shouted, 'That's what this monster did to this first soldier!'

Hearing the accusation, the officer swung the butt of his rifle around and thrust it into Firuz's back, hard, knocking him flat.

Hakim ran over to help him. Firuz sat up holding his back and glaring at the officer. 'I was talking medical!'

The officer raised his rifle again, but Hakim raised his hands over Firuz's back. 'Please,' he implored in Arabic. 'It's enough.'

The officer let his rifle swing around his shoulder, then lifted two of his fingers for them to line up again. It was all they were to do for the time being.

The whole episode proved to him that the troop thought they were still in danger. They all needed water to continue, and night would have been the better time to travel, but their position was still being threatened. They were heading north now, as if going around an area they thought was hostile.

As the sun neared its point of setting, the Iraqi troop again changed direction, now heading towards the horizon. They had been wise to travel this route. From the south the gray clouds of a skirmish were blowing in their direction. They were like animal trackers, trying to hide their scent and sound away from their prey.

Between two steep hills the troop finally came to a halt. The vehicles were set in a semi-circle, and men posted on the advance hill. The jeep pointed its machine gun at the prisoners, while the guards made them sit half-way up the rear hill in clear view. The Iranian medics were freed to treat the wounded again. The soldiers then began a more intense search of each prisoner.

Hakim cleared out the stones around them and lowered the exhausted and injured down to rest. He would have liked the same privilege, but duty came first. His face was sore, crackly burnt from the day in the fierce sun. He tasted his blood with each lick of his lips and longed for a cup of water to wet his chalky mouth. He massaged his wrists, getting the circulation flowing again to his numb hands.

The reconnaissance officer brought a few assistants with him over to Hakim. He kicked the soles of the broken-jawed soldier's boots.

'He needs to rest,' Hakim said in Arabic.

The injured man had enough strength to hurl any insult he could through his throbbing mouth, although he managed only to lisp and spit incomprehensible syllables. Hakim quieted him by firmly pressing his jaw shut and whispering a warning. He heard the officer say to his men, 'Check the doctor.'

Firuz stepped forward, but was pushed down by a guard.

All the prisoners were seated now except Hakim. His pockets were completely emptied. His watch was taken, and his keys. They handed him back his glasses. But the letter the officer took an interest in, trying to read it in the last light without a flashlight. His look at Hakim was as though he had discovered a hidden treasure. His yellow teeth glistened like a dog.

'Persian. You are Bahá'í.'

Hakim stared at him blankly. He neither admitted the accusation nor denied it.

'We have one of those Bahá'ís,' he shouted down the hill for his men to hear.

Firuz did not have to understand Arabic to guess the invective. 'He's not a Bahá'í! He found that letter, you stupid ass, on the body of a dead soldier your men plowed down!'

'Hold your tongue,' Hakim told Firuz. 'I'll tell them.'

The officer shook his head at Hakim, then popped a chuckle. 'Your troops killed the Bahá'ís.'

'I know,' Hakim said softly.

'What did you both say?' Firuz begged.

The officer crumpled the paper and tossed it to the ground. Firuz bent forward to retrieve it. A medallion fell out from beneath his shirt, catching the eye of the officer.

The officer bent down and pulled Firuz up by his chain, as another soldier pressed his gun against Firuz's back. In one pull the officer snapped the medallion off his neck, then with the back of his hand smacked Firuz down, cutting him across his cheek with the medal.

Then the officer spoke in clear Persian. 'All you Iranians have are Bahá'ís, Armenian Christians and Jews. This is why your Revolutionary Leader is losing the war!'

He laughed with his men, heading back down the slope to his

commander. Hakim bent down and picked up the letter, uncrumpled it, then refolded it neatly, and reverently kissed it before sliding it into his shirt pocket again. He went over and sat down beside Firuz to tend his wound.

'Someone's going to think you're Bahá'í if you act like that,' Firuz said, cautioning him.

Hakim found his vial of methiolate in his bag and doused a gauze bandage, then pressed it against Firuz's cheek. 'Would it matter?'

'No-ah. AH!' Firuz took the pad himself and dabbed it on his own face. 'I'd still be your friend.'

'And I,' slurred the toothless soldier.

The irony of their fealty made Hakim feel uncomfortable. He merely nodded. 'I'll remember that if I ever become a Bahá'í.'

'It would be better if you could produce a miracle and get us out of this hell,' said another blindfolded soldier.

Firuz clarified Hakim's station in life. 'He's a doctor, not God.'

Another prisoner spoke out. 'You forget, God is on our side.'

'If there is a God,' said another, disconsolately.

'If,' Hakim agreed, looking out to the distant night flares of war beginning again with its rumbling explosions. He got up and reseated himself a few steps up the hill to be alone. The guards saw his action, but did nothing. They could still see him.

He stared up at the sky above to the face of the full moon. He had said 'if', which bothered him. Who was he to say 'if'? He slipped his glasses on and brought out the letter. He had to strain to read, but the moon was bright.

'My dear Tahirih,' it began. His heart pounded. He questioned his mind why he was unable to read it calmly. It was only a letter.

He read, 'My dear Tahirih, Forgive my weakness of pen. I am unable to write how strong my love is for you. My heart fills with joy as I recall our few years together. In each pebble of sand I see the clear reflection of your countenance, as though you were present. Is this a sign of my ardent prayers to be beside you; is this the longing of Majnun for his Layli?'

What Iranian was not familiar with the spiritually intoxicated lover, Majnun, who thirsted for the presence of his beloved Layli? It brought memories to Hakim of the verses related about Majnun being found by other men as he sifted through the sands of the desert, tears flowing down his face:

*They said, 'What doest thou?'*

*He said, 'I seek for Layli.'*

*They cried, 'Alas for thee! Layli is of pure spirit and thou seekest her in the dust!'*

*He said, 'I seek her everywhere; haply somewhere I shall find her.'*

However much Hakim knew that this poem of mystical lore was not about the bonds of mortal love, it still reminded him how much he missed his wife.

He remembered his lessons, and how he had learned that Bahá'u'lláh likened this passage to the search one makes for the presence of his true Beloved. Ziya was a glint of light to his search.

A cooler wind made the page waver in his hand. His eyes read swiftly across its letters.

'Never be sad that our bodies are separated by distance, for it is evident that at all times our souls are near each other and attached through all the realms of God.

'. . . Forgive my shortcomings always. Pray for me, whatever may befall us out in this land of waste, pray that we all are protected from the steel of our enemies, who would turn us away from that for which we were created.'

The prayer remained to be read. Hakim's body shivered. It wasn't the cooling weather. It was that he knew the prayer. He wasn't battling his mind to read it, it was the fear his heart contained. His trembling came from there, forewarning him of oncoming detoxification.

'. . . By Thy glory, O Beloved One, Thou giver of light to the world! The flames of separation have consumed me, and my waywardness hath melted my heart within me. I ask of Thee, by Thy Most Great Name, O Thou the Desire of the world and the Well-Beloved of mankind, to grant that the breeze of thine inspiration may sustain my soul . . .'

Why was he feeling such pain wreathing through his body? He was dead.

'. . . Thou seest, O Lord my God, the tears of Thy favored ones, shed because of their separation from Thee, and the fears of Thy devoted ones in their remoteness from Thy Holy Court. By Thy power, that swayeth all things, visible and invisible! It behooveth Thy loved ones to shed tears of blood for that which hath befallen the faithful at the hands of the wicked and the oppressors on the earth.'

Hakim's head sank deep against his chest. He crushed the letter to his heart, unable to finish, unable to supplicate through His words to be shielded by the bounty of God. The tears streamed down his face. 'O God, forgive this miserable soul.' His head hit the ground before him, his body shaking.

A whistling rocket streaked across the sky and suddenly exploded only hundreds of meters in front of the encampment, igniting the night around them. The Iraqi soldiers scurried into position, firing into the darkness. The shell smoke blew over them, adding to their frantic movements. The guards tightened up the prisoners for security, huddling them into a smaller area.

Unexpectedly, another rocket imploded, this time near the base of the rear hill near the captives, hurtling shrapnel and sand everywhere. Then more rockets. And the prisoners broke free, scattering, at which the guards opened fire on them all.

Hakim sat still in his daze as the bullets whizzed by his ears. Firuz and the broken-jawed soldier ran up the hill in the smoke searching for him, while others ran over the top to safety.

The reconnaissance officer advanced up the hill with his assistants, firing at everything that moved, calling for reinforcements. The machine-gunned jeep rolled up, only to be exploded into flames by a direct hit from a shell.

Firuz saw the officer and his men coming. Desperately, he hurled stones at them, swearing God's revenge on them. The high-pitched streak of another rocket sent him for cover, but there was Hakim only a few more feet away. He lunged on top of him protectively, knocking him flat. The shell slammed into the hill between them and the soldiers, covering them in a mass of dirt and rubble.

'Get up!' Firuz dragged Hakim up the hill. 'You're not dying here. Neither am I!'

Hakim had been so forcefully directed that he knew he should be getting up the hill. His feet instinctively found their balance and he ran to the top, to the waiting soldier. Then he remembered Firuz. 'Come on!' he called back, unable to see him through the clouds.

Firuz ran along, distracting the fire from Hakim's direction. Then he froze; he had run into the aim of the reconnaissance officer's rifle.

Hakim, now seeing them both, was too far away to do anything. He shouted powerfully, 'Firuz!'

Another explosion rocked them to the ground. As the rain of

debris settled, Firuz looked for the officer and his men, but all he could find was the meteoric hole sizzling. Nothing remains after a direct hit.

'Firuz! Firuz!'

Hakim found him – relieving a dead Iraqi soldier of his water canteen.

'Some soldiers, huh,' Firuz said, still panting, heading up the hill with Hakim to the broken-jawed soldier. 'They obviously are not from this region. The wind changes direction when the sun sets.'

Hakim wasn't going to argue with him. He was just thankful to see him still miraculously alive.

'Now all we have to do, Doctor, is get back!'

'We have to,' slurred the broken-jawed soldier, as they slid down the other side.

'See if you can get us a more reasonable job, will you, Doctor? Somewhere possibly more sane. I'm beginning to understand why my mother doesn't like my kind of work.'

'By the Almighty God, I'll take care of that,' the soldier said, promising.

'Don't abuse our fortune,' Hakim warned them both. 'God doesn't hand out miracles freely.'

Firuz put his hand on Hakim's shoulder. 'Let's stay with this God. He's worked wonders so far.'

Hakim pulled Firuz forward, somewhat playfully. 'Don't talk, run!'

# CHAPTER 9

# Heroes' Recompense

Amin disregarded the watch he was repairing. He was sitting in the right position to view Mitra. If her mother could only see the streaks she was leaving on the front of the glass case she had been told to clean, he thought, amused. And she was using the most filthy rag.

'Is it almost ready, sir?' the woman asked impatiently.

Amin turned to the customer with Asiyih. She was wrapped from head to toe in black, though her olive jowls stood out, drooping with age. 'Patience, Khanum, patience. It will be a few minutes more in the ageless plan of existence. Patience. So you can continue what you were saying to Asiyih Khanum.'

He pulled the small magnifying lens, which was attached to his working glasses, over his right eye, and searched through the back of the watch, then added, 'And pick out a nice watch for your dear husband while you're with us.'

She ignored his pitch and went back to chatting with Asiyih.

Amin was pleased with that bit of attempted salesmanship. He was trying. And the sales needed to be better. The shop wasn't exactly a profitable business for his brother's family, although he was doing everything he could to assist them.

He made the work appear much more difficult than it actually was, and enjoyed a glance over his counter to see how Mitra was getting along.

Saffa sneaked in through the open front door, catching the attention of his mother and mouthing the words 'twenty tumans'. She nodded, pretending to be listening to the woman before her.

'Saffa,' Mitra called, without turning from the other counter's glass.

They all noticed her mess.

'How could you see me through that,' Saffa said, holding back a laugh. He wiped it clean for her, and showed Mitra her reflection. She turned away, not happy.

'Come on.'

Saffa took her to the back room and closed the curtained doorway.

Amin was proud of Saffa. He had at least tried to cheer his dispirited sister. He was proud of all of them. Another time he might have spoken against Asiyih and Saffa for spending their small earnings on gifts for a birthday. But Mitra needed cheering up. And God wouldn't mind the custom he thought, especially with what this family had been through for His sake. And their motives were pure.

Amin's unmagnified eye could see Asiyih clearly through the simple glass. He had grown to admire her, no longer seeing her as the wife of his brother, but as a shining example, a Bahá'í in her own light. What she had endured would have withered most people. It was as though she had bloomed in winter. Her clothes were now vibrant, full of color. And the henna she applied to her fast-graying hair brought back to light a lustrous sheen of red-brown color. Even her speech was alive, a source of encouragement to all.

'Please, continue, Khanum,' Asiyih said, now that her children were gone.

'Well, as I was saying . . . It looks like they are not going to issue or renew passports for any of the Bahá'ís. And with the coming food rationing, which we will have to get at the mosque, none of the Bahá'ís will be given their allotment unless they recant.' Her initial whispers crescendoed into full volume.

'Where did you hear all this from?' Asiyih asked earnestly, looking over to see how Amin was doing, only to find him listening to their conversation.

'The other friends, Asiyih. All Iran knows this. You should pay attention, Asiyih Khanum – and I told you that your children would be thrown out of that fanatical school.'

Asiyih watched Amin pop the batteries out of the fine watch and replace them with fresh ones. He came over, pressing the back on firmly, and adjusted the time.

Asiyih turned back to her friend. 'The administrators had no alternative. You know, one of Saffa's teachers put up a fight against his superiors and resigned his post in protest. It was the Ministry of Education that gave the commands.'

'Puh, puh, puh! I don't listen to politics, Asiyih Khanum.'

'Nor gossip,' Amin said, writing up the bill.

Asiyih smiled, shaking her head at Amin.

'I don't gossip, sir,' huffed the old lady. 'And if I happen to hear that some souls are escaping over the mountains of Azerbaijan to Turkey, or across the deserts from Zahedan to Pakistan, I didn't start the rumor. Truth is truth.'

Asiyih had heard this before, yet couldn't fathom escaping from Iran, risking one's life. 'What about their loved ones?'

'If they can afford it, they take their immediate families with them, Asiyih,' she said. 'If I had one hundred thousand tumans, I would take my family too.'

'All you need is fifty tumans,' Amin said, handing her the bill and the watch. 'And you can escape from this shop through the front door – without having to purchase another thing.'

She checked it thoroughly, even rattling it to see if it still kept time. She put it on her arm like an over-sized bracelet, and pulled her chadour sleeve down to cover it.

'Thank you, Amin. I must be going. Remember what I told you, Asiyih.'

'Yes, thank you, Khanum.'

'*Khoda Hafez.*'

'*Khoda Hafez,*' they both said, watching her leave.

Amin took off his glasses and rubbed the arch of his nose, then unfolded his plan. 'Now that Saffa's back, I'll take Mitra to my house. Then I'll drop her at your house before you close shop.'

'Thank you, Amin. That will give us enough time.'

Amin fetched Mitra out from the back. Asiyih gave her a kiss good-bye.

'Make sure that you lock the door, if Uncle Amin brings you home before we arrive.'

Mitra wasn't smiling.

'There's going to be a surprise,' she revealed, trying to brighten her up.

Mitra just nodded, as if listening to an order. She took her uncle's hand and went out into the bazaar with him.

Two men across from the shop were watching intensely as Amin and Mitra came out. They turned around when Amin glanced over to their direction, showing him the back of their army jackets, and pretended to be engaged in buying a watermelon at the stand before them. Out of the corners of their eyes they watched the man and child walk toward the entrance to the bazaar.

'If I have to turn around one more time like that because you're afraid someone will recognize you . . .' Firuz warned Hakim.

Hakim handed Firuz the underweight watermelon he held in his arms. 'Shut up, Firuz.'

'Why don't we just go to your brother-in-law's shop. I could use a discount on a new watch.'

A shopper came near the two, taking a second glance at Hakim. Hakim pulled out a cigarette and lit up, which made the man shrug off any idea of recognizing him.

'For someone who wanted to come home, you certainly don't want to be welcomed back. Were you that bad a surgeon?'

'I'm nervous, all right!'

Firuz stared at the shop-owner, who wanted to know what he was going to do with the watermelon in his hands.

'You call that a watermelon? Rubbish!' Hakim said, and walked away. 'It's the end of the season.'

Firuz was having a tough time. End of the season or not, it was still a delicious-looking watermelon he was surrendering. He gave it back and shrugged, blaming it all on the man he was with, then turned and caught up with Hakim. They moved closer to the outside of the shop.

'Jamshid must be in the back,' Hakim said aloud to himself.

'Who?'

'My sister's husband.'

Firuz noticed that other people seemed to be talking about them. 'If we keep loitering, the Pasdars are going to think we're up to no good. And I've had enough. I'm hungry. Let's go in the shop, or to your house.'

'That's it,' Hakim said, then checked his watch.

'What, what?' he asked, excited by Hakim's enlivened response.

Hakim pulled out a billfold of money and stuffed it into Firuz's hand. 'Go out and buy everything for a feast; meat, cheeses, vegetables, sweets, everything.'

'And where are you going off to?'

'Revolutionary Guard headquarters – for civilian employment. I'm supposed to meet a Commander there.'

'And what about me!' he shouted after him.

'Get plenty of mutton!'

'I meant a job. Remember who helped wire up the jaw, too?'

'I remember.'

Hakim came back and gave him some more money, just in case. 'Get a large lamb.'

'Hakim? What happens if the parliamentary father unwires his son's jaw?'

'Hope there are vacancies in Iraqi hospitals. Get the food and I'll meet you by the taxi stand in an hour. And don't stand around. The Revolutionary Guards will know you're up to no good.'

Firuz watched Hakim vanish through the shoppers. 'Did I hear humor? I'm rubbing off,' he said to himself, turning toward the watermelons. 'There's hope yet for the doctor.'

Hakim's taxi rushed through the afternoon traffic. Each building they passed brought back memories to him. Outwardly the place hadn't changed much, but the people were much more somber, there was no life in their appearance, the atmosphere was depressing.

He had mixed feelings about being there. He didn't know what had happened to his son, where he was, how the others would receive him. He would have to find a way. Firuz would help.

The taxi pulled in front of the refurbished building, which was surrounded by an army of Pasdars, some of whom became attracted to the taxi when Hakim began arguing about the outrageous fare. The driver finally gave in to what he could get, glad to get rid of his passenger.

The Pasdars directed Hakim where he needed to go. At each section he was searched. Even the women and children were searched as well, by other militant women. It was quite a sight to get used to – women in centuries-old coverings in modern times, with modern-day weaponry slung over their shoulders.

A Pasdar called out to Hakim, 'This way, Doctor.'

He didn't like the sight of the place. It reminded him too much of the time he had been led to the empty room to see his wife. He fantasized having a hidden hand grenade and pulling its pin at the appropriate moment when he reached his destination, taking with him all the corrupt and evil officials he could imagine. He wanted to get in and get out as quick as he could before he suffocated.

Hakim was sent into an office.

'Dr Hakim Irani,' the voice at the desk said, reading his name.

It was a voice he had hoped never to hear again. Isfahani. He hadn't changed much. His face was a little harder in its features, the eyes a little colder, the stature a wee bit more despotic, more gray at the temples, but it was Isfahani. And there was one very important change: Isfahani was sitting in the Commander's chair.

Isfahani re-introduced himself and had Hakim take a seat.

'It's an honor to meet an Iranian war hero,' he said, with a smirk, offering him one of his cigarettes. Hakim surprised him with one of his own. They were both the same brand.

'Commander Rashti sends his regards to you, Doctor. I'm sure you remember the Commander, and how he remembers you.'

Hakim devised the vision of tying both Commanders to a pack mule and kicking it into a live minefield.

'He has received instructions that I should endeavor to take all measures available to secure your every wish – to serve your country, that is. By the way, Doctor, did you read today's paper?'

Isfahani was playing it cool. He wanted to determine how much the doctor had changed, and if he could still serve his purpose. He removed a copy of the paper from his drawer and dropped it open for the doctor to see. Hakim glanced down, read the headline, then looked up indifferently. He knew what he had done.

Isfahani flipped through the pages to where the article continued and exposed a picture of Hakim and Firuz in a solemn pose beside the broken-jawed soldier, and his father, an Iranian parliamentary figure.

Hakim hated Isfahani's boyish smirk. He concocted another scheme where he was Isfahani's judge, letting Isfahani choose the type of his execution. Hakim would become his willing executioner.

'It's a noteworthy picture,' Isfahani remarked. 'Ayatullah Rustami suggested that an article to follow up your bravery and escape was a proper way to inspire the region.'

Hakim emptied his thoughts of violence. It solved nothing. And he had had enough of this man's nonsense. 'You have received my letter, no doubt,' he began factually, 'requesting my "desire to serve" in a city hospital.'

Isfahani's attempt with the newspaper proved the doctor's resilience to him. He folded it up and threw it aside. 'Yes, Doctor. I have.' He studied Hakim's face more carefully. It was stronger, more defying, a different type of adversary. It challenged Isfahani.

He brought out a stamped letter and showed it to Hakim. 'I have already found what I believe to be the perfect job for your qualifications. It's only a few hours away, in Khorramabad. I'm sure that the Ayatullah and Commander Rashti will approve – and convince our parliamentarian.'

Hakim nodded his approval, then smiled. 'Good. You'll see that Firuz Mostaqim is granted a position there as well.'

Hakim put out his cigarette and sat back.

Isfahani was slow to speak. 'I'm afraid that is out of the question, Doctor. He's not needed.'

Hakim leaned up and tapped the official document. 'We wouldn't want to be disobedient to our instructions, Commander?'

'Don't get cocky with me, Doctor!' he lashed out.

Hakim stood. 'From my hotel room here, I have spoken directly with our parliamentarian. He said I should call him back to tell him how pleased I was with all the arrangements the "Commander" would make with me.'

The doctor was thorough – Isfahani had to give him credit for that. 'I should be very upset, with you trying to usurp my responsibilities. But every time we meet, I always move up in rank.' He stood up, eye to eye with Hakim. 'As you may have ascertained out in the field, they wanted you dead, killed in action. I've always hoped that you would return. Allah seems to answer my prayers. Now it appears that they want to make use of their new-found hero, and I think you should be put to pasture, like an old horse.'

'Maybe you should have shot me that day. You could have been in Qumm right now, next to the Revolutionary Leader.'

'Wait outside,' he said, infuriated.

Hakim instantly obeyed.

Isfahani called to the Pasdar at his door. 'Keep the doctor there until I call for him.'

The guard shut the door, acknowledging the command.

Isfahani sat on his desk and dialed a call. The doctor was not going to make a fool of him.

'. . . Commander Rashti, please.'

He knew the Commander would steal the idea he had. Isfahani had to make it sound as though his own ideas came from the Commander, then there would be nothing to lose. As usual.

'Good afternoon, Commander. I've just spoken with Dr Irani . . . No, no. I did as you suggested. The newspaper didn't affect him either way. No, I would venture to say that our doctor's belief is mere survival now. Yes. He has accepted the hospital job. He's asked for the Jew to be with him and I think this is a good idea. I'm going to call the Ayatullah personally to recommend it.'

Isfahani's bait worked like a charm.

'No, no. If you would prefer to speak with the Ayatullah about the matter yourself, it would be much better presented. Yes, I think it's a good place too. I'll be able to check on him weekly and report his progress to you. That prison will be a clever starting point for the campaign – though we'll have to take our time using him . . . Thank you, Commander. No, please, it was all your ideas which suggested my insignificant words. It would be my honor to be your guest with the Ayatullah. Yes, soon. *Qurbani shoma*.'

He certainly would be in Qumm one day, as Rashti's equal, he thought, going out.

'All right, Doctor. You have your job and your Jew.'

There was a new plot brewing behind Isfahani's composed words. Hakim simply nodded. Isfahani led him out of the building.

'Don't worry, Doctor. I will always look after you. A just master always looks after his old servants,' he said, then clicked his mouth.

Hakim stopped and looked at him. 'You wanted to say something else?'

His voice was callous. 'How could any one like you, who has shamed his family, his friends, his belief, be worthy of being proclaimed a "hero", and still be so remote from God?'

The stab stunned Hakim, yet he didn't show the wound to Isfahani. After a moment he shrugged his shoulders and gazed deep into Isfahani's eyes. 'Welcome to paradise, Commander.'

Hakim got into a taxi and went across Kashan to the bazaar. He had merely altered the words Firuz had greeted him with when he entered the military camp, and used them on Isfahani. It made him see in some mystical way the cyclical patterns that governed reality, its never-ending cycles; the end in the beginning and the beginning in the end.

He found Firuz waiting outside the bazaar with all the groceries, told him the good news of their upcoming job, then left him as suddenly. There were a few things Firuz had not purchased that he wanted. Actually, he needed an excuse to go past the shop, which to his surprise he found closed. As he rushed to get back he nearly knocked over Saffa, who was coming out of the fabric shop with his mother.

Saffa saw the sporadic movement of the strange man maneuvering around them, saw him make his way out of the bazaar quickly, hiding his face.

'Pasdars,' he said in disgust, pressing the bundled package of cloth under his arm.

'What did you say?' Asiyih asked, disappointed with the tone of his remark.

'I said, "I wish we could buy a sweet for Mitra, too."'

'That's the most positive lie I've ever heard,' she said, shaking her head. 'God has provided us with enough gifts for today.'

She noticed how poorly Saffa was carrying himself. 'Walk with dignity. You are a Bahá'í.'

He straightened his body as he always did when he heard this phrase, then slowly fell back into his casual posture as they went back and forth from shop to shop.

'Why don't we walk somewhere else today, Mama. You're not really shopping – and they're not selling to us.'

'This is another way to teach the Cause of the Blessed Beauty. And we'll walk in the same area. After a few seeds are planted, the farmer waters them until they sprout.'

'The bazaar isn't fertile soil.'

They went past the butcher's and the bakery, at an easy pace. Whenever she looked at him, he quickly straightened. He said to himself, despising their condition, 'If Baba was here.'

A middle-aged woman dropped a parcel from her stack of goods at the feet of Asiyih, who quickly bent down and placed it securely on the woman's other packages. Their eyes met. Asiyih smiled at her, a smile which was returned, but then the woman turned away. She had wanted to say thank you, but knew who

Asiyih was and obviously didn't know what to say. Her eyes had shown Asiyih her gratitude.

'Now we can go home, Saffa,' she said happily.

Saffa paid their bus fares and sat down beside her. She watched for their stop, while he worried about how he was going to bring up the next subject. And before he had enough courage, they were off the bus and walking up the main street crushing the falling leaves beneath their feet.

'I was thinking,' he began half-heartedly.

Asiyih walked vigorously, which made him keep up and speak more loudly. She knew what she was doing.

'I was thinking that maybe – '

'Yes, Saffa?'

' – That maybe it might not be a bad idea to move. To Teheran.' He rushed to say everything he wanted before she stopped him. 'No one would ask if we were Muslim or Bahá'í. And we could sell the shop and I could open a new one. I know enough – '

Asiyih shook her head. Where her son got his ideas she didn't know. 'Do you want us to sell the shop to your Uncle Amin? What would your father want us to do?'

'Other families are moving,' he said defensively.

'Where are they running?'

'Mama. I'm not suggesting "running". I am thinking about Mitra and you.'

'Trust in God.'

'It's not that simple.'

'It is, dear.'

He kicked a pile of leaves. 'Uncle Hakim used to talk like that.'

She ended his rebellion with her strong gaze. 'Stop listening to your friends who increase your doubts in God.'

'I'm sorry.'

She touched his cheek, then put her hand on his shoulder. 'All these tests will pass soon. Be patient.'

When she looked away from him, he thought he saw a tear in her eye. It was his fault if she was saddened. He thought of something to cheer her up.

From an open trash bin he pulled out a newspaper stuffed on top.

'Put that back in the garbage,' she said softly.

'It's today's. And it's important to keep abreast of the latest news.' He opened the front page. 'See! Iranian troops kill 100 Iraqi soldiers.'

'If you're going to read, tell me inspiring news.'

He searched for the right story. 'Prime Minister calls for new confidence!'

She shook her head.

'Medics' daring escape in rescue of parliamentary leader's son? Food rationing to be implemented?' The stories were not interesting to his mother's ears. He got an idea and ruffled the paper, clearing his throat. 'Bahá'í Faith declared as sovereign religion of Iran?'

Asiyih turned. Saffa's face was deliberately hidden behind the open paper. 'Where does it say that?' she said with a smile.

Saffa heard her happier tone of voice. He went along with his reading. 'Bahá'í Faith topples Iran through the love of God. When asked how this was possible in such a short time, Mr. Saffa Danesh of Kashan replied, "Shielded with the protection of the Most Great Name of God, no dart of animosity could ever have penetrated the armor of this once persecuted community. And with their flaming arrows of love they rose to attack and pierced the hearts of the Iranian peoples, igniting within their breasts the fire of the love of God and unity!"'

'*Yá Bahá'u'l-Abhá!*' she said, then laughed. 'A poet!'

He threw the paper in the next bin and walked closely beside her down the alleyway to their home. His mother was right; there really wasn't any place to run, nor any reason to do so.

Asiyih held Saffa back with a sudden stop. Their front door was open.

Saffa calmed her. 'Uncle Amin probably left the door open.'

'Your Uncle Amin knows better,' she said, with a waver in her voice.

Saffa gave her his package and pushed the door open with his foot, then carefully peered in. It looked safe. The strong odors of onions, vegetables and steaming rice filled the courtyard as they entered. Someone had placed their grill on bricks. It was filled with kebab sticks of lamb, tomatoes and onions spitting over the coal fire. Asiyih went straight into the kitchen, Saffa beside her. Standing on a chair was Mitra, leaning over the stove and stirring a pot of bubbling stew.

'What are you doing?' Saffa asked her, as he and his mother

glanced all around the room. There were fruits and vegetables, canned goods, breads and sweets on every table top. Even the oven was filled with more meat cooking inside.

Mitra pulled out her stirring spoon and pointed at the mouth-watering meal roasting in the oven. '*Tass-kebab!*'

'Mitra, dear. Where did all this food come from?' Asiyih said sternly. 'Uncle Amin?'

Mitra shook her head firmly and pointed her stick to the courtyard, where an unknown man entered, hidden behind the weight of more packages of food.

'Who are you?' she demanded.

'Oh, I'm sorry,' he said, in a muffled voice, trying to make his way to a clear spot to put everything down. The bags dropped onto a table in the kitchen. Firuz wiped his blue jeans off and turned around. 'I should have knocked. I thought no one was home yet.'

He looked like a delivery boy, hoping that his order would be appreciated.

'I thought that . . . well . . . Firuz Mostaqim.' He politely introduced himself, looking expectantly at the door, realizing he was all alone.

'What are you doing here?'

'We were given four weeks leave, so we came first to Kashan to help out, then we're going to my family in Hamadan.'

Their blank faces told him he had only confused them. 'To help who?' Asiyih asked.

'Me,' Hakim said simply, as he came in behind them.

Asiyih turned; her legs became weak, her face paled. 'Saffa,' she said, covering her mouth.

Saffa's eyes were wide. It couldn't be his uncle – he was dead – but he wasn't. 'Uncle Hakim?' He rushed to his uncle's embrace, who kissed him hard on both cheeks, then looked over at his sister. She was still dumbfounded by his presence. 'Are you happy, Asiyih Khanum?'

'We thought they killed you, too!' Saffa shouted in joy.

Asiyih's gaze went to the floor. She couldn't face him. He should not have come back. Where had he been all these months without a word or a letter to them to tell them of his condition. She was so confused.

Hakim's fears of returning were confirmed. He had been away

too long, and his past acts still scarred his presence there. He tried to be cheerful and patted Saffa on his back. 'Help Mitra check the kebab.' He smiled to Firuz. 'Come, my friend. We have a long way to travel tomorrow.'

'It was my pleasure to meet you, Khanum,' Firuz said, then joined Hakim.

Saffa listened as the front door closed tightly. He was going to have to tell his mother something she might not like to hear, but he was the man of the house now.

'Now, what would 'Abdu'l-Bahá say?'

He went over to help Mitra. His mother had heard him, but said nothing. So he answered his own question and quoted,

*You must consider all His servants as your own family and relatives. Direct your whole effort toward the happiness of those who are despondent, bestow food upon the hungry, clothe the needy, and glorify the humble. Be a helper to every helpless one, and manifest kindness to your fellow creatures in order that ye may attain the good pleasure of God.*

Saffa gave the spoon back to Mitra. 'Uncle Hakim taught me that. He said that it was the Hippocratic Oath for a true Bahá'í.'

She was amazed at his memory. Her brother would have told Saffa that to get him to memorize the passage. She sighed, gradually looking up at her son. 'All right. Go and call your uncle back in.'

He crossed his arms and leaned back against the stove, not budging, then shook his head. 'No.'

She didn't expect his flagrant attitude at a moment like this. 'Next to obedience to God, young man, is obedience to your parents. And I am your Mother!'

'And "he" is your brother . . . '

Before she realized how far Saffa's utterance had moved her heart, her feet had carried her down the alley to stop Hakim and his companion. She was completely out of breath. 'You can at least stay for supper. With your friend . . . please.'

Firuz thought that must have been the most difficult offer this woman had ever had to make. He bowed out. 'Forgive me, but I should return to the hotel. I'm not feeling very well.'

'Don't play polite,' Hakim said.

'I'm not. I just think the food will taste better if you two enjoyed it alone.' He saw that he was right. Hakim wasn't arguing with him. 'Thank you, Khanum. Another time, perhaps.'

He backed away from the two. 'I'll wait up for you!'

Asiyih and Hakim looked into each other's eyes, then glanced away with nervous smiles. They had nothing to say to each other yet. And the street wasn't the place. Quietly, they turned together and walked back to the house.

Supper passed easily. Hakim kept Mitra and Saffa filled with tales of army life and his adventures. He excused himself from being 'forced' away so long and promised them all he would be much nearer to them.

After an hour of television, and when Asiyih sent the children to their rooms, Hakim was exhausted of his stories. Asiyih brought him a cup of tea, joining him in the warmth of the guest room. It all reminded him of the comforts of his own home, which was difficult to be near without the feeling of utter loss.

They stirred their cups of tea, sitting across from each other.

'Mitra will make a good cook one day,' he said brightly.

'Yes. We haven't eaten like this for months. Others can make use of what we have in abundance.'

It was like her to give away what was extra. 'But keep the sweets for Mitra's birthday gift?'

'We really shouldn't be celebrating her birthday,' she said with a bit of guilt.

'Nonsense,' he boomed. 'Mitra needs to be encouraged, so do you and Saffa.'

The way she looked at him, as if disbelieving him capable of being inspirational. Hakim wished he could vanish. Who was he, he wondered, when his sister was still steadfast and not he? He put down his cup. He had run out of idle chatter. It was time to speak with someone who knew his past. Yet it was so hard to step forward into an arena of vulnerability and open himself to the blows he had so long deserved. 'Asiyih. Before you ask.'

She thought he was going to burden her with all his guilt to feel exonerated. She would not do that for him. 'I'm not interested, Hakim.'

'Whenever I want to talk to you, you disregard the difficulties we're faced with, like overlooking someone's faults. This is different. Everything is not going to be fine.'

Conflict was all over his face. She tried to listen.

'I want to share my feelings with you, my pain, my loneliness.'

He rubbed his forehead. He wasn't making himself clear. He never did with anyone when it came to expressing his inmost feelings. 'And I tried a diary.'

'A diary?'

He sighed. 'Oh, it didn't work.' He looked at her, searching her eyes. 'Please, Asíyih, don't be angry with me.'

The plea in his voice ran chills through her breast. This was still her brother, but she didn't know him any more. It was hard to know anyone. She rubbed her fingers along the lip of her teacup, fighting within her the instincts to love and forgive.

'Why did you change the subject when I asked if Jamshid was going to be late?'

'Because it would have been hard to explain in front of the children,' she answered him simply.

'Is he in prison?' he said, guessing at her meaning.

'He was.'

She put the cup down and explained the events Hakim had missed while he was away. 'That was several months ago, after you disappeared. The Bahá'í committee he was appointed to needed to have an emergency meeting. They had heard that it was best to meet in groups of threes and drive around in a car to discuss their problems. They thought this would eliminate jeopardizing anyone's home.'

Hakim feared that Jamshid was dead now. He just listened. There was nothing else he could do or say.

'They were being watched all the time, and were subsequently all imprisoned. We never learned the charges. We went to see them, but the authorities denied having them. We received mysterious phone calls saying he had been sent to Evin, that his body was at the morgue for us to collect. It was cruel. And they did this when you disappeared too. It wouldn't surprise me to learn that he is dead. I don't know. I can only pray.'

She went out into the darkened courtyard. He followed and stood beside her at the shallow pool.

'Amin has helped out a great deal. He's even offered to buy the shop. And he teaches Saffa his father's craft when he's able to come around.'

Hakim had no wisdom to offer. His troubles and difficulties seemed to become smaller than the eye of a needle compared to hers.

'There has been talk of not giving food rationing cards to Bahá'ís at Naw-Rúz – time will pass quickly to the New Year. Will you be staying long?'

'A few days. I am to join Firuz with his family, then we are off to work in Khorramabad.' He shook his head. 'I'd rather be fighting another war.'

'Which war?'

'The one that rages in me.' Hakim chuckled to himself. 'Before a nation, we're a hero; in the presence of God, an apostate.'

She turned around. 'What are you mumbling about?'

'Newspapers. Nothing.' He came up to her. 'It's getting late. I should get back to the hotel.'

He didn't feel they had talked enough, but it would have to do. He didn't want to tire her any longer.

'I received a few letters from Payam. He's doing well.'

'Where is he?'

'He returned to Africa.' She paused, then said, 'He believes you're dead.'

'Let it remain that way, for now.'

She made it quite clear. 'You're not a hero to him.'

Hakim didn't wish to have the children overhearing them. He went back into the guest room with his complaint. 'Please, Asiyih. This is not the Heroic Age.'

'When is not the Heroic Age?' she said forcibly, following him. 'Should my Jamshid have renounced his faith because they threatened him, his job, his pension, his family, his life – a limb, a broken bone, his children? Did you think persecution was not part of the Cause of God – only in books or history?'

She had said it all. He sank back into the chair with a thud, then pounded his fist against his forehead.

She took a deep breath. 'I'm sorry. We've all been through a lot. Even the children.'

When he looked up, she was gone. He went out again to the darkness of the courtyard looking at his reflection in the pool. 'Hero.'

Asiyih returned to his side and gave him a letter she had kept for him. Hakim had the feeling it was Payam's, and didn't want to read what he had written. 'How did he get out of the country? He escaped, didn't he?'

'He thought about it,' she said. 'But when he went to the

airport, there wasn't even a question. By the grace of God, he flew back to Africa.' She pushed the letter into his hands.

'I don't want his letter.'

'It's not.'

Her answer disturbed him. She held his hands firmly. 'Come back to us when you can.' Her voice choked. 'Or write.'

Hakim couldn't say good-bye. He kept the letter, letting his hands slip from hers, turned, and went out into the night.

In the trash bin in the hotel room remained the thin rind of the entire watermelon Firuz had eaten for supper. He was alone, enjoying his bedside view of the televised news, watching the images of chanting mobs and angry clergy wailing and speech-making. The camera swept across the crowds, assembled in their thousands at Freedom Square in Teheran, waving their fists in unison at the demonstration.

Firuz matched their actions in sarcasm, and played on the chanting. 'Death to the Shah, Death to the Shah, Death to the Imperialists – Death to anything that moves!'

The hotel door unlocked. Hakim entered, apparently exhausted from his long evening. Firuz ceased his fun, rising to turn off the set. Hakim came over slowly. He dropped the open letter onto the table beside the TV, walked past Firuz and flopped down on the other bed, burying his face in the pillow.

Firuz switched the set off, then peeked into the open envelope, thinking it had to do with the way Hakim was acting. He pulled out the newspaper clipping within and read aloud to himself. 'Tragic Collision Kills Five. A mother, her two daughters and a grandson were killed instantly, police said, when their car lost control and collided head on with a clergyman's car last evening. The esteemed mujtahid, Mulla Ahmad . . . Ziya Rahbari . . . '

Firuz glanced down the rest of the clipping. The article was six months old, about the same time he had first met Hakim. 'Hakim, what does this article have to do with you?'

Hakim took his time to roll over. The pattern of the material he lay upon burnt into his face. He stared up at the ceiling, thinking about Firuz's question. 'Shall I tell you what really happened?'

Firuz sat on the edge of his bed.

'A woman, two of her children and her only grandchild, were killed for their beliefs. And a God-fearing mulla, who finally had enough courage to stand up against the horrible injustices of his fellow countrymen, was murdered. They were all burned beyond recognition to cover it up.'

Firuz believed Hakim was trying to tell him the truth. It would have made more sense to hear in the times of the Shah's SAVAK.

'It's a fantastic story. But what does it have to do with you being so upset?'

'Whenever I take a pen to sign my name, a pain shoots up my arm. And I hear my grandson scream, even though my name was changed.'

Firuz read the article again. 'If it's true. If that's true. Hakim, why didn't they kill you?'

'. . . Because I had no faith.'

All the points of the jigsaw puzzle fell into place. 'Then you are Bahá'í. And that letter you found on that dead soldier – the Iraqi officer was correct!'

Hakim massaged his eyes. 'I was Bahá'í.'

'What do you mean, "was"? A Bahá'í is a Bahá'í, like a Muslim's a Muslim or a Jew's a Jew. Wasn't your father Bahá'í?'

Hakim sat up, taking off his shoes. 'A Bahá'í's faith is not conditioned by his heredity.'

'True,' Firuz said, seeming to have known this before.

Hakim removed his jacket and shirt and threw them across the back of a chair. 'I chose my faith – survival. It was a lot easier than believing in God and recognizing His Manifestations.'

Firuz was getting excited about the conversation. He was going to solve Hakim's dilemma and suggested, 'Maybe your god wasn't God?'

'Don't get philosophical.'

'No, what I mean is: Show me one soul who claims to know God, and I'll show you a madman, an ignorant fanatic, or a Prophet!'

Hakim dressed in his pyjamas. 'For a Jew you "know" a lot.'

There was a smirk there that Hakim didn't appreciate.

'And why not? Everything I'm saying is in the writings of your Faith and mine.'

Hakim stopped dressing. 'What do you know about Judaism and the Bahá'í Faith?' he asked, challenging his ignorant claims.

'A lot! Now that I'm beginning to get a little insight into your past, it's about time you started to learn a little about mine . . .

About one hundred years ago, during the time of Bahá'u'lláh's imprisonment and final exile to the prison-city of Akka, Palestine . . .'

He paused from his story and addressed Hakim's wide-eyed stare. 'Surprised I know so much?' That shut Hakim's mouth, and he went on. 'My great, great-grand-uncle was a Jewish scholar, with extraordinary knowledge of the laws and traditions of Judaism. One day someone told him about the claims Bahá'u'lláh made. Like any honorable scholar, he set out to investigate them, or rather challenge them. Anyway, after some time, his ardent pursuit led him to embrace His Cause. His entire family became Bahá'í. And so all his descendants, my cousins, are Bahá'í. However, my great, great-grandfather, the scholar's brother, refused to ever speak to him again, or for that matter any of the family. They went so far as to move across the city to be away from their influence. Today it's just one large family. We are all Jews by race, but our faiths are different.'

Firuz waited for Hakim to speak. 'So. Are you surprised or impressed?'

'Neither,' he said, getting into bed.

The story sparked a few questions in Firuz, even if Hakim wasn't interested. 'I don't suppose you want to tell me about your ex-Faith now, do you?'

'Not now.'

Hakim lit a cigarette.

Firuz looked around the room. 'I can wait.'

'Wait.'

He lay back on the bed, glancing over at Hakim. 'Who knows. Maybe one day I'll go back home and live on the other side of Hamadan.' He thought seriously about his hint. 'I think from the little I know, if I ever chose to become religious, I'd probably become a Bahá'í.'

Hakim sprang up and threw his cigarette at him, which Firuz immediately stamped out on his bed. 'You never cease to amaze me, Firuz. Life with you has been nothing less than unbelievable. Do you have any idea what you're saying, you pigeon-brained donkey.'

Firuz jumped off his bed, and sat. 'Yes, Hakim. I know what I'm saying.'

'So, why don't you declare yourself a Bahá'í?'

'For the same reason you recanted,' he lashed back.

Hakim was ready to pounce on him for that, but Firuz stayed him with his accusing finger. 'Just because anyone, and I don't care who it is, says they accept all the great spiritual principles – and every Faith has the same ones – it doesn't mean that they are translated into reality and deeds.' Firuz held Hakim away. His breath was hard. 'And I'm not willing to die for embracing something I don't understand yet. And neither were you!' He backed away to the base of his bed and stood. 'What do you want to do? Strike out against the world because you were wrongly persecuted?'

'I was!'

'Who hasn't been? Pick up any Book of God! Look at the lives of any early followers – chased from their lands, thrown to lions, slaughtered, tortured – persecuted! No one can tell me they didn't know what they were in for when they embraced their Faiths.'

'There is a difference,' he said, pulling out the bed sheets to go to sleep. 'The social laws which governed the followers. They could recant in certain circumstances.'

'So. Un–recant!'

Hakim's arm went up like a judge rendering his infallible verdict. '*Kar ist kih shodih.*'

Firuz shook his head. 'Virginity, conception and death are irreversible.'

'Firuz. I broke the Law of God.'

'Very good . . . Can't you fall down? Can't you get back up? Who built the pedestal you fell off of, you or God? What do you want from life?'

'Faith,' he said.

'Then start again!'

Hakim's face went blank. All his anger was gone. Firuz thought he must have given him either a heart attack or the most frightening realization he could imagine. After six months, an infidel in the eyes of Islam, a Jew, was telling Hakim what his wife, a condemned Islamic heretic, had told him before her death: Start again.

Firuz's mind was churning. 'I'm starting to understand the whole thing now. Surgeon? Skilled and transferred to the front lines. What a proof of faith!'

'It's enough, Firuz,' he said quietly. 'Don't play psychiatrist.'

'You're the doctor. Symptoms: Patient feels in his yearning commitments, shame, fear, hate, anger, self-pity – maybe even to self-annihilation – emptiness. Attempts are made to rediscover, re-examine his human contract, seek confirmations and reality. These, my dear Doctor, are the signs of a seeker!'

Hakim pointed to the door. 'I've had enough of your nonsense. Get out of this room.'

Firuz grabbed his bag and jacket, then turned from the door. 'My diagnosis is correct. But I can't make the patient take his medicine.' He threw his bag back on the bed. 'I'll return for that tomorrow before I leave.'

Hakim gave up being argumentative. Firuz was right. 'Just sit down, Firuz.'

'You mean a lot to this crazy Jew!' he hollered at him. 'I've learned so much from your dedication, don't you think you can learn a little about something from a fool like me?'

'Then teach me, wise ol' Jew.'

'That was cruel.'

Firuz walked over dejectedly to the bed and sat, facing Hakim.

'Sorry,' they both said.

Hakim offered him another cigarette. Firuz showed him the one he had: the bent one he had put out on his bed.

'What does your father think of you?' Hakim asked.

'I'm a madman. I don't write enough, or come home enough. And why can't I find a wife at my age and settle down like everyone else. Then my mother worries that I don't eat enough . . . When do we start work, Hakim?'

'Now. I think I'm going to go tomorrow. I'll take the bus.'

'How long is it to Khorramabad?'

'Six, seven hours.'

Hakim looked at Firuz, who had a mischievous look in his eyes. 'Aren't you going to go home?'

'So I'll write my father on the bus and tell them how well I'm eating.'

'You are a madman!'

They kissed each other on both cheeks, laughing heartily, then got into bed. Firuz undressed in the darkness, whistling to himself.

'Thank you, Firuz,' Hakim said, thinking the evening over. 'You are going to make a fine doctor one day.'

'Thank you, Doctor,' he said, climbing into the sheets.
'Do me one favor?'
'Yes, Hakim?' he said, still gloating over his praise.
'Don't go into psychiatry.'
'. . . yes, Hakim . . .'

# CHAPTER 10

# The Prison's Diagnosis

Hakim pulled the curved needle through the skin of the man's buttocks to finish the last stitch. Firuz cut the excess thread then freed Hakim of his instruments to secure a patch over the wound.

There were too many of these types of injuries for Hakim. He might as well have been back at the Iraqi border, with the number of civil war wounds he was seeing. And this was not the first time he had sewn up the rough-looking character on the table in front of him. The crowd this one hung around enjoyed stabbing people.

Hakim snapped off his rubber gloves. 'Stay off this side for a few days,' he told the patient. 'And choose your friends more carefully, brother.'

'Yes, Doctor.'

Hakim had said that to him the last time. The next time they met would probably be for identification in the morgue.

Firuz followed the doctor out beyond the curtain, letting the nurses take over discharging the man.

'You're going to have a hard time explaining why you're late.'

'God punishes me enough, Firuz. I don't need you to remind me about the method in which I must face my retribution.'

They went out into the main hall, dodging through the waves of staff and patients.

'Ah, the wonders of justice.' Firuz mused on that thought. 'Even Moses kicked a rock and got justice. Which reminds me.'

Hakim saw that look of incessant questioning in his eye.

'You didn't say whether the Universal House of Justice was elected or appointed?'

'You're right, I didn't!' Hakim said flatly, then nearly knocked over a patient struggling on his crutches.

The patient apologized. 'Not you,' Hakim said, then pointed at Firuz. 'Him.' The patient then apologized to Firuz. Hakim threw his arms up and walked away from them, imploring God to send him back to the front lines. Firuz made excuses to the patient for Hakim, then ran to keep up. Hakim looked as though he was going to slap him, as he waved his hand at Firuz. 'Stop asking me all these questions!'

'But, Doctor. Who else could I ask in this city of cities?'

Hakim pulled his lab coat lapel out for Firuz to see his name tag more clearly. 'All this says is "Doctor Irani", that's all I know. Bother someone else with the appropriate label.'

Firuz snapped his fingers, knowing just the person. 'Commander Isfahani.'

Hakim ignored him until they came to his office door. 'How long has he been in there?'

Firuz glanced at his watch. 'Forty-five minutes. I guess we took too long.'

'It was a puncture wound.'

'Yes, but only nine stitches.'

'Five minutes a stitch overtime.'

'Like a soccer match: Hakim 9, Isfahani 45.'

Isfahani looked up from the desk as Hakim and Firuz entered. Firuz backed out to leave the two alone and whispered to Hakim as he pulled the door shut, 'The House is elected.'

Hakim would torture him later. 'I'm sorry to have kept you waiting, Commander,' he said turning to Isfahani, seeing the man was not in the best of moods. Hakim thought he must have developed ulcers by now.

'How's the patient?' he asked shortly.

'I think he'll live. He just won't be able to sit down for a while.'

Isfahani's face reddened. 'I am talking about last night's casualty.'

It was an honest mistake. Hakim worked a smile into his diagnosis. 'Well, our Warden is very blessed. If the bullet had been only two more centimeters to the left,' Hakim explained, showing Isfahani on his own coat the bullet's relationship to the heart.

Isfahani relaxed. 'Once again the odd duo save another important life.'

Hakim called out down the passage, disturbing Firuz's chat with a few nurses. 'Go see how the Warden is!'

Firuz left the pretty nurses and went into the intensive care unit. The attending nurse saw him coming. 'He's been up for about fifteen minutes,' she said, trying to close the curtain so Firuz wouldn't go in. He caught it, and slipped around the woman, then pulled the thermometer out of the bed-ridden Warden's mouth and read it to her.

The Warden's cheeks wobbled when he spoke to his rescuer, 'Thank you, Doctor Irani.'

Firuz shook his head, giving the thermometer to the nurse. 'Fine, Warden. All we need now is to get you glasses.' He patted the Warden on his arm, above the intravenous. 'You can thank the doctor later for performing his miracle, that God only knows saved your worthless life. Just rest. We'll have the nurse let your family in to see you.'

Firuz knew this older nurse detested him; she considered all Jews 'unclean'. He contemplated teaching her what he had pried out of Hakim about the Báb being the Promised One of Islam. He would have enjoyed telling her that he had become 'clean' by becoming a Bábí, which would have started another avenue of hatred. Then reason reminded him that Hakim would get into a lot of trouble on his behalf, so the vengeful fantasy would have to wait.

He went back to Hakim's office to report that the Warden's condition was stable. He opened the door only to discover that the two men were gone. It may have been nothing to worry about, but he had a strange suspicion something was sour. He searched everywhere, finally going to the admission desk. 'Did Doctor Irani go out?'

'Yes,' answered the nurse, talking simultaneously on the phone, 'with a Revolutionary Guard official.'

'Where?'

She got confused between the conversations. He pulled the phone from her ear and asked her again. 'Where?'

'The prison, for some reason,' she answered.

Firuz threw his lab coat off and found his jacket, then ran out. Hakim was in trouble – 'Out of the well and into the frying pan.' He shouted to the nurse's station he passed. 'I'll be at the prison.'

Hakim had accepted Isfahani's offer to see the other medical facilities of Khorramabad – in the Khorramabad prison. But he hadn't planned a guided tour of a select row of cells. It was immaculate – white-washed walls, scrubbed toilet holes. It was another of Isfahani's intrigues.

'This is a model prison,' Isfahani went on to say. 'Its infirmary's small, but efficient for the general needs of the prisoners.' Health depended on how long the new prisoners had to stay in their rat cages, Hakim thought. He wasn't about to start an argument, but asked anyway, 'I believe an old prison such as this has a lower level?'

'There is no need to go down there, the cells are disused.' Isfahani directed the prison guards to open the next cell for them.

Hakim cut their engagement short. 'Very clean? Is this what you want me to testify to? Why am I here, Commander?'

'Doctor, I brought you here to allow you to see with your own eyes the conditions of cleanliness and the justice of Islam.'

The prisoners stood to attention. Their garb was spotless.

'Very nice. Clean.' Hakim walked on past the cell. Isfahani gave the command to have it closed. Hakim turned back to him. 'How can I serve your career now, Commander?'

Isfahani showed him his empty hands. 'My desire, dear doctor, is that you'll keep performing the splendid job you are doing here . . . And to help these ignorant and misguided souls to remain healthy so that they can stand trial in our Islamic courts.'

. It was too obvious not to see through, Hakim thought, then said, 'I'd be a good example for the Bahá'ís you've incarcerated here.'

Hakim's name was shouted through the block. Isfahani recognized the voice. His plans would have to wait. 'Your Jew has come.'

Hakim shouted, 'We'll be there now, Firuz!'

'Are you safe?'

'Yes!'

'Don't jump to conclusions, Doctor,' Isfahani then said. 'I just want you to treat all the prisoners medically.'

'It's the Warden,' they heard Firuz shout.

'We're coming now. Get back to him!'

Hakim lowered his voice. 'You'll excuse me. There is a prisoner in the hospital who needs my help immediately.'

Isfahani held his stand. 'I think you understand, Doctor.' He turned and gestured for the guards to let them through the successive gates to the outside. Firuz met Hakim at the main entrance, put him in a waiting taxi and sent him speeding off towards the hospital.

'Why aren't you going with him?' Isfahani asked, coming towards Firuz.

'He can handle it without me.'

'What about the patient?' He was not buying his casualness.

'He's quite well.' Firuz turned to Isfahani. 'I was worried more about the health of the doctor.'

He had succeeded in getting the Commander's temperature up. He could have gotten himself killed for the stunt, or at least beaten to a piece of raw meat, but it was the only chance he could take to undermine Isfahani's air of authority.

'You think you are clever?' Isfahani asked, daring him to speak further.

'As we are the same age, approximately, I'll be honest with you.' Firuz took the challenge boldly. 'Don't play games with the old man's life. He's done more to serve his country than you or I will ever do. And that's not by political ideals, that's by practical deeds. And that's all I wanted to say. Commander.'

Firuz saw the lingering Pasdars behind Isfahani. One word from their Commander and he was theirs.

Isfahani shook his head. He was amused by the attempted bravery against the 'Commander'. 'You judge me too harshly, brother,' he began smoothly. 'We all have to play different roles. I am merely an aspiring guardian of our beloved Iran.'

'Who are you guarding it from, God? Or maybe from a weak man like Hakim, who once believed in serving God and country, pursuing his profession and treating people with kindness. Are you protecting our country from souls like that? Pick on someone else, Commander.'

'You make him out to be a holy soul.'

'No, just a damn good doctor.'

Isfahani glanced at his watch. 'You're brave for a Jew. It's a shame that you'll never understand what it is to be a true protector of Islam, from all the diseases of foreigners and infidels.'

'No. I wouldn't understand that even if I became a Doctor of Islamic Law.'

A car with more Pasdars pulled alongside them. Isfahani went to the front passenger door.

'My last question, Commander, as an infidel, is: Who will protect Iran from the faithful?'

He climbed in and shut his door, then rolled down his window. 'Our holy leader is the physician. And we shall see which of our physicians will lead us to the straight path of God.'

The car pulled away and Firuz stepped out into the street. He would be looking to prove Isfahani wrong in time, even if it meant walking a crooked path to God.

The week Hakim spent getting the Warden back to health was refreshing to him. In some way, the Warden's belligerence and argumentative qualities reminded him of Amin. He missed a good verbal bout with his sister's brother-in-law. His wits hadn't been tested by one his age in such an amusing way for a long time.

'Take it a little slower this morning, Warden,' he said, while writing out his progress report. 'You don't want to rush back to work too quickly.'

The Warden shuffled along the row of beds, a nurse at his side. 'You're right, Doctor,' he said, 'But if I ever catch that son of a –'

'You can worry about that next week.'

The Warden rested beside a bed, holding its side rail for support, huffing. 'You know the verse, Doctor. "Trust in God, but tie your camel." Well, I have already tied my camel for this week.'

He forced the nurse to take him back in Hakim's direction. 'Do you trust in God, Doctor? Forgive my impudence for asking a devoted Muslim like yourself, but these days I don't know what anyone trusts. Communists, Imperialists, Sacrificers, Fanatics – we have them all.' He pounded his fist on the cart Hakim was working on. 'Well, I believe in God and I trust that He punishes that mother – Oooh!' He clutched his paining ribs. Hakim assisted the nurse in getting the Warden back into his bed, propping pillows under his side to make him more comfortable. He kept a close watch on his heart beat, listening to his chest and lungs. The Warden calmed down.

Two prison guards were trying to get past the ward sister.

'I'm sorry, but it's the doctor's orders that no one is to see him.'

Hakim glanced over towards the noise. The guards may have had the awkwardness of youth, but they were determined to get by.

'Excuse us, Doctor Irani,' the taller one said, seeing Hakim. 'We need to speak with our Warden about an urgent matter.'

The second guard saluted, seeing the Warden in bed. Hakim wasn't too harsh. 'All right, as you are already within speaking distance, make it brief.'

The guards stepped up to the side of the Warden's bed, removing old uniform caps. Hakim motioned the nurse to come away with him, so as to give them some privacy.

'Please, Doctor,' said the first guard, stopping Hakim, 'it concerns you, too.'

'Yes, yes. Stay, Doctor,' the Warden said, moaning dramatically and holding his wounded side. It was the best performance of courage in the face of death Hakim had seen in a long time, better than the Ben Hur chariot death sequence at the cinema. What an impression it was making on the guards.

The Warden beckoned them closer for his final words. 'Did you find the mule? Did you get my message? Speak! What is it?'

The second guard looked to the first for support. The first guard wet his lips, thinking how to proceed with his information. 'There is a young man some Pasdars brought in as a suspect.'

'The assailant!' the Warden shouted, miraculously recovered.

'No, Warden. He's not the one.'

'You know this for a fact?'

'Yes, sir.'

'Oh.' The Warden sighed disappointedly, then mumbled curses under his breath.

Hakim coughed through his laughter. He was enjoying the show.

The first guard turned to Hakim. 'We came here because the prisoner's in pretty bad condition.'

'So why do you bother me! Can't you see how weak I am? If the infirmary can't handle him, have him sent with a guard over here for treatment by Doctor Irani.'

The second guard spoke out. 'Sir, I don't think that is possible.'

'So, donkey brains, take the good doctor to the prison. Use your undersized heads!'

The first agreed with the instructions, but had more to reveal before he could carry out the orders. 'We mean, Warden, sir, that the prisoner is being held in the lower cells.'

'We just thought the doctor could help,' the second guard added hesitantly, before the Warden could explode.

Hakim no longer enjoyed the show. He was in the next act.

And it was very possible that Isfahani was producing the entire spectacle, but his second thoughts told him that these guards were too naive to have contrived such a plot. He saw the Warden preparing to strip his men of their rank. His glance was enough to warn him not to get angry.

The Warden's wound was bothering him because of all the tension, so he relaxed and mumbled, 'Nepotism, Doctor! Can't even trust your own relatives amongst your men.'

'Would you at least entrust the doctor to our care?' asked the first guard.

'The one person I trust is the doctor! And he should examine your heads! Ooooh!'

'Don't raise your voice, Warden,' Hakim said. 'Doctor's orders.'

The Warden gave in. 'Take the doctor with you. But don't be long . . . Who'll look after me?'

Hakim pulled the curtain around for the Warden to rest. The guards backed to the ward door, and turned when it was opened, nearly colliding with the person who entered.

'Now what's happening?' Firuz asked, seeing Hakim surrounded.

'I have a case at the prison.'

'Is it a cough or indigestion?'

'Get my bag, Firuz,' he ordered seriously, and went past him with the guards. They went up the hallway. 'And get a gas lantern and a couple of flashlights, too. Strong ones. With extra batteries.'

Firuz pulled Hakim aside. 'What am I going to tell your sister when she comes? Isfahani has grabbed you again?'

'He doesn't know about this. Nor will Asiyih, will she?'

'He's suffered a few burns too, Doctor,' the guard said, thinking they were discussing the case.

'And get plenty of gauze, alcohol, jelly, everything.'

Firuz must have been stupid to believe this was legitimate but gave in. 'All right. Do you need me?'

Hakim went to his office to throw his winter coat on. It was getting cold outside. 'I don't want both of us in prison,' he said lightly.

'Who's going to answer my next question?'

Hakim came back out. He let Firuz wade through his thoughts.

'I suppose it will have to wait?' Firuz asked.

'Forever. Take care of our mule- and camel-kicked Warden.'

Firuz collected the instruments and medicines Hakim needed, then went back to check up on the Warden as instructed, only to find him entertaining an unexpected guest. He came up to them. 'Good morning, Warden. Commander Isfahani.'

Isfahani was in his usual form. 'Would you mind if I saw the Warden alone for a while. Business,' he said.

'Certainly,' Firuz said, investigating the trolley of food the nurse rolled up. 'I've decided not to stay for lunch.'

Isfahani made sure Firuz left before continuing the conversation. The nurse served the unappetizing meal on a tray for the Warden. They were both disappointed with the entree.

'Would you care to join me?' the Warden said, joking.

'Thank you, no. I'm considering having a large supper this evening. I'm asking Doctor Irani to join me.'

The Warden uncovered his food. 'Well, you'll have to wait.'

'Why, has he already accepted another invitation?'

'No,' said the Warden, devouring the tiny portions of chicken and rice. 'He had to attend to another prisoner.'

Isfahani smiled at the Warden's joke, and joked back. 'Which ward is the prisoner in?'

The Warden went on to his bowl of soup, then wiped his mouth as he finished, looking forward to his jellied dessert. 'At the prison.'

'The prison?' Isfahani had misunderstood. The Warden was not joking.

The Warden called the nurse over to take the tray, telling the Commander what he knew. 'It was a special case.'

Isfahani waited until the nurse took away his food. 'What's a special case, Warden?'

The Warden covered his mouth politely, cleaning his teeth with a toothpick. 'It seems the prisoner was a friend of one of my guards, and has been injured by some of your over-zealous Pasdars mistakenly capturing him as my assailant.'

Isfahani pulled the curtains around them shut. He wanted no one else to see what he was about to do to the Warden if he got violent. 'Where is the prisoner, Warden?'

The Warden pointed down with his toothpick, then glanced up at the infuriated Commander.

'Your assailant?! You . . . I thought it was made clear to you that Doctor Irani was not to be allowed there!' he yelled.

The nurse came over. 'Please, Commander. There are other patients in this ward.'

He ignored the woman. 'You know why the prisoner is there,' he blurted out without thinking.

'I don't know,' the Warden said, breathing hard.

'Commander,' the nurse pleaded.

'You could have ruined my past month's work here.'

'How was I to know? I'll see that – '

'No. Now I'll see to it.'

The Warden clutched his chest.

The nurse asked him again. 'Please, Commander.'

Isfahani saw the fright in the nurse's face, and remembered the Warden's condition. 'Don't die,' Isfahani ordered.

The Warden nodded his head. 'Yes, sir. Thank you.'

Isfahani left the Warden to the nurse. He went out. The doctor was there too soon, he told himself, that prisoner was already set for trial. It was too soon. He wasn't ready either. Or was he? he wondered. He went into Hakim's empty office and used the phone. He pulled out his pocket phone book to dial, going through the switchboard, then removed his cigarettes, a pad of paper, pen. As he got through, he spied the shoes of the nurses standing outside the door. He could see their reflection on the polished surface. They weren't spying on him, but he kept the identity of the person he spoke with unstated, to be cautious.

'His name is Arif Rouhani . . .'

Isfahani wrote down the instructions as he received them.

'Yes. They put him in prison here last night. Doctor Irani went to visit him about a half-hour ago . . . No, from what I gathered he'll live at the most a few more days, a week maybe . . . Yes, but if the doctor is not allowed down there, the prisoner will definitely die before you arrive . . . I arranged the day after tomorrow – eleven in the morning.

'The Judge, the Warden, the Mujtahid and myself,' he said, writing down the list of names he was given. 'Yes, I'll see to them, too. May I also suggest Doctor Irani?'

The reflection vanished beneath the door as the nurses walked away. Isfahani switched ears to listen. He was forced to obey what he was being told, but pointed out, 'Because I believe the doctor could get the prisoner to recant. Why? Because he's a doctor, and doctors hate to see people they're healing suffer . . . Yes. I understand that . . . '

He snapped his pen in half. 'Are we trying to wipe out their beliefs or their adherents! . . . Forgive me. Yes, I'll prepare everything. *Qurbani shoma*. *Khoda Hafez*.'

Isfahani hung up. He dumped the broken pen into the trash. His hand was full of black ink. He wiped it dry with a cloth. 'Clergymen.' He had to think hard about what he was supposed to do next.

# CHAPTER 11

# The Heart's Physician

What began to trouble Hakim was not the fact that there was a prisoner who needed attention, but why the guards beside him had specifically asked for him. Any doctor could have taken the responsibility.

They went down the cracking cement steps to the guard post in the lower section. They weren't able to see much. The few stringed lights were scarcely enough to let one even see where one was walking.

An old guard, bent with years, greeted them. The young men spoke intimately with him. Hakim let his eyes drift to the damp walls beside them. The smell was not pleasant. Somewhere above them there was a broken water pipe that was never inspected from below. As far as Hakim could see, the old place should have been filled in years ago. Evin prison was computerized, modern. This prison was out of the pages of history.

The old guard scratched his scanty white beard as he spoke with the others. The familiarity made Hakim wonder if this was not another of the Warden's employed relatives. The second guard turned to him. 'We can go through, Doctor.'

The first guard received the keys from the old man and pushed the wooden corridor gate open for them to go past. Hakim lit the gas lantern and turned it up full, illuminating the corridor walls ahead.

They went slowly. A rat scampered across their path from one cell to the next. Through the bars they could see that each cell was empty of prisoners. Hakim was satisfied enough to keep the strong light in the center of the corridor. He had no desire to disturb the other vermin that hid in the dark corners of the cells they were passing.

'It's the leak which attracts them,' said the first guard.

'We should send the Pasdars down here to shoot them all,' the other said.

'Is this your first time down here?' he asked them, knowing the answer full well.

'Not the first,' the second one said.

'How did you come to know of this man's condition?'

The first one explained. 'I knew his family, when my parents were working in Yazd. When I learned who it was who the Pasdars threw in here, I found out which cell he was dropped into. He's messed up badly, Doctor.'

The second guard pointed a flashlight towards the cell on their right. 'This is it.'

Through the iron bars they could see a soft light coming from the top center of the cell. There was a small barred opening up there, leading to the next floor up.

'I left the lid open so we'd know which one it was.'

As the second guard spoke the lid crashed shut, thundering, cutting off the little light they had gained.

'Hey!'

'Never mind,' Hakim said, putting the lantern on the ground. He took the flashlight and angled it through the bars to the now closed iron hole. He tilted the light down the black wall to the center of the floor beneath. There a figure lay in a heap, as though it had been dropped from above.

Hakim pulled the light back from the cell and illumined the door bolt and lock. The guards unlocked it with great difficulty. It hadn't been opened for years but at last the rusted bolt snapped open.

Hakim went in and knelt beside the prisoner, placing the medical bag to his side. He shook his head repeatedly as he assessed his state. His arm was viciously fractured at the forearm. There was an odor of burnt flesh and clothing from a charred wound in his shoulder. On his thigh, dried blood formed a pattern in his jeans from a blow by a deep tearing chain. And over his chest where his shirt was torn, there was a colorful bruise. The guards were right, it was bad. More like sickening.

'He can't be moved,' the first guard said sadly. 'He won't live much longer, will he, Doctor? I just thought you could make it a little easier. He was just wronged, that's all.'

Hakim took a deep breath. He would do what he could, but that wasn't going to be much. He doubted if even a hospital could do much.

He handed them his flashlight. 'I'll need a bucket of boiling water, some clean sheets, towels, and a few blankets. I'll do what I can.'

They thanked him and left him with the lantern at his side.

Hakim took his time, pumping up the gas pressure to its peak. He could see clearly now. The patient was a young man, maybe in his early twenties. He couldn't figure out what in the name of God this youth had done to deserve this, then lightly surmised that he was probably happy that someone had gone and shot the Warden.

The man began to mumble indistinguishably.

Hakim bent low over him. 'Son? Can you hear me? . . . I'm a doctor. I'm going to have to do something that may be a little painful, to help you. Do you understand? I want you to take a deep breath.'

The mumbling became intelligible.

'. . . We rely on none . . . save God.'

Hakim kept his eyes on the man's chest as he inhaled. His breath didn't seem to cause him much pain, nor cause him to cough. He made the decision to take care of his arm first. Hakim was sure that if he had survived all this punishment and the fall too, he'd be tough enough for the tortures Hakim was about to administer. He put his glasses on, then removed a pair of scissors from his bag and cut around the charred, exposed shoulder, throwing away the bits of cloth as he worked.

He began sweating profusely and wiped his brow with his coat sleeve. It was warm in there. He took off his coat to continue. There would be time to rest later. The quiet whimpers of pain kept his speed up. He had done all he could on the burn – it wasn't deep, but was most probably infected by the dirt and gravel he had been dragged across. He was going to have to wait for the guards to return before he could continue in that area. Then there was the fracture.

'If it hurts, let it out,' he said tenderly, filling a hypodermic with an anesthetic. He adjusted himself over the forearm and injected the medicine. At least the fracture hadn't broken the skin. He had the splint ready.

'All right, son,' he said, sitting up, 'Here we go.'

He took hold of the man's elbow with a firm grasp. The man's body flinched, anticipating the pain. Swiftly Hakim grasped his wrist. He squinted, his face grimaced as he snapped the arm into place with a twist. It was done. The man's body writhed upwards in agony reacting to the sudden pain and howled out before collapsing unconscious. 'Aaah. *Yá Bahá'u'l-Abhá!*'

Hakim stared at the still prisoner's face. A cold flush came over him, until he erupted deep from his gut. 'No!'

He released the arm and clenched his fists above his head as he rose, turning away. 'No!'

The two guards raced into the cell, slopping the steaming bucket of water between them onto the cell floor. 'What is it? What's wrong?'

'Why did you bring me here?' Hakim asked angrily. 'Why did you ask for me?'

'We just thought you could help,' answered the first guard, fearfully.

'You knew what he was!'

The first guard dropped all the materials he had in his arms. 'We didn't think a doctor like you would worry about that.'

Hakim swung away from them. It wasn't fair, he thought bitterly. It wasn't fair. He wasn't a Bahá'í. Why was he still being tested by God?

The guards looked at the prisoner's still face. 'Is he dead?'

Hakim wanted to run, to hide, bury himself under a mountain. His breath was short, rapid with his thoughts. If he ran from all this, he reconsidered, then he wasn't a doctor. He remembered the soldiers he had found with Firuz, lying face down in the sand. What had he done for them? Here was a patient. It shouldn't matter what he was, or where he came from, or how he got there. Hakim was a doctor. It was his duty.

He turned to the guards. 'He's not dead,' he said, under control. 'Put the towels beside him and open them up. We're going to have to move him now, while he's still unconscious, so I can continue . . .'

The guards brought in more buckets of water, placing them beside Hakim, who now rested against the side wall of the cell, his glasses crowning his brow.

'We brought you some more fresh batteries too,' the first guard said, replacing them in their flashlight.

The second guard looked over at the prisoner, now at ease beside Hakim and sleeping on his side on the cushion of blankets.

He noticed how much work the doctor had done. The splint, tape and gauze explained all that.

Hakim was too tired to look at his watch. 'How long has it been?'

'It's just past dark,' the second answered. 'You should retire for the evening.'

'So should you two. I'll stay till he wakes.'

'I am tired,' the second guard said to the first, admitting it.

The first guard nodded, then said to Hakim, 'The old man down the passage knows you're still in here. All you have to do is call. The doors are all open. This one is not exactly going to escape.'

'Thank you, Doctor,' said the other.

Hakim managed a drooping nod. 'Good-night.'

'Good-night,' they said, going out.

Hakim looked into the corridor. The light never changed; everything was quiet. Time had vanished from this place. He leaned over his patient and pulled the sheeted blanket up over his side. The movement woke him. Hakim sat back on his knees, looking into his eyes, waiting for them to focus.

'. . . Where am I?' he whispered voicelessly.

'Tell me how you're feeling?'

The man tried to focus his vision on the person who towered over him. Hakim put his glasses on properly.

'I'm in prison,' the man said, finding enough strength to smile.

Hakim nodded, waiting for the man to tell him how he felt.

'. . . I'm in great pain – all over. Yet I feel very happy.'

Hakim could understand the medical symptoms, but the spiritual comment was a waste of the man's breath. He wasn't in the mood for 'happy' patients; it was no doubt a clever ploy to get him to ask 'and why are you happy'; he wasn't interested in starting. The physical pain was going to be there with the young man for the rest of his life. Then Hakim remembered: the prisoner would only have a few more days, if they had already meted out a death sentence. He picked up all his debris. It was enough for one day's work.

'Are you a doctor?' slowly asked the man.

'Supposedly.'

'Why did they allow you to help a Bahá'í they are most likely preparing to execute?'

Hakim closed his medical bag. 'They probably thought I would enjoy an extra few hours' practice.'

'I see,' the man quietly replied.

Hakim pumped the lantern full, then went to the cell door. The man tried to sit up. Hakim strode over. 'Don't move! . . . Just lie as you are. You need to rest.'

He did as he was told, seeing how concerned the doctor was.

Hakim didn't like the man's gaze; he was trying to read his soul. So he added, 'And let those stitches in your leg close. Can you breathe? And don't lie. Cracked ribs are serious.'

'Yes,' he answered calmly. 'Will you be back?'

'Morning and evening,' he said firmly, detailing his responsibility. 'You'll need antibiotics and a change of dressing to keep those wounds clean from infection.'

The man thought the instructions were finished, but the doctor filled his ears with more warnings.

'And if you need anything, you're to call out. I'll make certain that the corridor guard comes. He can call me if there's an emergency.'

The man's eyes were strong, clear. Hakim had to keep darting from his stare, but was drawn by their magnetism.

'Now rest!'

'Thank you for your kindness, Doctor.'

Hakim turned out the lantern. He was free to go. He had said everything he needed to say.

The man was confused; why was the doctor shuffling in the darkness to get out of the cell? He heard him kick over his medical bag, mumble, then pick it up.

'Are you afraid of me?'

'What?'

Hakim pulled the flashlight from his bag and switched it on.

'You seem uneasy, Doctor. Is it because I am Bahá'í?'

Hakim answered with a nervous chuckle. 'Young man, I am at the stage in my life where I am afraid of no one.'

'God?'

Hakim flashed the light into the man's face like a weapon, making him squint from its brilliance. 'Do you have any idea that you've been accused of attempting to kill a prison warden?'

'I'm a scapegoat.'

Hakim was about to give him a good lecture, but refrained and

149

said instead, 'Go to sleep.'

'What do you know about the Bahá'í Faith?' he asked, persisting, trying to see the doctor beyond the ring of light.

'If I wanted to investigate the Bahá'í Faith,' he said with a huff, 'I certainly wouldn't –'

'– Arif –'

'– come to – What?'

'My name is Arif. Arif Rouhani.'

Hakim finally realized he was shining the light in the man's eyes and switched it off. 'I don't want to know your name.'

They were in the darkness again. Hakim accidentally kicked the lantern over, misjudging its place, then relocated it and lit it again.

'Maybe it would be better, Doctor, if you could send someone who is not afraid of being near Bahá'ís.'

Hakim found his bag. 'I'm not afraid of being near Bahá'ís. I'm a doctor and I'll take care of anyone who needs my assistance! – It's because you're relatively well that I'm going to ask that another doctor be sent instead in my place. And good-night!'

Hakim removed himself from the cell. He couldn't get over the impudence – the feeble attempt to get him to speak about the Bahá'í Faith. He heard the man begin to chant, even knew the prayer himself. Ha! Ziya used to chant that prayer to the children. He called out into the dark hall ahead. 'Guard!'

Awakened from the shadows, the guard came forth jingling his keys, and stood in front of the already unlocked corridor gate. 'Is everything all right, Doctor?' he asked with a yawn.

The chanting stopped abruptly. Instinctively, Hakim turned around and ran back to the cell. The guard pushed the gate aside and followed the doctor. Hakim knelt beside Arif, whose frame had become still. Slowly his eyes opened, gently glancing up at the doctor. 'I will live only if you return in the morning.'

Hakim gazed into his dark eyes. With a quiet breath he nodded his promise. He would leave a note to Firuz telling him where to find him.

Hakim was using the last spare set of batteries to help him see now. The gas in the lantern had been completely used up during the night. It was his mistake not filling it up originally at the hospital. Arif was propped up by a wedge of blankets against the wall, watching as the doctor sat beside him, dabbing gel on his shoulder burn. He tried to be light. 'You should have shaved this morning, Doctor.'

Hakim glanced coldly over his glasses for a moment, then carried on with his work. Arif smiled, listening to the doctor's near inaudible muttering as he examined the festering shoulder wound more closely. Arif went on talking to himself. 'I, on the other hand, couldn't find a mirror in this grand hotel to shave in.'

'I should pull more dead skin off,' he said more clearly.

Arif covered the torch light with his other hand. 'If God permits, you can continue later, but not now, Doctor.'

Hakim acceded. He put away his ointment jar in his bag, then removed his glasses and said seriously, 'You need to be under hospital supervision. I need to take X-rays if I'm going to continue.'

Arif shook his head. 'You and I both know this is my hospital.'

'You don't have to die!' Hakim snapped harshly.

'No. I don't have to die. But it is not exactly my say.'

'No, but you're resigned to dying here.'

'The only thing I pray that I am resigned to is the will of God.'

He wasn't in any humor for his piety and challenged him with a short gaze. 'You're awfully young to claim to know the will of God.' He was going to show this idealist the reality of this nether world. Almost unfairly, Arif closed his eyes, and became quiet.

Hakim felt satisfied that he had shut him up. Arif could have never answered his question, nor would he have been a match for his knowledge. The man obviously had to resort to prayers. 'God's Will', Hakim thought with a huff, how could a mere adolescent know the will of God, when he didn't know it himself after thirty more years' experience.

Hakim reprimanded himself. He looked at Arif's young face. Thirty years of the world made no difference to God. All that mattered was one's last moment. Of all of the people he could learn from, here was one who might hold the key to the questions he was unable to unlock for himself. How he wished the man would stop what he was doing, and for the love of God, answer his burning questions.

Arif looked at his painful shoulder, then over to the doctor. 'I am not capable of satisfying your queries with my own words,' he said sincerely, 'I can only quote from One beyond all mention and praise.'

Hakim sat down near him, allowing himself to enter his school. He set aside his inner turmoil to hear what precious passage Arif would offer. The words flowed melodically and with power from his voice:

*Having created the world and all that liveth and moveth therein, He, through the direct operation of His unconstrained and sovereign Will, chose to confer upon man the unique distinction and capacity to know Him and to love Him – a capacity that must needs be regarded as the generating impulse and the primary purpose underlying the whole of creation . . .*

Hakim was spellbound. Had he not read these words before? Yet the youth before him was opening doors to expanses he had never been able to explore, though he had always thought he had. In the back of his mind deeper questions burned, warning him of his vulnerability, cautioning him that no one could understand God.

Arif's glance fell to the ground. A tear fell from his cheek as he too felt carried away by the sublimity of the verses. He pressed his memory to recall a prayer:

*All glory be to Thee, O Lord my God! I bear witness for Thee to that whereto Thou Thyself didst bear witness for Thine own Self, ere the day Thou hadst created the creation or made mention thereof, that Thou art God, and that there is none other God beside Thee. From eternity Thou hast, in Thy transcendent oneness, been immeasurably exalted above Thy servants' conception of Thy unity, and wilt to eternity remain, in Thine unapproachable singleness, far above the praise of Thy creatures. No words that any one beside Thee may utter can ever beseem Thee, and no man's description except Thine own description can befit Thy nature. All who adore Thy unity have been sore perplexed to fathom the mystery of Thy oneness, and all have confessed their powerlessness to attain unto the comprehension of Thine essence and to scale to the pinnacle of Thy knowledge. The mighty have all acknowledged their weakness, and the learned recognized their ignorance. They that are possessed of influence are as nothing when compared with the revelations of Thy stupendous sovereignty, and they who are exalted sink into oblivion when brought before the manifestations of Thy great glory.*

Hakim was afraid. He felt suddenly stripped naked before the world, fearful of his own reality, of being remote from God.

Arif was more entranced by his own utterances, enraptured by the love burning within his breast:

*As a token of His mercy, however, and as a proof of His loving-kindness, He hath manifested unto men the Day Stars of His divine guidance, the Symbols of His divine unity, and hath ordained the knowledge of these sanctified Beings to be identical with the knowledge of His own Self. Whoso recognizeth them hath recognized God. Whoso hearkeneth to their call, hath hearkened to the Voice of God, and whoso testifieth to the Truth of their Revelation, hath testified to the truth of God Himself. Whoso turneth away from them, hath turned away from God, and whoso disbelieveth in them, hath disbelieved in God. Every one of them is the Way of God that connecteth this world with the realms above, and the Standard of His Truth unto every one in the kingdoms of earth and heaven. They are the Manifestations of God amidst men, the evidences of His Truth, and the signs of His Glory.*

Hakim covered his eyes, feeling the throbbing pain in his brow. And Arif went on:

*This is the King of Days, the Day that hath seen the coming of the Best-Beloved, Him Who through all eternity hath been acclaimed the Desire of the World.*

Hakim covered his ears, pulling the hairs at his temples.

*Great indeed is this Day! The allusions made to it in all the sacred Scriptures as the Day of God attest to its greatness. The soul of every Prophet of God, of every Divine Messenger, hath thirsted for this wondrous Day . . .*

*So loud is the call that reverberates from the Abhá Kingdom that mortal ears are well-nigh deafened with its vibrations. The whole creation, methinks, is being disrupted and is bursting asunder through the shattering influence of the Divine summons issued from the throne of glory . . .*

'ENOUGH. Please, I beg you,' Hakim cried out.

His head spun in confusion as he stumbled to his feet, near to fainting. In one action he swept up his medical bag and staggered out into the corridor. He had to get away.

Arif slowly opened his eyes. He looked towards the cell door. The doctor was gone. The verses he had recited by heart should have inspired the doctor to recognize who Bahá'u'lláh was, by His own Words. Then he understood. He had spoken too much and overwhelmed the doctor's soul. Ashamed, he felt God would never forgive him for this act, and cried.

The plate of soup and strips of bread remained uneaten. Arif sat in the fading light with his eyes closed, quietly chanting prayers to himself.

As he made an effort to regain a full breath, he pressed his hand against the bruise over his ribs, trying to lessen the pain. He felt he was no longer alone, and opened his eyes. There at his cell door was Hakim, wearing the same soiled clothes from the morning, still holding his medical bag at his side.

It seemed like ages had passed for both of them.

'I didn't expect you to return,' Arif said.

'No. Nor did I,' Hakim said meekly.

'Yes . . .'

Hakim took a step in, still uncertain whether he should be there.

'How long have you been standing there?' Arif asked him.

'A half-hour or so. I don't know.'

He remembered why he had come and went over to Arif, not prepared to say anything else, but to carry on with his treatment. He pulled the blanket off Arif's side and was shocked to see that the leg wound's stitches had opened.

'You were sitting on your knees?'

'Yes. Until I couldn't endure the numbness. I'm sorry.'

Hakim went to his bag and pulled out a packaged syringe and needle. He was going to have to start all over again.

Diligently he re-dressed all the wounds, muttering his disapproval as usual.

'This will have to do until morning.'

He glanced at the uneaten plate of food. 'I think, if you ate that, you'd get sick.' His joke brought a smile to Arif's face.

'I'm sorry,' Arif said, apologizing immediately.

'Don't worry. I'll give you some more vitamins and antibiotics to hold you over.'

'No. I mean about this morning.'

'Oh. Yes.' Hakim covered his error. 'You shouldn't be sorry about that. You shared what you held most dear.'

Hakim tried to be honest with him, in his own way. 'I suppose my colleague, Firuz, would say that I left so abruptly because what I heard affected me.'

Feeling he had said enough, he got to his feet. He was ready to go home. He hadn't slept much the night before, and the whole day he had locked himself in his office, thinking about everything

154

that had been said. He hadn't come back just to tend the wounds, really, he had returned to tell Arif what he was feeling. 'I was frightened,' he admitted. A chuckle escaped. 'How I wished to God I could have been buried in the depths of the earth rather than carry the weight of all those verses.'

Arif had to put his head down to rest. He closed his tired eyes.

Hakim put his black bag back down and wiped off his sweaty palms as he paced along the iron bars. 'You know, all my life I have memorized verses from all the Holy Books of God so that I could answer every question that was posed to me – intellectually. Yet I discovered now that I never questioned my own arguments in my heart. They were always the logical irrefutable explanations that no one could disprove. So I was satisfied.'

Hakim wandered over beside Arif, and leaned against the wall, slowly sliding down until he squatted beside his bedding. 'I'm only a medical doctor, yet no Muslim could better my knowledge of Islam, and no Christian could withstand my proofs for the validity of the station of Muhammad, and no Jew could deny my proving the manifest reality and splendor of the station of Jesus.'

Hakim took a breath from his words. He'd never spoken about this with anyone, but had to say it to Arif. 'I may have felt shame when I turned away, but never fear. Shame enough to kill myself – not because of God – because I couldn't face my loved ones, my friends, the world. My world, rather my own imaginings. But when one begins to feel the "fear of God", where can one run? What refuge is there for a soul to seek? Where could I hide?' He paused, reflecting on his own words. Then added, 'I spent the whole day today in a stupor. If I prayed it was not to be forgiven, not for my own salvation or personal gain, but because, because . . .'

He glanced over to Arif, who had quietly fallen fast asleep. He leaned over and pulled the blanket up over Arif's chest, and said, 'Because there is no one to truly impress, is there? No one to truly trust, no one to ultimately love, no one to finally know, no one to absolutely fear, save God. *Yá Bahá'u'l-Abhá*. May my miserable life be a sacrifice for His loved ones!'

He sat back against the wall. He knew Arif hadn't heard a word of what he had tried to tell him.

'O God. I feel more vulnerable now than I've ever felt before in my life. But. I'm not afraid . . .'

155

# CHAPTER 12

# The Beaten Path

The morning light poured through the window blinds of the hospital office. Alone, Firuz paced impatiently in front of Hakim's desk wearing out the same strip of carpet, glancing frequently at the phone. He kept his tan fur cap on and his thick winter coat buttoned up, ready to go to the bus depot if he had to. He wasn't supposed to be the one to go. That was Hakim's duty, not his. But he wasn't at home. And the prison guards were emphatic that the doctor hadn't come to the prison. Firuz was worried. He could just see himself meeting Asiyih Khanum and her children and having to explain to them that he had no idea where Hakim was.

Firuz heard the door open without a knock. He turned, blasting Hakim, 'Where have you been?'

He dropped his angry expression, feeling the fool. It wasn't Hakim: it was Isfahani who had entered.

'Where's the doctor?' Isfahani casually inquired.

'You tell me.'

'I asked you a simple question.'

Firuz guessed right through the Commander's charade, thinking, who else but Isfahani could pretend to be looking for the doctor when he had him hidden away somewhere. 'Really? He's in prison, isn't he?'

'The doctor is not at the prison. I gave explicit instructions this morning that the injured prisoner was to have no visitors, none at all.'

That was the exact story the prison guards had told him. Firuz didn't know what was going on. It was better to pretend he knew where Hakim really was. It would keep Isfahani's suspicions to a minimum. 'Then he's already gone to the bus station to pick up his family.'

'And where are you going?'

'I'm the assistant to the welcoming committee.'

Isfahani stepped out. 'Tell the doctor I want to see him; before I return to Kashan tomorrow.'

'Very good, Commander. I will.'

Firuz went to the desk and scribbled a cryptic note to Hakim, telling him to stay put, or he'd tell Asiyih that he had forgotten she was arriving. Then he wrote in bold letters: YOU DIDN'T FORGET DID YOU? DID YOU??

Hakim lay comfortably asleep. His eyes didn't feel any warmth of morning light urging him to awake. He imagined he could hear the sweet melodic chanting of the imprisoned Arif, which stirred his thoughts, reminding him to bath and shave before he went back to that pit. He stretched well, and rubbed his half-frozen nose. He opened his eyes. The darkness seemed unfamiliar to him. He pushed his back off the stone-cold floor. The blanket which covered him fell into his lap.

The chanting still continued.

The realization came hard and swift. He had slept in the cell all night. There was Arif, sitting on his knees, facing in Hakim's direction. He finished his prayer and said, 'Good-morning, Doctor. I hope you slept well.'

Hakim wasn't dreaming. He was in prison. He fell back against the wall, still mystified. 'Good-morning?'

He gave Hakim a few minutes to compose himself, then asked, 'Do you dream, Doctor?'

Hakim scratched his head and combed back the few upstanding strands. He answered automatically. 'I never really remember my dreams. Just everyone else's.'

'We were blessed with the most beautiful visions, dear Doctor. Shall I tell you?'

There was a glazed look in Arif's eyes, as if he could see through the walls far into the distance.

Hakim merely nodded. There was not much else he could do.

'I dreamt that you and I were sitting beneath a majestic tree. Behind us was spread a verdant emerald-green valley of grape vines, beneath an arc of towering snow-tipped mountains. From the slopes a sapphire-blue river ran its course down past our tree and flowed into a sea far beyond our view. I knew it was an ocean, because I could hear the rhythm of waves pounding against the unseen shore.

'Oh! and there were so many God-intoxicated men who sat with us, people out of the pages of history, enjoying the shade of the tree's umbrella.

'A nightingale perched upon the top-most bough warbled its enchanting song, vibrating the limbs of the entire tree. One red fruit shook free and dropped into your hands. Its perfume was heavenly; a bouquet of jasmine and roses.

'I remember that you chose not to taste its nectar. You only admired it, deciding rather to save it. All the other fruit which had fallen was already collected by those around us. I desired to climb to the highest limbs to pick what ripened fruit remained. I prayed that I would be guided by the nightingale's direction.

'By the mercy of God the nightingale understood my plight and untwined the most succulent of fruits. She hovered above my head then released it to my longing hands. I kissed the beloved fruit and rendered thanks to God, then ate of its essence which consumed my being. Unable to remain in its mortal shell, my body fell to the earth like a wind-blown leaf. The nightingale called me to its abode and my soul flew up towards its nest.'

Arif looked at Hakim. 'Now I don't wish to remain in this fleeting world of dust any longer.'

Hakim had listened attentively. He was caught up by the similarities between this dream and the near-same one Isfahani had shared with him months earlier. Only in Isfahani's dream, he remembered the fruit became overripe, rotten, mashed into pulp to become nectar. There were so many allusions, so many symbols to decipher. The nightingale, tree, ocean, fruit – life, sacrifice, suffering, death, the Most Great Spirit. It raised questions, deep questions.

'If Bahá'u'lláh really is the Promised One foretold in the Books of all the Messengers, then why must His followers suffer?' Then asked, expecting the perfect answer, 'And what is the difference between sacrificing oneself and sacrificing one's self for others?'

Arif was overwhelmed. He wondered how his words had prompted these questions, then looked up at the doctor. 'These are the questions which you have dreamt about, aren't they?'

He considered the point seriously. 'Maybe they are.'

Arif didn't have the perfect answer. He only said, 'Seek out the Writings of Bahá'u'lláh.'

'Don't you know?' he asked, disappointed by the terse suggestion.

Arif restrained himself from quotations. He spoke from his own understanding. 'One of the universal principles brought by Bahá'u'lláh for this age is the power of independent investigation, so that no man will blindly follow the knowledge of his forefathers or accept that which is contrary to the exigencies of this Day. The path begins with search – striving to be in accord with God's will for all mankind, and not with our own selfish desires. I guess this is one reason why the followers of Bahá'u'lláh, too, must suffer. We begin to know the battles we must face when we embrace the Cause of God, battles from within as well as from without. We are armed with the Writings of God to fight hate with love, ignorance with knowledge, injustice with mercy.'

Hakim had heard this so many times. 'Not all Bahá'ís do that. Hate for love, sacrifice – '

'Don't look at the followers of light, of Bahá'u'lláh, look to the source itself, the Manifestation of God, and His Writings.'

Hakim was not pleased. He had set his hopes on instant enlightenment, not the arduous journey of traversing the 'seven valleys' throughout an eternity.

Arif tried to move his numbing leg beneath, then felt the stitches tear in his thigh. Under the blanket he pressed his hand over the area, hiding his agony from the doctor. His thought was clear and he said, 'A person only sacrifices when he is in love.'

Hakim noticed that Arif was squeezing his thigh where he had bandaged it. He untangled himself from the blanket. 'I told you, you cannot sit like that. Do you want to damage your stitches? And how did I get this blanket? I told you to keep warm.' He stretched Arif back out on the bedding, then covered him.

Arif sensed that his last comment had gone unheard. Something inside stopped him from repeating himself. He watched Hakim go through his bag, pulling out his medicines and talking to himself, reprimanding his body for sleeping there that night. Arif spotted an envelope and a pad of paper among the things the doctor pulled out.

'I'll have to go back to the hospital to get more supplies.'

'Forgive me, Doctor, but may I borrow that pad of paper and the envelope.' He saw the question in Hakim's eyes. 'I want to write to my parents and tell them I'm in your care.'

Hakim was staring at Arif's wounded arm, so Arif waved the other.

'This one's still good to write with.'

'You're going into the hospital today, if I have to raise an army to get you there.'

Arif took the writing material from him. 'Doctor?'

'Yes?'

'Would you mail this letter when I finish?'

'I'd rather send for your parents to take you home!'

'Just giving them this page will suffice.'

Hakim glanced at his watch. 'O my God. What's today? Ten o'clock. Oh no. My sister. I forgot. And don't move!'

'Yes, Doctor. I won't.' He watched him collect all his things and replace the flashlight with more batteries.

Hakim stood the flashlight on its end and lit up the ceiling. 'I won't need this. The guard knows my call in the darkness and just lets me through while he goes back to sleep. I'll be back as soon as I can.'

He suddenly stopped his hurry. There was another question in his mind. 'Ah.' He was more serious. 'Could you say – it's difficult for me to ask this, but – could you say a prayer for me?'

'If you'll remember me in your prayers, too.'

They both made their promises and Hakim disappeared down the corridor, shouting, 'And don't move!'

Arif waited for the doctor to pass the creaky corridor gate, then coughed violently, shivering from the pain across his chest. He longed for the executioners to put him out of his misery. He angled the blank paper on his good thigh and in the design of a circle wrote:

*Though my body be pained by the trials that befall me from Thee, though it be afflicted by the revelations of Thy Decree, yet my soul rejoiceth at having partaken of the waters of Thy Beauty, and at having attained the ocean of Thine eternity. Doth it beseem a lover to flee from his beloved, or to desert the object of his heart's desire? Nay, we all believe in Thee, and eagerly hope to enter Thy presence.*

'Surprise!' Firuz called out as he threw open Hakim's door. Asiyih, Saffa and Mitra looked in from behind him.

'I thought you said he'd be here,' Saffa said, gazing into the empty office.

Firuz added to his excuses, leading them in, 'He's probably making his rounds still.' The note he had written was missing from the desk. 'But', he added brightly, hoping that it was Hakim who had taken it and not the cleaning girls. 'He is here.'

'Thank God,' Asiyih said.

'Oh, Firuz!' a nurse said, passing the open door, then peering back in. 'Doctor Irani is looking for you.'

'Such alluring breath! May God bestow wealth on your impoverished family! Go tell him I'm in his office.'

The nurse took the time to smile to the others in the room.

'Go, go, go,' Firuz shouted, clapping his hands to get her to jump and do her duty.

'Who's Doctor Irani?' Mitra asked glumly, then sat down on the couch beside her mother.

'Your uncle, dear,' Asiyih said, pulling off her hat and coat.

Saffa busied himself with the array of medical charts on the walls, studying their details.

'Firuz!' Hakim bellowed from the hallway.

Mitra ran out of the doorway. Her gloom disappeared. 'Uncle Hakim!'

'Mitra!' Asiyih wasn't quick enough to stop her. She stood holding only her coat.

'Who's this Khanum?!' exclaimed a jubilant Hakim, still in the hallway. 'Kiss? . . . That's my Mitra! Are you happy? Are you well, my little Mitty? Mice eat you!'

He came around the doorway, holding giggling Mitra in his arms.

'Uncle Hakim. You need to shave,' she said, scolding him, rubbing his rough cheeks. She jumped down and ran towards her mother.

Saffa followed, coming up to his uncle and kissing him on both cheeks. 'You do need to shave.'

Hakim wiped Saffa's charcoal upper lip with his finger. 'So will you soon!' Hakim glanced at Asiyih. She seemed startled by his appearance, and so he stunned her further. 'Are you happy, Asiyih Khanum?'

She wasn't stunned; she was dumbfounded. 'Yes,' she finally said, then smiled embarrassedly, having to ask, 'What's come over you?'

Hakim looked at Firuz, who was gawking at him too. 'Where is that Isfahani?'

'I don't know. He was looking for you earlier. Where were you last night?'

'At the prison,' he said simply, watching how his nephew was so captivated by the medical charts. The boy was going to be a doctor one day.

'This morning?'

'Yes, Firuz, this morning.' Hakim smiled at Asiyih, showing her that everything was all right, absolutely typical, all in a day's work. But she couldn't believe that anything was normal, not sure what had come over him since the last time she had spoken with him.

Firuz put his inquiring mind to work. 'They let you in?'

'They let me out!' Hakim went over to his phone. 'Hello, hello.'

'If you're calling Isfahani, he's not there. Some guerillas bombed their headquarters, we heard on the radio.'

Hakim hung up the receiver. 'I want you to get him out of prison. His leg looks septic. And I want chest and arm X-rays taken as soon as he's brought in.'

'Who's this?' Asiyih asked.

'A young man in the old prison,' Firuz said to her, then went back to Hakim. 'Isfahani has left explicit instructions that no one is to be allowed near him.'

'That has never stopped you before. Go to the Warden. Use your genius.'

'We released the Warden yesterday, remember?'

'I know that – go to his office and tell him the man needs surgery immediately.'

Firuz saw how confusing this conversation had become to Asiyih. He nodded too soon to Hakim, who took the gesture as a sealed agreement. Firuz was still trying to figure out what was happening himself.

Hakim took Mitra by the hand, making small talk and laughing with her, then turned, letting Saffa come and join them, taking them out. Asiyih didn't know what to say. 'That man was not my brother.'

The strangest thought came to Firuz's mind. 'You know. If I assessed the situation correctly, I'd swear the man had fallen in love.'

'At his age, who with? Layli?'

It was only a thought. He shrugged. 'God only knows.'

Hakim popped his head back in, looking at the two bewildered souls, then said to Asiyih, 'Coming?'

Asiyih was inclined to believe Firuz's notion. There was something about Hakim that made her believe her brother was actually Majnun, crazy and intoxicated.

Hakim disappeared from view. She went out after him. Hakim yelled back from the hall to Firuz. 'And make sure you call me when he's prepped!'

'The man is Majnun,' Firuz said to himself, contemplating what he was supposed to do. 'He's completely out of his mind. Don't worry, Firuz. It's going to be easy. You just walk up to the prison gates and have them open before you like Moses with the Red Sea.'

The prison gates didn't part quite so easily, nor were the prison guards influenced by the magnificence of his voice. Firuz tried another way of getting himself inside – desperation.

'Look. All I know is that there is a patient in there under the care of Doctor Irani.'

The 'rocks' were completely unmoved by his story, detaining him while other prison visitors were sifted by. Firuz glanced back to see if his followers were still behind him. There was the ambulance driver in his vehicle reading the newspaper, waiting for his command. Firuz envisioned a call to attack and drive to the cell, but pleaded instead, 'Then could I please speak with the Warden? Please?'

One guard gave in and made the call from his post booth.

Firuz signaled to his driver, he'd return in a moment. The guard in the booth came over to Firuz, shaking his head to his companions.

'What do you mean "no"?' Firuz said, shaking his head, too.

'The line's busy.'

'Well then, get me an escort to his office, by the mercy of God. You want me on my knees begging?'

The head of the guards went over to some Pasdars who were having a break and told them the story, glancing over at Firuz regularly.

'I'm Doctor Irani's assistant!' he shouted to them, pointing to himself. 'The one who took care of the Warden. The bullet hole is five centimeters beneath his left ventricle – the lower left portion of the heart.'

The people around him were staring as he demonstrated on himself how the bullet went in and where it had lodged.

Whatever he had said got him in. The medical bag he carried had to be handed over to be searched. The Pasdars who were leading him to the administrative block went through all the items in the bag as they walked. Firuz did not disturb them, staying a step behind to look around.

As they passed an intersecting hallway, Firuz caught a glimpse of two strong men, Pasdars dressed in their khaki uniforms, dragging a slumped body from a room. His own escorting Pasdars turned at the next corner, which gave him the opportunity to double back for another quick look down the other passage. He returned just in time to watch a black-robed clergyman of high dignity thanking another official. Then two more proceeded out of the room – the Warden and Isfahani.

'Hey!' one of the Pasdars yelled to the other, finding themselves alone. They drew their hand guns and ran back around the corner.

Firuz leaped ahead as he heard their fast-traveling footsteps and knelt over one knee, crouching on the floor.

'What are you doing?' one of them shouted, ready to shoot Firuz through the head.

'I'm tying my shoe lace,' he answered, not looking up.

The angry Pasdar squeezed Firuz's arm, bringing him up, then jabbed him in the stomach with the nozzle of the gun. 'Don't ever do that again or I'll blow your guts out. Understand me, brother?'

He pushed Firuz against the wall, then put his gun back in his belt. 'Move.'

This time Firuz led the way, being ushered directly to the Warden's office. He was lucky to be walking away just gasping for breath. There was no doubt in his mind that what he had just caught a glimpse of was important enough to have him disappear.

They sat him in one of the office chairs, keeping an eye on him until the Warden returned. It struck Firuz that he could be in more danger than he had first realized. The Pasdars may have not questioned if he had seen anything, but if Isfahani should return to the office with the Warden, he was going to have a lot of explaining to do. Isfahani had already warned him that no one was permitted to see the prisoner and here he was, come to get the man to the hospital? This could well become the perfect set-up for Isfahani to see to his dismembering. . . . Firuz was beginning to understand the wisdom of obligatory prayers.

The Warden stepped into his office, looking ragged.

'What are you men doing in my office?'

Firuz was pleased to see that the Warden was alone. The Pasdars beside him straightened up.

'This doctor came to see you,' said one.

Firuz stood to explain, aware that the Warden knew who he was.

'That's no doctor!' shouted the Warden. 'What are you doing here?' Perspiration was pouring from the Warden's face. He wiped his brow and neck, waiting for his answer. Firuz noticed how he was clutching his slowly healing side.

'Doctor Irani has requested that I see if one of the prisoners can be moved to the hospital for immediate surgery.'

'We have facilities here,' he said brusquely.

'Yes, Warden, but he made it very clear that this case was extremely serious.'

'Young man. No one in this prison needs to visit any hospital for treatment, and to this God is my witness! Now who let you in here?'

The Pasdars fidgeted, making it obvious to him, then added, 'And they'll show you out.'

The Warden took Firuz's arm. As he spoke Firuz noted his foul breath. It was not lack of cleanliness, but from an upset stomach, as if his whole insides were turned out. It must have had something to do with what he had seen in the hallway, Firuz thought to himself.

'You can tell Doctor Irani that his patient has been transferred. He won't need to worry about him any more. Do you understand?' Firuz nodded, suddenly feeling sick to his stomach. He did understand. And he had the task of telling Hakim the man's foul fate.

When he got back to the hospital he stayed in Hakim's office. He left his winter coat on, having the feeling that he would have to go out again soon, even though the hours ticked by. He poured himself another cup of tea, waiting.

Asiyih came in and switched on the overhead light,

illuminating the dusky room. She had obviously found who she was looking for. 'Hakim said you would be here.'

'Where's Hakim? I mean, the doctor?'

She didn't understand his question. 'He was here after lunch . . . How did the operation go?'

He didn't say anything. He just bolted across the room, guessing what Hakim had done.

'Where are you going?'

'To stop him! Excuse me, Khanum, I'll explain later.'

Leaving Asiyih, he ran down the main corridor, out the emergency entrance, and jumped into the passenger side of an ambulance.

'Drive to the prison,' he instructed the driver, who peered over his newspaper.

'Again? Now what's wrong?'

'It's Doctor Irani.'

It sounded serious, so the driver put away his paper.

'Lights,' Firuz called out, getting the swirling red flasher to go on.

'Is he ill?' the driver asked, pulling out the vehicle and speeding up the main road.

'No, but it's an emergency.'

'I hope it's exciting.'

Firuz was not interested in hearing the driver's fantasies. He held on to the dashboard as they swung around a corner.

'Do you know how some of the chosen Committee members of our government got to the Revolutionary Guard Headquarters in Teheran in the past months?' the driver went on. 'By ambulance. That's because they killed all those people where the political headquarters was meeting.'

'Wasn't that exciting enough for you?'

The driver drove through a red light without looking, nearly hitting a car, but carried on the conversation undisturbed. 'Murder isn't clever. I'm talking about saving lives. That's why the ambulance driver in Teheran is living an exciting career.'

Firuz kept his eyes on the road until they neared the prison.

'You have to be very clever to be a good ambulance driver,' the driver said, obviously thinking himself the type.

Firuz melodramatically braced himself for the imminent crash, then said seriously, 'All right. Drive through the prison gates, we're going to get him out by force.'

The driver glanced at Firuz. 'Are you mad?'

'Drive! and don't stop.' He held the wheel steady for the driver, who kept trying to figure out if this was for real. They were almost at the gate. Firuz was leaning against him as though he was going to turn the wheel and throw the ambulance right into the massive iron gates. Then he shouted, 'Look out!'

The driver slammed on the brakes, screeching to the curb.

'Was that exciting enough?' Firuz said angrily, then threw the door open and got out.

He put his hands immediately in the air. The guards' weapons were directed at him in fear. 'It's just me!'

The security lights flooded his face. 'What do you want?' someone hollered.

Firuz stepped cautiously up to them. 'Did Doctor Irani go inside?'

'You'll wait till he comes out. It's only the Jew!'

Everyone calmed down. The lights moved away.

Firuz ignored their added remark. He wanted to know more about Hakim. 'You said "out"?'

'He was let in to see one of the prison guards,' said one.

'Look. I'm his assistant,' he began, then shut up abruptly as he caught sight of Hakim's shadowy figure inside coming towards the gate, walking with another guard.

The driver came over to the gate as well and peered through. 'Is he all right?'

'We'll find out now.'

Hakim was speaking with the young guard who had first told him about the injured prisoner. 'When did they take him away?' Hakim asked solemnly.

'Mid-morning, Doctor. What did the old guard want to speak to you about?'

'Just the towels and blankets left behind. He asked if they were the prison's or the hospital's property. I told him they were a gift from the hospital.'

The two stopped at the gate and shook hands.

The young man was despondent. 'He shouldn't have been convicted of attempted murder.'

'Yes.' Hakim choked. 'Thank you for letting me through. Good-night.'

'Good-night, Doctor,' they all said.

Hakim walked into the driver and Firuz as he came out. The gate locked behind them.

'All right?' Firuz asked, searching Hakim's eyes.

'Yes,' he said in a hushed voice, leading them to the vehicle.

'Will you be needing the ambulance, Doctor?' the driver asked.

'No. Send it back. I want to walk home tonight.'

'We'll walk,' Firuz said, putting himself in.

Hakim stared into Firuz's eyes, questioning his motives.

'The streets aren't too safe at night to walk alone. All right?'

Hakim conceded, and Firuz nodded to the driver, who switched off his emergency lights, got in the ambulance and drove back towards the hospital.

Firuz kept pace silently beside Hakim, watching shop owners leaving their places of work to go home, careful that the way Hakim traveled would not meet with trouble. There was nothing he could do but pray that God was protecting them both. He felt safer when they got past the hospital. The neighborhood was better. He was not going to disturb Hakim's thoughts, seeing on his face how deeply affected he was by the prisoner's fate.

The brighter stars were now visible. The call to prayer echoed from the amplifiers on the mosque towers. A light haze rose from the homes' burning fires. It was cold enough to snow, though the east wind came from the clear mountain sky.

Hakim brought his hand out of the warmth of his pocket and pressed his coat flat over his chest, feeling the envelope he had placed there for protection. It gave him a lot to consider.

There was no way to know if Arif was dead, but a piece of himself had died. Hakim had felt this feeling before when others close to his heart had departed from this realm of clay. He hoped the young guard would be able to find Arif's family and tell them their son's fate before he would have to. He would hate to be the first to tell them.

'I need a break,' he finally released.

Firuz kept his silence, letting Hakim breathe.

'Amin has made an offer to buy Jamshid's shop. Asiyih and Saffa both want to keep it, but they need more help.'

'God always takes the best souls from this realm at such unexpected times,' he thought aloud. 'The remainder of us struggle until beaten out . . . And I'm beaten. I want to start again.'

Hakim stopped before entering the front door of their acquired place, a small government house arranged for them by Isfahani. He smelled the food Asiyih was preparing for supper.

There was something deep inside which made Hakim desire to assure Firuz that the world hadn't become darker to him. There was a reality to this world and a purpose – he was just beginning to realize it was still possible to search after it and find it. It had all begun with Firuz challenging him. He didn't know how to say 'thank you'.

He looked at the ground. There was something he could say, that possibly both of them could now understand:

> *Were it not for the cold,*
> > *How would the heat of Thy words prevail,*
> > > *O Expounder of the worlds?*
> *Were it not for calamity,*
> > *How would the sun of Thy patience shine,*
> > > *O Light of the worlds? . . .*
> *When the swords flash, go forward!*
> > *When the shafts fly, press onward!*
> > > *O Thou Sacrifice of the worlds.*
> *Dost Thou wail, or shall I wail?*
> > *Rather shall I weep at the fewness of Thy champions,*
> > > *O Thou who hast caused the wailing of the worlds . . .*

# CHAPTER 13

# In the Month of Questions

Hakim and Saffa spent the entire morning in the back room of the shop polishing all the brass and copperware they could find to clean. The old wooden worktable proved the best place for the messy job and the ideal spot for Hakim to be alone with Saffa for the first time since he'd been back in Kashan. He wished the two of them could return to the days of intimacy, when they spoke constantly of life's great mysteries. And this was his chance, though he didn't want to be the first one to start the conversation. He wanted Saffa to feel, without any prompting, that he could confide in his Uncle Hakim once again.

The hours passed without a word from Saffa. So Hakim went on with his part of the work, whistling, coughing and chanting a few popular melodies which he knew Saffa liked. Not once did Saffa look across the table at him. And he waited, keeping himself rolling in patience with the phrase, '*The wise are they that speak not unless they obtain a hearing.*'

Then he thought to himself that if there really was a plot to see who could refrain the longest from speaking to him, his nephew was now in the lead.

'Saffa?' Amin called from the front, then stuck his head through the curtains to find him.

'Yes, Uncle Amin,' he answered instantly.

Hakim wondered why his nephew didn't fall at Amin's feet and thank him for saving him from his torture of vowed silence.

'I'm going,' Amin informed him. 'If you need me I'll be at my shop.'

'Yes, Uncle Amin.'

Hakim was inclined to blame Amin for devising a plot against him, but reconsidered: Amin's one good quality was that he was not a vengeful character. He opened his mouth to say good-bye, but Amin had already departed. He watched the curtain sway until it settled on the floor. Hakim tried reminding himself of

170

Amin's good qualities. Anyway, Amin was very busy this month. Then again, everybody was busy to Hakim this month.

He plopped the old toothbrush into the milky cleaning solution, splashing half the liquid on the table. Saffa glanced up: he tried not to look beyond the spill. He was not to say anything to his uncle and had managed to hold his tongue thus far. He was not going to let this incident get him to speak either. He swallowed that thought hard, then told himself that it didn't matter if Uncle Hakim was getting upset, he was doing what he had to. The Law of God demanded it. He went back to his meticulous polishing.

Hakim put down his brush, then slid the metal tray he had finished scrubbing towards Saffa to dry. He looked around him, seeing that he had finished all the pieces. He was just going to have to sit there patiently; then he took a deep breath. 'Finished,' he said easily. The time of being patient had ended. 'So. After all this, I could use a good walk,' he said, taking a quick, invigorated breath, ready for the exercise.

There was no response from Saffa.

Hakim glanced up at the ceiling, staring for the moment at the canals of cracked paint. 'I love the fragrance of fresh snow. And it's better than this cleaning fluid . . . Saffa, why don't you and I go up to the Gardens of Fin for the afternoon and – '

'No thank you, Uncle Hakim,' he said briefly.

Hakim definitely detected the nervousness in Saffa's voice from having to speak to him. He was not going to let him get off that easily. He cleared his throat. 'Firuz wrote that he's gone home to his family too. For a rest. He said he had a surprise for me when we get back to Khorramabad.'

Saffa completed the piece he was working on and picked up the metal tray his uncle had just finished.

Hakim was deliberately being ignored. He didn't want to get angry about it, so he dipped his brush into the solution instead, watching the whirlpool of mud he was creating. 'I think Firuz is going back to medical school to get his degree. I admire him. You have to be someone special to make it in medical school. It's tough. Very hard. Very difficult. Very, very, hard.'

Hakim reached for a brass vase across the table and soaked it with his brush.

'I've already cleaned that,' Saffa said.

Hakim gave it back to him. 'I know. I saw some oxidation –

And I remember that you were going to go to medical school?'

Saffa wiped off the vase, thinking about his uncle's last words. He did want to go to medical school, but how could he, he thought. 'You have to be in school first,' he said, then slapped his mouth closed.

Hakim slammed his brush down. 'Is it so terrible to talk with your uncle? And you've avoided my company almost the entire time I've been back, as though I've had some contagious disease.'

Saffa wiped his hands off on a rag, standing up. 'I have to go,' he said, then left the room quickly without an explanation.

Again Hakim found himself staring at the waving curtain. 'God, what did I do?'

Asiyih heard the words from the back and saw how much of a hurry Saffa had been in to get out to the bazaar. She was in the middle – she understood the frustrations of both sides, but she was not going to interfere. Hakim was going to have to learn why his family wanted nothing to do with him.

Saffa came back inside. He went over to the free counter, then made himself busy rearranging a display of watches. He saw his mother's questioning stare. 'Too many fanatics all over the place. And I forgot my coat.'

She saw in his face how disturbed he was. Saffa had never walked out of his uncle's presence so disrespectfully.

'Why don't you take your father's books out and study?' she suggested.

Saffa bent down and pulled out a book from beneath a stack of papers in a drawer.

'In the back,' she said, pointing to the curtain.

'I'm fine here.'

'Obedience is a virtue.'

'Mother. It looks better when there is a man up front,' he said, reasoning with her, then saw her surrendering plea.

'Please, dear.'

He had lost many battles by that stare and soft voice. He closed his book, then glanced to the front.

An elderly man in a long heavy coat pushed the door open, cautiously entering. He held his cane like a weapon, more than for balance. 'Good-morning, Asiyih Khanum,' the man said cordially, moving towards her counter. He hadn't noticed her son.

Saffa put his book back down on his counter. He wasn't going to have to go now that his mother was busy with Aqa Gulshani. And he wanted to hear what the old man had come for.

'*Alláh'u'Abhá,*' he said, greeting her softly. His throat was groggy from a cold he had obviously succumbed to.

'*Alláh'u'Abhá,*' she said. 'We haven't seen you for quite some time, Aqa. Are you well?'

'Yes, very,' he said, then sneezed. He wiped his nose with a handkerchief before confiding his story. 'I was visiting my family in Teheran. Things there are becoming very bad, Asiyih Khanum. The communication between the Bahá'í friends has broken down to a standstill.'

He glanced back, feeling he was being watched, then saw Saffa and covered his heart, mumbling his greetings. He turned back to Asiyih. 'Is that Jamshid or Saffa?'

'Saffa,' she said with a deep breath. Aqa Gulshani had been away and didn't know.

'Looks as strong as Jamshid.'

Aqa Gulshani's eyes were sharper than hers. He had seen a likeness in her son that she had only hoped for. Jamshid would have been proud of him, she thought.

Aqa Gulshani pulled a weighty purse from his pocket. 'I brought something to sell to Jamshid – Oh.' He seemed to remember hearing about Jamshid's disappearance. 'I'm so sorry, Khanum.'

'Amin will be in tomorrow.'

'No, no, no. I trust you. If this was a carpet shop, I would sell you all my silk rugs too.'

He placed the purse in Asiyih's palm without disclosing its contents. 'How much is it worth?'

The heavy weight pressed her hand against the glass top. She opened the string top and slid out three antique jewelled pocket watches into her other hand. They were hand-carved with gold and gem chips laced into a design of rare craftsmanship. 'They're beautiful,' she said, admiring the detail.

'Solid gold,' he said proudly.

Hakim came out to the front in time to see the man Asiyih was waiting on cover her hands with his handkerchief to hide what she held. It took a second for him to recognize the man. 'Aqa Gulshani?'

'Yes,' he said, taking a little longer to recognize Hakim. 'Doctor Rahbari?'

Hakim extended his arm to greet him. '*Alláh'u'Abhá.*'

'*Alláh –* ' he said cheerfully, then frowned, stopping before kissing the doctor's cheek. 'You're not a Bahá'í.'

Hakim's glowing countenance dropped. Out of the corner of his eye he saw Saffa nodding his head, agreeing with Aqa Gulshani's statement. Asiyih saw her son's action too. She quickly changed the atmosphere and gave Aqa Gulshani back his handkerchief. 'You two are old friends. Now tell us why you've brought us these heirlooms.'

Aqa Gulshani was reluctant to speak. 'I'm afraid I shouldn't be here, with Hakim present. Nothing personal, Doctor . . . But because my mission is of an important nature, I will direct my dealings to you, Asiyih Khanum. That will make my presence here acceptable before God.'

He put away his handkerchief, giving his nose a quick swipe.

Hakim ignored the words. He didn't want to go through another fight to discover why he was being universally excommunicated. He looked over at the watch pieces.

'I want to know what these are worth.'

Asiyih lifted the weight in her hands. 'Saffa, bring me the magnifying glass. Aqa Gulshani, we will only be able to guess. We need my brother-in-law, Amin, to find out their current value.'

Saffa put away his father's book and went past his uncle into the workshop, returning with a strong magnifying glass, and stood on the other side of his mother.

'Go ahead,' she told him.

Saffa had never seen such pieces. He took each one to study. His father had told him of these types and what they were worth, but to actually see them came only once in a lifetime.

Aqa Gulshani stood in front of Saffa so no passerby could see what was being looked at.

Hakim asked, 'How long have you been hiding these, Aqa?'

Aqa Gulshani was not going to look at him. 'I haven't been hiding them.'

Asiyih could see Saffa was having difficulties figuring out their exact worth. 'Give an estimate, dear, if you can.'

'About one hundred thousand tumans.'

'Aqa. If you're sincerely interested in selling these, I know a man who would go so far as to give you gold coin value instead of paper money,' Hakim said.

'Gold coins?' he asked, looking up at Hakim. 'Gold coins?'

'It could be arranged.'

'That would be fine. As long as I get money.'

Hakim was suspicious of his selling the rare pieces. Aqa Gulshani had no need of more money. There was something that was being undertaken by the old man that was not clear to Hakim yet.

Asiyih had the same curiosity and asked, 'Why are you selling these?'

'We've decided to move from Kashan.'

'To Teheran?' she guessed.

'No. More to the east. I have a nephew out there – Hessam.'

'Yes, Hessam,' Hakim said, agreeing with him. 'I think I remember him.'

Asiyih didn't like the tone in her brother's voice. He was up to something.

'Isn't he an engineer out in the great desert, near Zahedan, if I'm not mistaken?' Hakim asked.

Aqa Gulshani fumbled for his handkerchief and blew his nose. 'Yes, yes. Well. I must be going. I will trust you to complete the affairs, Asiyih Khanum.'

'You are welcome to join us for supper, Aqa,' Hakim invited.

'I'd rather not. Business only. Asiyih Khanum, add the purchase of a small clock. Just in case.'

Saffa wrapped the watches up in their case and handed them to his mother, who in turn gave them to Hakim.

Aqa Gulshani used his cane more like a walking stick again and went out. '*Khoda Hafez*. I'm trusting you with my life.'

Without Asiyih or Hakim noticing, Saffa disappeared into the back workshop. Asiyih turned to Hakim for some answers. 'And why would he be moving to his nephew's place in Zahedan when his entire family live in this region?'

Hakim bounced the weight in his hand. 'Because Aqa Gulshani is going to try and escape across the desert into Pakistan,' he said simply. 'He has no nephew in Zahedan. I was just doing a little investigating.'

'May you be wrong,' she said, shaking her head. 'Where is he running to? To get himself killed by some cut-throats and left to die. Thank God, Payam didn't have to go out this way.'

Hakim was thankful for that too. The journeys over the mountains to Turkey or across the desert to Pakistan were both life-risking. Many had gone, but no one knew how many had been injured, robbed or murdered.

'I think Aqa is just trying to escape the persecutions here. I suppose that he feels he has more to gain by taking this chance. Do you remember when the Universal House of Justice sent Hands of the Cause, Counsellors, and other representatives throughout Iran to implore us all to take our professions, our funds, our dedication to the Cause, to leave Iran and pioneer to other lands. We didn't listen. Maybe we were too attached to something here – the future of our land, our loved ones, work, home. It's no good now saying, "If we had only known."'

Once again her brother was telling her more about the reality they faced than she herself had considered. His review of the situation, seeing the loving guidance of the Institutions, made her wonder if she had been too hard on Hakim. Maybe he had failed because of his own weaknesses and not because he desired to give up his Faith?

'Asiyih. I'm sure the Universal House of Justice doesn't approve of such actions. All we can do is try to make it easier for those around us to endure their hardships. This evening I'll go visit Ali Quli.'

'Is that whom you meant to see for the funds?'

'He owes me many long-standing favors. I'm sure he knows how to handle these affairs.'

'He has too many fingers in too many affairs. Haven't you learned to stay away from dark characters like that?'

'He could do a righteous act.'

'I don't think we should get involved.'

'Asiyih, too many are suffering death, starvation, are grief-stricken, recanting, disappearing. I have to do something. What will happen to people like Gulshani if we don't help each other?'

'Let it be his choice if he wants to run from injustice and difficulties. God sends us these tests for our perfecting.'

'It could be our choice to make sure he's given a chance to survive so he can pass his testing.'

She snapped, 'You are just feeling the guilt of your own past actions!'

This was his day for a thousand wounds, he thought as he was about to defend himself. Then Saffa threw the curtain open, dressed for the wintry outdoors.

'Where are you going?' she asked.

'Away,' he said coldly.

'Why are you so angry?' she continued, stopping him from getting away without an explanation.

Saffa couldn't look at either of them. As far as he was concerned he never wanted to see his uncle again. 'Because now he's speaking for the Universal House of Justice.'

'What are you talking about? Your uncle and I were only giving our opinions.'

Saffa was not too old to be put in his rightful place, and Hakim had had enough of his attitude. 'Son, why did you nod your head when Aqa Gulshani said he shouldn't be talking with me?'

'Because he spoke the truth.'

'Who says you shouldn't talk with me?'

His uncle's voice boomed through his ears. 'The Writings.'

Asiyih gasped. 'It doesn't say you shouldn't talk with your uncle.'

'He broke the Covenant.'

The implication was serious. It explained to Hakim the attitude of those around him. He saw the shock on Asiyih's face and heard the tremor in Saffa's voice. How well he knew the fears of the reality of that statement. Asiyih never would have said that; if she had believed it, she never would have allowed him near herself or any member of the family.

He put his hand on her shoulder. 'Let me be alone with him for a few moments.'

Asiyih went out without a word to her son. She found a secluded corner in the back and sat and prayed while the two talked, hoping to God that everything would be cleared up.

Hakim wasn't angry with Saffa, he just wanted to talk it all out. When he looked over at him, Saffa's gaze was still to the ground. He spoke quietly. 'You have accused me of something very grave. But can you prove your charge?'

'I am not even allowed to be in the same room with you, let alone speak with a Covenant-breaker.'

Saffa put all his strength into his convictions. It hurt, but greater than his love for his uncle was the Law of God. And what he said was in accordance with the teachings of Bahá'u'lláh. Ironically, it was Uncle Hakim himself who had taught him that Covenant-breaking was a spiritual disease so virulent that to be near a soul declared as such would cause even the spiritually-minded to be consumed.

Hakim had to conclude that Saffa was being influenced by someone else. Everything had been fine between them, until he had come to stay with them. 'I think you've been listening to backbiting gossip. In fact, you too have broken the laws of Bahá'u'lláh by performing this shameful deed.' He knew Saffa would weigh his words. He had taught him that backbiting was one of the most grievous sins: Bahá'u'lláh had said it was 'accursed' of God. It quenched the light of the heart. Hakim wanted Saffa to feel the guilt of his own actions.

'How?' Saffa asked, glancing up quickly. 'I'm telling the truth.'

'And how do you know the backbiting is true? Did our National Spiritual Assembly tell you this, or did it come from the Universal House of Justice?'

Saffa knew his uncle was treating him like an ignorant child, which he wasn't. He had read the Writings on this point and argued back, 'No. You know that you can't come to a Nineteen Day Feast, can't serve on an elected or appointed institution within the Faith. And you can't give to the Fund or even vote! You've lost all your rights as a Bahá'í.'

Saffa had studied. He was no longer a child who could be filled with knowledge to parrot back information. Hakim was going to have to treat him maturely, like the man he was becoming.

'You're right, Saffa. I can't do those things. But may I ask you one question? Can a Muslim or a Christian participate in any of those things?'

'They're not Bahá'í.'

Saffa had answered his question. 'Nor am I,' he said painfully. 'I lost my faith. That's why. Breaking the Covenant implies something far worse than breaking a law of God. Both of us have broken laws, of different seriousness, but not the Covenant.'

Saffa was not yet convinced.

'I can prove it, if we go to the Writings. Do you have your father's books here?'

Saffa was willing: it was the only place to go. He nodded. 'I have a few of them here.'

'Any Tablets of 'Abdu'l-Bahá?'

'I believe so,' he said, searching behind the other counter where he had hidden the volumes. He brought them all out.

'It's wiser to take them in the back.'

Saffa agreed.

The two made their way to the workbench and cleared it clean, then sat on opposite sides, getting their passages ready to prove their points. Asiyih kept to the shadows. They both seemed nervous to her: though their words were strong, the investigation was not easy for either one of them.

Hakim put on his spectacles and searched through the pages, glancing up at Saffa as he spoke. 'Do you know why Bahá'u'lláh repeatedly wrote in certain Tablets about the appointment of 'Abdu'l-Bahá as the sole Interpreter of His laws and teachings, and made him the Center of His Covenant after His ascension?'

Saffa was used to the verbose and complex questions of his uncle: they would not confuse him. 'Because 'Abdu'l-Bahá was His eldest son and the only one He trusted.'

Hakim shook his head. 'He was made the "Center of His Covenant" so that unlike past religions, the Cause of God would be able to withstand the severing winds of division from within by the Covenant-breakers after the ascension of the Manifestation of God, from being split into sects like all the other religions. No past religion of God has had in writing the explicit provisions of the Pen of the Manifestation for this unique station.'

Saffa showed his uncle what he had read before, from the book he had opened. 'Here. 'Abdu'l-Bahá has written: "Firmness in the Covenant means obedience, so that no one may say 'this is my opinion', nay rather he must obey that which proceeds from the Pen and Tongue of the Covenant."'

Saffa smiled proudly, and waited for his uncle to comment on that.

'Isn't that obedience to what is revealed by Bahá'u'lláh?' he asked, considering seriously what Saffa had read.

Saffa swallowed. His Uncle Hakim was not playing with him, but was honestly listening to what he was saying, and, more important, to what the Writings were saying. Saffa reread the passage, then nodded; he agreed with what his uncle had gleaned.

Hakim pulled out a series of folded sheets from the back of another book; Jamshid had obviously considered it important to place them there. Hakim glanced through them until he found something.

'Listen to what the Universal House of Justice has written, the Institution which Bahá'u'lláh called into existence as infallible. "Bahá'ís themselves are commanded by Bahá'u'lláh to investigate truth independently, to 'see with' their 'own eyes, and not through the eyes of others'. Every Bahá'í is at liberty, nay is urged, to freely express his opinion and his understanding of the Teachings, but all this is in a totally different category from that of a Bahá'í who opposes the clear Teachings of Bahá'u'lláh."'

'The two quotes aren't conflicting. They support each other.'

'True,' Hakim agreed.

'Then I'm sorry about what I said about you voicing your opinion, Uncle Hakim,' he said, partially closing his book. 'But we still haven't distinguished between breaking a law and breaking the Covenant.'

'We're coming to that, we're coming to that,' he said, tapping his finger on the next sheet. 'The Universal House of Justice defines specifically what Covenant-breaking is: "When a person declares his acceptance of Bahá'u'lláh as a Manifestation of God he becomes a party to the Covenant and accepts the totality of His Revelation. If he then turns round and attacks Bahá'u'lláh or the Central Institution of the Faith he violates the Covenant."'

'Then who determines who a Covenant-breaker is?'

Hakim opened his mouth to answer, then looked back to the book for the original. 'It goes on to say that only the Universal House of Justice can make that final decision.'

'And if you recant?'

Hakim put the book down. 'You haven't attacked Bahá'u'lláh or His Institutions, you've just failed under pressure. I've never signed anything like that, or said as much.'

Hakim closed the book. He looked into his palm, then massaged his cold hands.

Saffa could see what the investigation was doing to his uncle. But they had to continue. He buried himself in his book, then looked up. 'Uncle Hakim. Do you want to become a Bahá'í again?'

The question was like asking a double amputee if he wanted his legs reattached and to walk again. His whole being searched now for certitude, for constancy. His heart longed for the inspiration to cry aloud his declaration of faith, though his mind told him that not his words, but his deeds, were the proof to God. He could have written a letter to the National Spiritual Assembly explaining his failure, humbly imploring to be reinstated, but the government of Iran had now dissolved their National Spiritual Assembly. It was to the Universal House of Justice that Hakim knew he would ultimately have to write and seek their decision. How could he answer from his heart the sincere innocence of his nephew's question?

'If you teach me a little about the Bahá'í Faith I'll be able to stand up and pray for forgiveness, as a Bahá'í,' he said in a whisper . . .

'Uncle Hakim, I too will pray that God accepts your prayer.'

Hakim covered his tears with his hand.

Saffa looked over to his mother, hearing her sniffling. 'I'll try to be more obedient. I'm sorry.'

She shook her head, staying where she was. She had seen enough to make her believe both men were growing in their faith.

Hakim looked at Saffa. 'I will too.'

The two embraced, weeping like children.

'I'll try and teach you, uncle. Teach me too.'

'Do you still want to become a doctor?'

'You know I do.'

'Then we'll teach each other how to become doctors to humanity, spiritually and bodily.'

Saffa nodded his promise on Hakim's shoulder, then wiped his face and stood back at arm's distance. He laughed.

'What?' Hakim asked, smiling.

Saffa shook his head. 'You're going to have to go through all this again – with Uncle Amin.'

Hakim burst out laughing. 'O God!'

Aqa Gulshani got word that his order was ready and rushed to Asiyih's shop. When he entered he saw that Saffa was busy with a sale to a young couple. He straightened himself as best he could and made his way with his cane to the other counter, then cleared his throat and said, 'Is my clock ready yet?'

Saffa was embarrassed before his customers, and excused himself to say, 'What clock, Aqa Gulshani?'

'What clock?' he said, with a nervous laugh. 'Yes. Where is your mother, Saffa?'

'In here!' Hakim called out from the workshop and came out wearing an old smock. 'Good-morning, Aqa Gulshani.'

Saffa went back to serving his customers.

'Good-morning, Doctor.'

'Please. Come in the back. I'm just packing your clock now.' Hakim parted the curtain for him to pass through, then closed it, whispering as they walked to the work bench, 'I procured an excellent deal for you.'

Aqa Gulshani clapped his hands for joy. 'May the blessings of the All-Merciful surround your very being,' he whispered back excitedly. 'How much do I owe you for the clock?'

'The price has already been deducted.' Hakim reached up to a shelf and pulled down a clean jar of fruit preserves. 'Those pocket watches were part of a rare set. We got forty-two thousand tumans each. It was the best anyone could do on the black market.'

Aqa Gulshani looked at the jar Hakim handed him. 'What's this?'

'Your gold.'

'What!'

Hakim gestured for him to keep his voice down. 'The coins are in the preserves.'

Aqa Gulshani did not find this amusing. 'I hope that you have an explanation for this unseemly joke.'

Hakim took the jar from his hands and slammed it down on the bench. 'Listen to me, Aqa Gulshani. I know full well what you are planning to do. Your nephew Hessam is overseas. Zahedan. Ha.'

Aqa Gulshani's face flushed a deep red. 'What does that have to do with trading three hundred thousand tumans worth of watches for a bottle of preserves?'

'Who are you planning to visit in Zahedan?'

'A friend,' he answered, not being intimidated. 'A Bahá'í friend.'

Hakim shook his head, pulling out a slip of paper to hand to him. 'Don't jeopardize an innocent man's life with your scheme. You can safely stay at this address. The landlord there has been informed of your expected arrival. He can be trusted as well as any "relative" or "friend".'

Hakim hadn't closed the curtain as tightly as he imagined. He saw the figures of the customers leaving through the front door.

Aqa Gulshani was outraged. He folded the paper and slipped it into his pocket. 'What are you trying to suggest?'

'If you want to get across the patrolled border to Pakistan with money, any Bahá'í – '

'How will they know I'm Bahá'í?'

'Is your memory so short? The National Bahá'í Center was completely divested of its contents when the Revolutionary Guards had its offices ransacked. They are looking for any excuse to kill any Bahá'í. And they have the files to know who is who.'

Aqa Gulshani became quiet. He wiped his nose.

Hakim relaxed. 'If a Bahá'í travels with a passport and a large sum of money, without a doubt he'll be robbed and executed on the spot.'

'I'm just going for a visit,' he said, more weakly.

'Aqa. That is between you and God. But if you are going to try and escape on your own, or try and reunite with your loved ones overseas, please listen to what I have to say.'

'I am Bahá'í.'

'No one has suggested otherwise, my old friend.'

Aqa Gulshani took a seat. 'I didn't mean . . . I'm frightened, Hakim. Each day it grows worse. The men with open arms in the streets. My family, children – my wife, and I may never see them again. It's our only chance. I must try. For my wife's sake. I'm not a very strong Bahá'í. If they arrested me, I wouldn't survive their grueling tortures – I . . .'

Hakim slid the jar over to him. 'Ali Quli is waiting for your passports. He'll mail them. If they are confiscated, well, we tried our best, and the rest we will leave to the will of God. Keep this jar with you. And bring some other gifts so this doesn't stand out.'

'How much will I have to pay him?'

'One hundred thousand tumans.'

'I'll sell my carpets. The bank can issue me traveler's checks.'

'Aqa. The bank is not going to give you thousands of dollars for your tumans. You're not going on a scheduled trip.'

'I should have left before the revolution. And how do I know that they won't cut my throat and take the money when I'm at their mercy in the desert? Answer me that, Doctor Rahbari?'

'Ali Quli said that he'll hold the money in trust until you reach

Pakistan. Once there, another man who knows Ali Quli will pay off our Zahedan friend. They've done this before.'

Aqa Gulshani reached for the preserves. 'Why are you doing this?'

Hakim took off his smock. 'Because you wouldn't listen to the advice of a non–Bahá'í who would tell you to remain here and face the tests of God.'

Aqa Gulshani stood up and declared, 'This is the most Bahá'í thing you have done.'

'Don't you dare compare the Cause of Bahá'u'lláh with this act!'

Saffa threw the curtains open, which startled Aqa Gulshani into giving the jar back to Hakim. Saffa came over and handed him his wrapped clock. Hakim put the preserves back in his other arm.

'Thank you. It's a beautiful clock,' he said loudly towards the front.

Saffa smiled. 'There's no one else here, sir.'

Hakim escorted Aqa Gulshani out. As he was about to close the door to keep the draft out, Asiyih rushed in excitedly.

'I just met a woman who asked me to give her a book on the Faith!'

'Really?' they both said.

'Isn't it wonderful! We have to have her for supper,' she said and ran back to take off her coat.

Saffa looked out the door into the bazaar. To him there were so many like Aqa Gulshani who were trying to cling to their lives and possessions, to get away from the persecutions and hardships. Then there were others like his mother had met, who knew what the Bahá'ís were faced with, and yet fearless of the consequences they were still investigating the Cause.

Asiyih came back up front. 'Hakim, what happened with Aqa Gulshani?'

'Others will come after him.'

'I still don't agree with what you're doing.'

She came over and stood next to him, looking out the door, hoping for a customer. The floor heater between them warmed their legs.

'And I don't agree with what they are doing,' he said. 'The only service we are providing is to put them into contact with

184

trustworthy people. That's all. We can't make them persevere.'

She sighed, thinking about the woman she had just met. 'I wish we could all see the light at the end of this dark tunnel and be content with the calamities around us now. O God, if the mullas or the Revolutionary Guards find out.'

Saffa raised his voice, 'Let them come.'

'You!' Asiyih said, swinging around. 'I should have your uncle send you and your sister to your aunt in Africa.'

'You can send Mitra. But you need me.'

'Your uncles and I can handle the shop without you.'

'Who will clean up my room?'

Hakim laughed. 'Is Uncle Amin teaching you how to do that too? Asiyih,' he said aloud. 'Come to think of it, Mitra will have to remain too. She cooks a delicious thick stew.' He rubbed his round stomach, as it was getting about time for lunch. 'And we have to keep our employees well fed.'

She was outnumbered. 'Then I'll go to Africa. But before I go, both of you lazy men to the back and clean up that mess. There are empty preserving tins all over the place.'

Hakim and Saffa headed to the back.

'Can we strike, Uncle Hakim?'

'No,' he chuckled. 'Then we wouldn't get lunch.'

The shop door opened and a bearded man entered, wrapped in a thick winter coat and scarf. He meandered up to the unattended counter, seeing a younger woman on the other side viewing merchandise.

Hakim sat in Amin's chair, reading the newspaper, while Asiyih helped the woman. He let the man who had come in browse for a while, more interested in overhearing what the woman was talking to Asiyih about.

'But where do I go to get a passport?' she asked.

'I don't know, dear. You are not going to get a passport so easily. And don't talk about seeing someone to make you a false one. That is against the law. Bahá'u'lláh wouldn't like that.'

There was something about the tilt of the man's head that made Hakim think he had come more to overhear than to buy. Come to think of it, he had seen him lingering around the shop before. Hakim got up and stood behind the counter, saying nothing. The man looked more closely at the watches.

'We're still going to try, Khanum,' the woman said.

'Tell me,' Hakim bellowed across the room, getting the man's quick attention. He spoke to the woman. 'Do you like that watch, Khanum?'

The woman glanced back at the watch Asiyih had taken out of the case for her to see more closely. 'It's all right, sir.'

'Well, think it over with your husband. We can let you have it less twenty-five percent.'

'Good,' she said, agreeing, although she was a bit confused.

Asiyih didn't like the way Hakim was booming. There was trouble. She put the watches away. 'Thank you, Khanum. Remember what we said.'

The woman nodded, comprehending at Asiyih's tilt of the head telling her to leave. '*Khoda Hafez.*'

Hakim said forcefully, 'May God guide your business trip. You'll make more in your venture than we do. It seems everyone is merely "looking" these days.'

Hakim called the wandering-eyed man's interest back to himself. 'Can I help you?'

The woman left. The man stepped from the counter. 'No. I've seen enough.'

Saffa came into the shop with Mitra, passing the man going out. Their ears, noses and cheeks were bright red. Snow powdered their clothing.

'What was that?' Asiyih asked Hakim, summoning Mitra over to remove her gloves and scarf.

Saffa knew. 'The creep who's been watching the shop for the past week.' He pulled off his hat, combing down his hair, then knocked the snow off his cap.

It was one of Isfahani's thugs, Hakim thought. He must have been spying on him all the time. 'It is enough with Ali Quli. He is not as wise as I once knew him to be with his spending. If people want help they can go to him directly, but we'll stay away from him completely. We'll have to find another way of helping the friends. I don't want anyone to go to prison or whatever for my stupidity.'

'*Yá Bahá'u'l-Abhá!*' she exclaimed, glad to be rid of the entire affair.

Hakim was going to have to visit Isfahani soon. His holiday was almost over. Everything had a beginning and an end. Even

186

history, he thought, repeated itself until a lesson was learned. The trouble was, most people usually learned a lesson after they got burnt. Hakim had been roasted on the fire enough for one lifetime.

# CHAPTER 14

# Pursuing Watchmen

Isfahani had his expected guest be seated while he finished his personal phone call. He was not too impressed with this assistant chosen for him, nor did it appear that the man was overwhelmed by the set-up he was being placed in. Isfahani wasn't concerned about the simplicity of his makeshift office. Headquarters at the theological school next to the mosque was the safest and the most sensible place. He wondered if his office shattered the young man's vision of the prestige of being a Commander. This man was far younger than he himself had been when he first became an assistant. Acne still scarred his face, which reminded Isfahani of adolescence, but made the man look hard. He must be hard, to have moved up in rank.

Isfahani cut his conversation short. He took the file the man had brought with him and went through it.

'Wives are the same, Husayn,' he said to him, taking a hit of his cigarette.

The man looked at him coolly. He was aware of how to treat a Commander of the Revolutionary Guard – with respect, but with a sense of one's own self-worth, if one wanted to make an impression. 'Yes, Commander Isfahani.'

By the looks of the reports, Isfahani was getting an educated assistant. He wanted to hear how well he presented himself. 'You're married?'

'As it says in my records, Commander,' he said, indicating the file.

Isfahani glanced up. 'I asked you.'

The challenge Isfahani gave him in his stare was not met by subservience. The returning gaze was defiant, not to be subdued by intimidation. After a moment Husayn lowered his gaze, avoiding a conflict. Isfahani was pleased, though he knew that had they been on equal terms this one would never have backed down.

'Yes, Commander. I am married.'

He went on. 'Children?'

'None.'

Isfahani put his elbows on the table, then slid the file aside for the time being. He stroked his mustache. 'Tell me about her.'

The Commander was being informal, so Husayn crossed his legs more comfortably. He maintained his air of smoothness. 'She was a fellow student at Teheran University. A much better student than I,' he said, proud of her. 'All my friends desired her for their wife.'

'And you won.'

He smiled pretentiously. 'Of course.'

'If she was as sought-after as you suggest, then you must have made a few enemies of your friends?'

'They found others, Commander. This one I won.'

It was like bargaining for a slave, Isfahani thought, wondering what arrangements Husayn had made with the girl's family to accomplish his seemingly callous goal. It was possible that he was probing in an area that was too personal. If his Commander had done the same to him at first, he would have adopted the same curt attitude. He eased off and leaned back in his chair, referring to the file. 'Why is it that you had no interests in the Marxist or Leninist movements at school?'

'Islam is complete. It encompasses politics and not vice versa,' he answered, then added, 'I am told that you also remained aloof.'

'On the contrary, I studied their movements well. I learned how to squeeze the nectar from their rotten fruit and use it for my purposes.'

Husayn studied Isfahani's face seriously, then said, 'Then I will have to learn, too.'

'You will,' he said, going on with the interview. 'Have you ever dealt with enemies of Islam, traitors to the regime, urban guerrillas – on an intimate level?'

'Not on such an intimate level as yourself, Commander,' he said, praising him. 'I even understand that as an Islamic Sacrificer you were able to get one of the daughters of a Bahá'í to recant her faith and marry you.'

It was a score: privileged information that Isfahani was not ready to be hit with. It was an unwise move so early in their game

189

of chess, attacking his queen with a pawn. Isfahani would show him the danger of insulting his kingdom.

'You come highly recommended by Commander Rashti. And he has entrusted me with your noble education. I am instructed to make you my Assistant.'

As Isfahani dropped his cordial tone, Husayn sat back up.

'If you ever argue or question my command, no matter how highly approved you come, I'll make sure that your next assignment for the glory of Iran is laying your life down in an Iraqi minefield. Don't take me lightly.'

'I don't, Commander Isfahani.'

A knock came before the door opened. A Pasdar stepped in. 'Forgive me, Commander. Ali Quli is waiting to speak with you.'

'Has the doctor arrived yet?'

'He's right here, Commander.'

Isfahani stood up and led Husayn out of his office. 'I want you to go with this Pasdar. One of our more respectable citizens is dabbling in things he's about to get burnt with. I'll join you presently.'

Isfahani then instructed the Pasdar as such, then added, 'Send in the doctor.'


Hakim's plan as he entered the office was to get one more month's extension out of Isfahani, and he knew how to achieve it. He removed his cap as he came up to the desk.

'Come in, Doctor. Tea?' Isfahani offered, having had a tray prepared for two. He gave Hakim a steaming full cup.

'Thank you, Commander. How's my replacement working out at the hospital?'

'Doctor Dana is fine. Please, have a seat.'

'Very good,' Hakim said, taking a chair. He slowly sipped his tea with the Commander, he wanted him relaxed, then said, 'I waited until you were here in Kashan to make my application.'

'For what, Doctor?'

'Another six-month extension,' he said with ease, ready for Isfahani's loss of hospitality. 'The children are out of school. My sister needs to earn an income, as her husband's past services to the government, his pension, have been made invalid, because he's –'

'One month.'

Hakim acted surprised by the interjection, then bargained.

'Three.'

'In one month you are to be back in Khorramabad at the hospital. I'm in a good mood. My wife is going to have my son.'

'Many congratulations, Commander. Wonderful,' he said. 'I need at least two months.'

'One. Good-day, Doctor.'

'Very well,' he said, having pushed the Commander far enough. He swallowed his last drop of tea, placed the cup on the tray, then left. He had got his month.

Isfahani was pleased with his handling of the doctor. He picked up the phone. He was overdue in calling the Ayatullah, and spoke about the doctor's visit.

'Yes. Doctor Irani requested another month here. As yet I've had no unusual reports about his activities.'

Isfahani poured himself another cup of tea and pulled Husayn's file over to glance through while he continued to talk.

'Closely? I am, Ayatullah. Yes, I too would like to know if he is merely here to help his sister and family . . . No. I have no idea what was in the letter the prisoner passed on to the old prison guard to give Doctor Irani. But I am quite certain it has to do with his extension. We will let him tighten his own noose.'

He sat up like a proud peacock, listening to the Ayatullah's favorable words. 'Yes, we were able to uncover the Marxist dissidents' stronghold. Thank you, Ayatullah. It was you who refined my abilities . . . I would be very honored to be your guest . . . *Khoda Hafez.*'

'Pasdar!' he called out, placing the phone down on the receiver.

The bearded man who had been watching Jamshid's shop entered. 'Yes, Commander?'

'What do you have further to report?'

'So far, nothing more, sir. But by my life, the doctor is involved in illicit activities against the Revolution.'

'Don't use grand words, just get me proof. Stay with him even if he goes to the toilet.'

'I will, Commander.'

Isfahani followed the Pasdar out, going over to the place where Ali Quli was being entertained. He entered a room lined with sandbags, which blocked the outside window. In the row of chairs along the side sat Husayn with Khurasani, who was enjoying a little chat with him, and another Pasdar who was making sure that Ali Quli was comfortable in the center isolated chair.

Khurasani rose when Isfahani came in, followed by everyone else. He gave Isfahani a torn-open manila envelope with seven passports inside. It had never reached its intended destination.

Isfahani turned to the accused. 'Do you know what the penalty is for forging exit visas, Ali Quli?'

'I'd like to know who planted those in my house, Commander,' he said, dripping a pool of sweat.

'Think hard,' Isfahani suggested.

Ali Quli saw Khurasani coming towards him massaging his strong hands, which immediately opened his mouth. 'It was Doctor Rahbari.'

Khurasani turned to the new assistant. 'The stew thickens.'

Husayn called Khurasani closer and whispered aside, 'Who is this Doctor Rahbari?'

'He made Assistant Isfahani a Commander. And the Commander made him an Islamic Hero.'

Husayn had only heard of a Doctor Irani. 'And Doctor Irani?'

'The same. Who knows what title the doctor will set upon the Commander's shoulders next?'

Husayn watched the Commander more closely, thinking about his own career and his chance to move up. Isfahani was glaring at Ali Quli. He threw the passports in his lap, knowing him to be lying to save his own neck. 'These are intercepted Marxist passports!'

The Pasdar pushed Ali Quli's chair against the sandbags, taking the passports. Ali Quli looked at Isfahani. 'Yes, but I help Bahá'ís too.'

His slip was an unexpected surprise to Isfahani, who put the pieces together.

'I mean, he helps Bahá'ís!'

Isfahani swept his hand commandingly. The Pasdar picked up Ali Quli by his throat.

'I have lots of money,' he said, gasping.

'Had,' Isfahani declared. 'Remove him. Throw him in prison for trial.'

Khurasani let the Pasdar and Ali Quli out, then turned back to Isfahani. 'You like examples, Commander.'

'It serves my purposes,' he said shortly. 'Confiscate his

property. See if there is anything else in his home.'

He glanced at the absorbed Husayn. 'I've been too lenient with the doctor. He has been to Ali Quli's a few too many times.'

'What do you propose to do?'

'We should be investigating his brother-in-law's shop.'

'It's Friday night,' Khurasani reminded him. 'After I hear the Mulla's sermon, I will bring you all you need.'

Isfahani agreed. 'Don't get carried away.'

Husayn wanted to be part of the discussion. 'Ayatullah Rustami once said, "Poisoned blood is always poisoned."'

Isfahani put him in his place. 'Our aim is to find the source of the poison and sever the viper's head, Assistant. Nothing more. Nothing less. "Justice," Mulla Ahmad once said. May God advance his station. And ours.'

Hakim left the small lamp on over the desk in the guest bedroom, where an envelope lay, its drying ink glistening. He went to see if Mitra had fallen asleep beneath the thick blankets of his bed: she had, mouth open and all.

For a moment her peacefulness let him forget the cares of his day at the Revolutionary Guard headquarters or, while in the shop, hearing the troubles facing the Bahá'ís throughout Iran. He should have been numb after hearing the hundredth arrow of hate shoot through his heart, but he couldn't cast out of his mind the stories he had been told, wondering what the world thought when it only read, in comfort, of an elderly couple set alight with kerosene for their convictions, or how an unknown assailant put a bullet through the head of a world-renowned physician because of the doctor's faith. Hakim envisioned the pleas that must have been made by the fair-minded around the world, the documents signed asking that the carnage be stopped. But how many, he wondered, actually understood how their life-blood that was spilt was a bounty from God. Did man forget to search for purpose, he wondered.

Amin had told him long ago about an elderly Bahá'í who had freely given up his faith to help teach the Muslims about the Cause of Bahá'u'lláh. And there were many more who had been forced to recant, whom few spoke about. There was a Bahá'í in Teheran who had recently recanted, like him, under pressure. Hakim didn't know the reason, he just prayed that all those who were being tested held fast to the Covenant, and that those who failed came to realize the true extent of their loss.

He thought of Bahá'u'lláh's own half-brother, whose perfidy and lust for leadership had led him to break the Covenant of God to such a degree of abasement that he had perverted the Holy Writings, ordered some believers killed, and poisoned Bahá'u'lláh, which had left Him with a shaking hand until the end of His life. And still the Manifestation of God always sought to forgive him, should he have repented. How great was the sin-covering eye of God. One hundred years later His followers were giving sweets to their executioners. The martyrs' families were teaching His Cause with great eloquence at the funerals, kissing their deceased loved ones, taking last pictures beside their fallen bodies with joy on their faces. Was this the way for God-fearing people to behave? Hakim marveled at the thought. Did they see clearly the purpose of this realm and revel in their joy at serving so exalted a Cause, he wondered.

The only purpose he had left was perceived by Isfahani and his worldly plots. Hakim had so far to return to God in penitence. Maybe Isfahani and his pursuing watchmen would, like the angel of death, or rather the angel of life, lead him to the presence of his Beloved.

Hakim looked into the closet and rummaged through the top shelf, trying to see the titles of a row of books, searching for something to read. He accidently knocked a clothes hanger to the floor. Bending down, he picked up an old jacket and dusted it off.

His hand brushed over the front, and heard the wrinkling of paper. He reached inside and discovered the sealed envelope he had placed there for security. He had forgotten all about Arif's letter to his parents.

'Uncle Hakim! Uncle Hakim!'

Saffa burst into his room, exhausted from his run in the cold night air. 'They've burnt down the shop!'

Hakim tossed the letter on the desk. 'Where's your mother?'

Asiyih rushed in and removed her wrap.

'What's happened?' he asked, bringing her to the bed to sit. 'Are you both all right? Asiyih?'

'There was nothing we could do,' she said, whipping off the scarf from her hair. 'We went to the bazaar, to the bakery shop. The baker's wife invited us there to tell her more about the Faith.

We spoke for a few hours. And when we came out we heard the mob coming. Saffa and I went to investigate more closely. They yelled "Bahá'í" – this and that,' she told him, not repeating their foul language.

'We were lucky that they attacked this late,' Saffa said, going over to his waking sister.

Hakim thought about the timing. 'It must have been planned. Ali Quli was imprisoned early today.'

'They were masking their search?' Saffa asked, wondering.

'They'll find nothing, Hakim. We've done nothing wrong.'

'No, you haven't,' he said, reassuring her, then leaned up over the desk and slipped his new-found envelope away in a drawer. He took the other envelope, now dry, in his hand and sat down beside her again, talking of other matters first. 'The little we've saved will sustain you and the children for the meanwhile. All the money we earned was by sales. That's the truth . . . I've been granted another month's leave, but it's time for me to return to medicine, to the hospital.'

He took her hands. 'We can sell what remains to Amin. He can rebuild the shop if he wants to. I'm sure Jamshid would agree that this is the best.'

Hakim turned to Saffa, who considered his uncle's suggestion, then nodded to them both. Hakim met Asiyih's gaze. 'I want you to all come to Khorramabad to live.'

She shook her head firmly. 'We can't leave, Hakim.'

He understood. 'Then come for a short while. For me? At this time it's important for us to be a family. And there are enough Bahá'ís here to serve the community actively. Only for a short time.'

'God willing,' she said softly.

That meant she would come. Hakim turned back to Saffa, with a questioning look.

Uncle Hakim was not asking him his opinion, he was telling him in his silent manner that he wanted to be alone. 'I know. Come on, Mitra,' he said, lifting her into his arms.

'You can put her in my bed to sleep now,' Asiyih directed him. They watched how easily Saffa carried her and the dragging blanket out.

Hakim spoke frankly with her. 'I have to go away. To deliver a letter which I promised I would do personally. I'll call Firuz, he should be back in Khorramabad by now. Tell him you're arriving. He'll give you the keys.'

They were both looking at the letter on the bed between them.

'The letter has nothing to do with sending anyone's passport. I promise.'

'God willing.'

'Yes. God willing.'

She hesitated, then asked, 'Is that the letter?'

He put it into her hands. 'No.'

She read Payam's name on the envelope, wondering what this had to do with what they were discussing.

'I've read all the letters he's sent to you,' he confessed. 'All three.'

'Men don't write that often,' she said, defending his son. 'But they write well when they do.'

'Sometimes I wonder if he ran away from here, instead of wishing to pioneer there.'

'Both. I think when you're twenty-five years old you try to assert your independence, like all sons do, but Payam also wanted to prove his dedication to the Cause as a pioneer, in some far-off land.'

'Didn't he run away from his family?'

She sensed his searching. 'Then why did he choose to pioneer so close to our sister and his cousins?'

'Did he run away from me?'

'No, Hakim. You're like every father looking for an excuse to take the blame.' This was all about Payam's leaving after he learned what Hakim had done. She tried to be more encouraging. 'His work called him back. You understand that. You taught him that value.'

'I guess so.' He touched the envelope in her hands. 'I want him to have this in case – What I mean is, I can't write to him now.'

He smiled to himself and revealed his passing thought. 'I remember Mama used to tell us, "Next to obedience to God is obedience to your parents!"'

Asiyih smiled too. How often she used the same phrase with Saffa. They both shook their heads, then sighed.

'And don't tell me I'm talking nonsense. Just give this to him, like you knew when to give me Ziya's letter.'

'You're crazy,' she said, then put her hand against his arm, becoming serious with him. 'If you read his letters then you know how much he sincerely loves his father. Because he knows the loneliness and anguish you've been through.'

Hakim buried his head in her lap, crying. 'I love him too, Asiyih, I love him too.'

The bearded Pasdar obeyed his orders at all times, even following Hakim a few days later away to the city of Yazd. He checked into the same hotel where Hakim was staying, overheard the phone call made to arrange to see the Rouhani family, and followed in a second taxi to wait out the doctor's meeting.

Hakim was aware that he was being followed, ever since he had had the meeting with Isfahani in the school at the mosque. He didn't worry about it. There were more important things to consider.

When he arrived at the Rouhani residence, the feeling of an awful purpose struck him. Here was a family living in the comforts of a well-furnished home – a well-to-do accountant and his wife about to have their lives shattered with the news he brought them.

He was met at the door by Arif's mother, a short dark-haired woman dressed in the latest of fashions. She was weak of voice as she led him into their modern guest room and served him a cup of tea. She called her busy husband from his study. The masterful chanting of a songstress spun on the turntable, soothing them until Mr Rouhani came in and wisely turned off the set.

Hakim let the two sit down together, then gave the father his son's letter. It was like presenting a written apology to a family waiting outside a surgery theatre to hear the formal results, like telling them of the failure of their son's operation. Compared to the stream of grief he felt for Arif, the parents' torment was like an ocean. His eyes wandered to a shelf, seeing a photograph of the family together on a trip. They had four children, it appeared, two sons, two daughters.

'He was a good son,' the father said, with a heavy sigh.

'An angel,' his wife wept, 'he was an angel.'

'His Holiness Bahá'u'lláh knows his heart, my love,' he said, comforting her in his arm, then turned to look at Hakim. 'Was he steadfast, Doctor?'

There was no doubt in Hakim's mind as he assured them with a

197

simple nod.

'*Yá Bahá'u'l-Abhá!*' he said, with a sigh.

'An angel,' she continued to repeat. 'He was an angel.'

Mr Rouhani brought his wife a box of tissues. 'My son wrote that the doctor who would be bringing this letter was very special and that we should render thanks to God for his loving-kindness to our son. I'm glad this letter told us what happened. So thankful to you for traveling so far. Last night, I dreamt that a messenger would be delivering great news to free us from our difficulties. And today you have come bearing this glad-tidings.'

Hakim stood to take a closer look at their children's picture. It was best to stand; he had sat through enough significant dreams.

Mr Rouhani wiped his nose. 'He was very strong in his love for everyone, all cultures, all faiths. He never hurt anyone. Even as a child when the other children used to taunt him about his faith, or tried to make him fight for his beliefs physically, he used to find a way to fend them off with his words. I can remember many times he would come home with bruises which he hid, never telling us who had inflicted him with such blows. Arif even defended his older brother.'

Hakim put Arif's school picture down, and lifted the other son's frame.

'He was a special gift to our family,' the father said to himself.

Hakim put the picture back on the shelf. 'Arif was a special soul to mankind.'

'He was an angel,' she re-affirmed.

'Where are your other children, sir?' Hakim asked.

'The two girls are studying for their matriculation at a school in India.'

'God willing,' she said.

The husband nodded. 'Of course, with the current situation, you are aware that we can't send money out of the country now to pay for their education.'

'I'm sure the school understands that,' Hakim said. 'And your other son?'

'Zabih? He's in the same city as Arif . . . was. He's married, and has two small children.'

'That's an unusual name,' Hakim said, knowing what it meant.

'It's Arabic for "Sacrifice",' the father explained.

'Yes,' Hakim said politely.

Mr Rouhani offered Hakim a second cup of tea, which he refused.

'We haven't heard from them for quite some time. I wrote to him a short while back, telling him that we were planning to move to our cousin's winter home in Zahedan.'

Hakim winced in his chair. He thought he'd never hear anyone mention that city again in that way.

'Would you like some more tea?' asked his hostess, composing herself.

Hakim's gestures stopped her from rising. 'No, thank you, Khanum.'

He hated having to say this to the man. 'I don't think Arif would have come with you to your cousins.'

The father understood immediately what Hakim was hinting at. He let down his guard. 'No. I suppose you're right.'

This was not why he had come there, Hakim thought. But he was just going to find out how far the Rouhanis had gone. 'Are you visiting a known cousin?' He pulled out a pen from his coat, anticipating the answer, and wrote out a name and address on a slip of paper.

'Not exactly.'

Hakim reached over and gave him the slip. 'Write to this cousin. Tell him you're coming for a short visit. He's a trustworthy friend who understands these matters.'

Mr Rouhani took the paper. 'We won't go unless Zabih and his family come with us. He is my son.'

Then his wife added, 'We must all go together to India.'

Hakim put away his pen. 'I know. I'll do my best. Leave as soon as you can. In fact, immediately. You'll need hundreds of thousands of tumans to pay for all the protection and passports. And you'll have to pay for your son's family as well.'

'Money is no problem. It sounds like you have done this before?'

Hakim wondered if all the poorer Bahá'ís would consider the same act if they had the money. 'I don't support this undertaking, Mr Rouhani. There are armed helicopter patrols constantly over the desert.'

'I've heard that many people have escaped in cars encased in concrete slabs to travel over the terrain safely.'

'That is not "safely". However you may travel it won't be

easy.' Hakim stood up. 'What if your son wishes to stay?'

'He won't if you tell him we are going.'

Mr Rouhani excused himself from the room. Hakim wandered over to the window near the front door. He saw the taxi, knowing that the bearded Pasdar was still inside. Mr Rouhani returned with his passports, helplessly. Hakim was going to have to help him. 'Do you have any stamps, and an envelope?'

Mr Rouhani led him to his study. Hakim had never done this before, nor did he really want to now. He found some cardboard squares and scissors, then created two similarly weighted envelopes for delivery. He had Mr Rouhani fill in the names and addresses he told him, then put one away in his coat pocket and held the other firmly in his hand. 'If I am questioned for being in possession of these, your lives will be in immediate danger.'

'I will arrange everything today. We'll leave tomorrow.'

As they joined his wife, Mr Rouhani felt he had to explain, before the doctor left their home. 'We want to come back to Iran, but it's important that we be with our family. After India, we'll seek refuge in Canada or Australia. They both are offering political asylum to the Bahá'ís.'

Hakim didn't need to hear their excuses. He wasn't God, and there were no clergy to confess to in the Faith.

She sniffled. 'Oh, may God exalt your station for your kindness. If you could only appreciate what it is to be a Bahá'í today in Iran.'

'Yes.' He had no other words to say, nor would he judge her comment. He went out, in full view of the Pasdar, and made sure that he was followed back to the hotel, freeing the Rouhanis from the watchdog.


Hakim brought his luggage to the hotel lobby and checked out at the front desk. He asked for a taxi, and left the envelope he had held all the time at the desk for the clerk to deliver for him. He went outside into the cold, knowing that it gave the Pasdar the chance to intercept the envelope.

The taxi brought him to the bus station. He sat himself in an open area, waiting to see what the Pasdar was going to do next.

The Pasdar saw where Hakim was clearly seated and slipped into a phone booth. The next time he looked up the doctor was gone. Hakim looked at him from the next booth, dropping in his coins. The Pasdar quickly turned away.

Hakim enjoyed deliberately embarrassing him. He even overheard the name – 'Commander Isfahani.'

Hakim got through on his own line. 'Hello. Can you hear me? Yes? This is Doctor Irani . . . Good, good, nurse. How are you? Is Firuz there? All right then, could you have him meet me at the station late this afternoon . . . Thank you.'

He spoke quick enough to beat the warning bleeps telling him his time had run out. He glanced over to the quietly talking Pasdar, who had his back to him against the booth, and slipped away. He headed towards the café to grab a bite to eat. As he passed a yellow mail box he made sure he was not being watched and opened his coat, dropping the envelope in, then went on to the café. He bought a coke and a fried egg with bread, then went and sat on his bench. He had never liked the dubbed James Bond movies he had taken Payam to see as a child. He was unable to believe anyone could be as cool as Bond was in the face of danger. Now he was convinced that Bond had never lived past the age of thirty, but had died from stress. It was easier to believe in the Walt Disney characters: the heroes were afraid of everything, and the audience died – of laughter.

Hakim was finished starring in the title role of 'Donald Bond'. The producer would have to find another sitting duck for a sequel.

# CHAPTER 15

# Reunion

The journey back to Khorramabad seemed timely to Hakim, this time not controlled by Isfahani's designs, but rather moved by an unseen force which willed his movements through space. In his deepest thoughts he longed to understand the reality around him, like the ant which was trying to unravel the most abstruse passages of the Qur'án. But one had to sincerely yearn to achieve that.

He became filled with a sense of longing. A different type of longing, more of a feeling, which he hadn't felt in the past year. A feeling which he could not remember in his last fifty years. He envisioned having to traverse the oceanic waves which threw him across his mind, or plunge into the depths of his heart to discover his answers. He wasn't afraid of drowning. How strange, he thought, he had always associated fear with longing. Maybe having fears was a reality of this material world. It made sense. He had always striven to alleviate a fear when he was being tested; he yearned when he wasn't able to offer others the comfort of his hospitality, wasn't able to attain a desired ambition, wasn't able to stop the world from taking his loved ones from him. These fears were bound to the physical world. Now he had to search to tie himself to the spiritual realm. Could there be fear where he longed for spiritual achievement, sought to comfort spiritually, or wedded himself to spiritual relations?

It was difficult to imagine. This was like trying to express the taste of something sweet on the tongue which unlocked landscapes, fragrances, and the imagery of a thousand realms, yet escaped all sense of description in words. And it had all to do with returning to Khorramabad.

The sound of bursting air snapped from the brakes of the bus beneath Hakim's seat. His deep thoughts jarred back to the reality around him. The rumbling engine downshifted into its lower gears. They were entering Khorramabad.

Hakim rubbed the icy frost off the window beside him and peered out, recognizing the familiar streets near the hospital. The station wasn't much farther on from there. Firuz would be there to greet him. He looked forward to their reunion very much.

Hakim glanced around the crowded bus, whose passengers were beginning to become alive, collecting their overhead parcels into their laps. His spying Pasdar was there as well, as inconspicuous as he had always failed to be.

Hakim tried to press his mind back to his deep thoughts, but they were as if erased, his mind blank. Maybe his forgetfulness was attributable to old age, he thought lightly with a smile to himself. A chill ran down his spine, raising the hairs on his neck. He was beginning to understand. His brow raised, as he came to realize that he was feeling 'happy'. No, he told himself, it was more than that. He was content, resigned; he felt, he felt – free. 'O my God,' he whispered, 'I'm free.'

His heart began to swell with his shaking breath. Answers to questions he hadn't even begun to raise flooded through his breast. He was talking about 'detachment'. All his quest for leadership, for being someone to admire, all the false airs for proving his piety – were shadows, not reality, he was beginning to see, convinced now that he was the greatest of fools.

He wanted to dance in the aisle and scream like a madman that he was cured of his rheum. There was no longer any need to impress his friends, his loved ones, his associates, not even himself. It was a wonderful feeling.

'My God, am I happy,' he said loudly with a deep breath, then chuckled a belly laugh. The bundled man seated beside him glanced at him as though he actually were insane. Hakim tried to stop laughing, though the man's crooked expression didn't help. 'Forgive me, sir,' he said, covering his heart with his hand. 'I'm just happy to be coming home.'

The man shrugged, then shook his head. He wanted nothing further to do with the man beside him. Hakim calmed himself down by looking out the window at the approaching station. He was ready for that crazy Firuz.

The bus made its wide turn into the depot and aired its brakes to a complete stop. As the bus door pulled open Hakim made his way to the front with his luggage in hand, stopping at each step to look over the waiting crowd, searching for Firuz.

On the top of a pylon base Firuz stood waving his gloved hands. He glanced down at a petite young woman beside him, muffled warmly in a woollen scarf and thick coat. 'There he is. It's Hakim! Doctor! Doctor! Hakim!'

Hakim heard his name being hollered and wove through the crowd towards the call. Firuz took the woman towards a clearing, then ran out to Hakim, who dropped his bag. The two men embraced heartily, clamoring, 'Hello, hello. Are you well, are you happy?'

The woman kept herself back, not wanting to disturb their long-awaited reunion, yet obviously pleased to see the two together.

'You look wonderful, Hakim,' Firuz said gleefully. 'Aside from those bulges under your eyes, you've lost weight!'

Laughing, Hakim teased, 'Oh, I should slap your face!'

Hakim noticed the still, womanly figure keenly watching them. His face lit up suddenly. 'God willing, this is the surprise!' He rushed Firuz and lifted him in his arms. 'I think, Firuz, it is you who have gained weight!'

With a mask of mock seriousness Firuz straightened his clothes, then looked over at the woman in question. He turned back to Hakim. 'Is she with you?'

She shook her head, not amused at his poor joke. He lovingly called to her. 'Come, Maryam.'

She came up beside him. Hakim liked the way she carried herself. He could see a strength in her character that was a good balance to Firuz's playfulness.

'May I finally introduce Doctor Hakim Irani.'

The introduction was like presenting one royal family to another until Firuz made it more familiar. 'Maryam Mostaqim, my wife,' he declared proudly.

'*Qurbani shoma*, Maryam Khanum.' Hakim's eyes welled. 'Wonderful. May the blessings of the Almighty surround your marriage and grant you the fruit of many children.'

'Thank you, Doctor,' she said quietly.

'So, Hakim!' Firuz clapped his hands to uncharge the emotional atmosphere, then reached for the doctor's luggage, only to have it wrestled from his grasp.

'No, no, please. Let me, Doctor.'

'No, no. I insist, Firuz. Let go.'

'Don't play polite in front of my wife. It won't work. I already told her how lazy you are.'

Caught offguard by the humor, Hakim laughed and released the bag into Firuz's care. 'I wouldn't want Maryam Khanum to get the wrong impression of her husband.'

'Thank you, Doctor. This way.'

As Hakim followed them out, he spied a group of Revolutionary Guards looking towards the off-loading bus. He knew they were waiting for their bearded comrade who would be reporting back to Isfahani. Hakim was going to have to do a lot of explaining when they were in each other's company again. But he was not going to get Firuz involved with it at all.

'Have Asiyih and the children arrived yet?' he asked.

'Yes. I put them in the Traveler Hotel near the hospital. With me already moved out, there still wasn't enough space for them in your small place. They wanted it that way. And don't worry, it won't cost us a cent. We treated the proprietor's wife, so they're doing us a favor.'

'I should know your antics by now,' he said, shaking his head. 'And the hospital?'

'Doctor Dana is good, but not as good as others I've worked beside.' He shook his finger at him, taking out his car keys. 'I just remembered it's against my faith to backbite or flatter anyone's inflatable ego.'

'Really?' Hakim said, then patted Firuz on the head.

He stared at the officially marked hospital car Firuz had in his possession. He should have known that Firuz would find a way to get it on loan. Firuz unlocked the back door and threw the suitcase in. Maryam followed and shut the door. Hakim began to argue about the seating arrangement, then saw what she had done and said to her, gently scolding her through the closed window, 'One of you is enough to contend with.'

Before Firuz opened the door for Hakim, he changed his light mood and said seriously, 'I have something important to say. I've learned that some of the missing imprisoned Bahá'ís in Teheran were found in the last few days fortuitously, buried in unmarked graves in the "infidels' cemetery".'

It seemed possible to Hakim. 'Any word about the imprisoned friends missing from Kashan?'

He shook his head. 'Nor about Asiyih Khanum's husband. It was Saffa who confided all this to me.'

Hakim nodded, then got into the car.

Firuz drove the car down the main street, considering what words of wisdom he could offer Hakim in comfort. Finally he said, 'I'm sorry, Hakim. I'm just beginning to understand the whole madness in this country about the Bahá'ís.'

'It's difficult to understand,' he said, pondering it himself.

'Well, we do bring it on ourselves.'

That was all Hakim needed to hear out of Firuz's mouth to remember how irritating he could be at times. He wasn't going to berate him in the presence of his new wife; instead, he took the fatherly approach. 'Firuz dear, don't start with me in the middle of the street.'

'I'm serious!'

'Good, good,' he said, trying to overlook the comments. Firuz had no idea what he was saying, he told himself, and it was going to be proved without anyone becoming argumentative. 'Dear, how do Bahá'ís bring this upon themselves?'

'By choice.'

'What choice?' he asked, losing his temper.

'By choice,' he said again strongly.

Maryam sat back in her seat and closed her eyes, silently praying.

Hakim calmed himself down. 'You're not making any sense, Firuz.'

'My people are Jews, true?'

'True. So?'

'If a Jew is brought before the Revolutionary Court as a Zionist, he is a Jew. Bang. No discussion, finished.'

'Finished?' Hakim asked, confused by his logic. 'What does that have to do with the Bahá'ís?'

'What does that have to do with the Bahá'ís?' he said, miffed that he was not understood, then spelled it out. 'They have a choice.'

Hakim was still not getting his reasoning.

'Look,' Firuz said. 'If a Bahá'í is pulled into court all he has to do is renounce his faith and he's free. A Jew can't do that. And that's what I mean by choice.'

As far as Hakim was concerned, there was no argument, except

206

that Firuz had a lot more to learn about life. 'That's some choice, Firuz. Live in remoteness from God, or suffer death.'

'Suffer martyrdom.'

'That's not a choice,' he said explosively. 'What do you think martyrdom is?'

Firuz shrank away as he turned the car up another street. 'I don't know. All I know is, that if people are willing to get killed for what they believe in, then there's either mass hysteria or some profound truth that others want to fanatically destroy.'

Hakim had heard enough, and looked out the window. 'I liked you before, when you drove a jeep. You didn't ponder such great mysteries, you just drove.'

'You can be grateful to me later. Remember who brought you out of the desert.'

'Thank you, your Holiness Moses.'

Their eyes met, and they apologized simultaneously, even arguing, then laughed at their old ways.

Maryam opened her eyes and saw Firuz glance at her in his rear view mirror and wink. She smiled.

'As your faith is, so shall your powers and blessings be,' he said, quoting to her, but received a warning stare.

He pulled the car along the curb to a stop. 'Hotel Traveler,' he announced. 'You can take your own bag from here, Doctor.'

'Aren't you coming in?' he asked, unclasping his seat belt, then looked back at Maryam for an answer.

'No, thank you, Doctor. We are still in the midst of getting settled,' she said apologetically.

'Yes, one of the staff decided to move to Teheran, so I –'

'I can imagine,' Hakim said, then pleaded to them both. 'Come in. Please.'

She smiled. 'Perhaps later. After you've visited your family.'

'Is Asiyih staying?' Firuz asked.

'We'll see what God has planned.'

'And you?'

Hakim got out of the car. 'Are you going to keep asking me all your questions?'

'No. I'm going to tell you a few answers.'

Hakim said, shutting his door, 'Then I'd better stay.'

Firuz jumped out into the cold and put Hakim's suitcase on the curb.

Maryam rolled down her window. 'Firuz?'

'Beloved?'

She smiled with her deep brown eyes. 'Take the doctor's bag in
. . . Firuz?' she said with a purr.

'You've married a callous monster, Maryam Khanum,' Hakim
said, reaching for his bag. Firuz began his reluctant yet firm battle
for its control.

'No, Firuz, don't worry . . . Oh!' he said, releasing the bag
suddenly into his grasp, remembering. He took out a slip of paper
from inside his coat and put his glasses on. 'Find a Zabih Rouhani
and family. They live somewhere here in Khorramabad.'

Hakim stuffed the note into Firuz's pocket.

'Is it urgent?'

'I promised his parents it would be my first concern.'

'All right, Hakim. It will be my first concern tomorrow,' he
said, then dropped the bag in front of the hotel entrance.

He ran back to his car door. 'Oh. Wear a black tie tomorrow to
work. Isfahani is supposed to be due to arrive and, according to
the gossip, with a new assistant.'

'Just find Rouhani,' he said, turning back from the half-effort
Firuz had made to bring his bag inside. 'You did marry a monster,
Khanum.'

'Thank you, Doctor. I like him too.'

Hakim watched Firuz get behind the wheel to chauffeur his
princess, then laughed. 'A perfect match!'

As Firuz started the car, Maryam called out, 'Doctor! Please
come tomorrow night for supper with your family. It will be a
modest celebration.'

'Bring gifts,' Firuz shouted as she closed up the window. 'It will
be our first Intercalary Days together.'

'Good,' Hakim said, waving good-bye as the car pulled off. He
watched with delight how slowly Firuz was driving. He wasn't
driving like a single man any more, more like a prospective father,
which was possible, he thought.

He went towards the hotel entrance and picked up his bag. The
notion of having a party made him reminisce. Intercalary Days
brought good memories to him.

His smiling expression suddenly fell. What he had heard was
not possible. With a sharp turn he searched up the street to spot the
car. It had already vanished from view. He must have misheard

208

Firuz, he thought. He could not have said 'Intercalary'; he must have said something else.

Hakim paced for half an hour in the hotel hallway outside Asiyih's room, thinking of other words that sounded like 'Intercalary'. There was no similar word that went with 'Celebration'. Maybe Hakim had heard Maryam say 'Intercalary'? Whoever said it, a Bahá'í celebration was not a Jewish celebration. This marriage was not as *kosher* as it appeared. He would throttle Firuz to find out in the morning. Now he had more pressing concerns: his sister.

He knocked and she answered immediately, letting him in without a word. They were both at a loss even to say hello.

What could he do? Inspire her to be on fire with the love of God? Give her a sedative? When he glanced into her eyes, he saw her silent anguish searching for an answer. What was he to do?

His arms slowly stretched out to her, and she came into his embrace. He held her close, rocking her gently, letting her wail. He felt her pain, and, more important to him, however unworthy he thought himself, he felt needed by her.

He gave her his handkerchief, speaking softly, 'We must not be sad over Jamshid's disappearance.'

She sniffled, shaking her head. 'Why couldn't they find the missing believers in our city?'

'Thank God that they happened on the graves of those few friends in Teheran,' he said, scolding her to be cheerful. 'Now the whole world will learn of their glorious fate, what they suffered for being Bahá'ís and remaining steadfast in the face of persecution. And one day we'll know Jamshid's fate. Remember that the clergy in the days of the Báb said His remains were consumed by dogs. Bahá'u'lláh had them kept hidden for sixty years. Look at His Shrine on Mount Carmel. Who would have believed it? Now Bahá'u'lláh is keeping Jamshid's frame hidden. The whole world will know his glorious fate one day too.'

'I know, Hakim,' she said, folding up his handkerchief. 'I just can't bear to imagine what he may have suffered.'

He took her hands. 'It doesn't matter what he suffered. It matters that he was steadfast. When you get to the next realm of God you can ask him to recount his stories of certitude.'

'You're right, I suppose,' she said, sniffling.

209

'Suppose?'

She caught his excited stare.

'What kind of a lover of God are you? Even in the glorious Qur'án it says, "He who doesn't believe in an afterlife is not a believer."'

Asiyih nodded instinctively, still mesmerized by his face.

Hakim swallowed, then looked down. He wondered where all that 'fire' had come from. When he looked again into her eyes, they were revitalized, strong, and he could see what was hidden in her heart. 'You want to go back home?'

'There is so much to do for the Cause there.'

For a moment he had thought he could protect her for eternity, guard her from a world of sorrows. But it was himself he was protecting, he thought, pleased that he could learn from the gentle lesson.

'Stay for a while, then we'll send you home.'

She gave him back his handkerchief. 'Will you come?'

'No,' he said, thinking carefully. 'I'm happy here.'

Hakim noticed that Saffa and Mitra were sitting in a corner playing backgammon. They had been there all the time, watching, listening. Their faces were sad. 'Come,' he said, calling everyone over to the lounge. He removed his glasses and brought out his prayer book from his bag.

Asiyih sat beside him and listened to him pour his heart into his chanting. Someone had told her that Hakim had fallen in love with Layli. Now she was ready to believe it was true. It was the only explanation for his enraptured state.

The few prayers sustained his energy through the night, allowing him to keep a watchful eye over Asiyih and the children as they slept. At sunrise, he didn't waken them for dawn prayers, rather slipped out over to his residence and prepared himself for work.

Freshly dressed, he exchanged his jacket and cap for his lab coat in his hospital office. He was pleased that not much had changed, and that his office was neat for his return. He sat himself in his chair and waited for Firuz, ready and armed with just a few deep queries.

Firuz entered the trap cheerfully. 'Good-morning, Doctor Irani. Welcome home.'

'Did you find what I sent you for?'

Firuz stopped. Hakim seemed angry to him; he'd thought this might happen. 'I'll go out and come back in again . . . Good-morning, Doctor.'

'Firuz!'

'In one evening?' he asked, then noticed Hakim's tie. 'That's red.'

'Well?'

His attempt to change the subject had failed. 'No . . . But Maryam is investigating.'

'And that's another thing. Come in and shut the door.'

'All right. But we can't talk long. Our Revolutionary Commander is waiting in Doctor Dana's office. He wants to see you now, now.'

The door closed. Firuz brushed the loose strands of hair off his lab coat to pass the time as Hakim began to pace. He had to do something to keep from laughing. He knew full well what this was all about and couldn't wait for it to be exposed.

'What religion is your wife?'

Firuz burst out. 'What do you take me for, a hypocrite? Haven't I always investigated the reality of something before – '

'Don't raise your voice with me, just answer the question!'

'She's the same faith as I am!'

'How – oh.' The words Firuz used registered in his mind. 'Oh.'

Pleased that he had quelled the attack brilliantly, Firuz repaired to the door to leave, then clarified his declaration of belief with the utmost simplicity, to eliminate any further misunderstandings. 'We are Bahá'í.'

Hakim lunged forward, catching Firuz off his guard, and pulled him back into the room, slamming the door. 'Are you insane?'

Firuz fought free. 'Majnun? Yes!'

Hakim blocked the door, pointing. 'You're a Jew!'

'Really?'

They stared at each other, breathing fire.

'And I'm proud of it,' Firuz added defiantly. 'It's my heritage. That never can and never will change. But my faith is Bahá'í. That I chose.'

'You! Do you know what you've "chosen"?'

'Lower your voice!'

'What do you want to be? A martyr, a saint, or a hero?' he asked through clenched teeth.

Firuz took a deep breath. He hadn't come to fight. 'You don't have to be a saint or a martyr, or even a hero to become a Bahá'í. You just have to try to be sincere. To be a seeker, yearning after God.'

The look of disbelief in Hakim's eyes made Firuz ruffled. He hated sometimes being treated like an ignorant fool. 'Maybe, if more Bahá'ís took the time to choose their faith on a daily commitment, they'd remember the purpose of being a Bahá'í and become more saintly.'

'What's that mean?'

'You know full well what that means. A child isn't a Bahá'í because his parents are. He must investigate the reality of this Cause, like it says in the Writings of Bahá'u'lláh. Then he can embrace the reality of religion and not follow the mere dogmas of his forefathers.' His arms flew out as he lectured Hakim. 'Look at the other faiths, our beloved country, the world. Everybody always fights over names to follow or not to follow. The names all originate from One Reality. My God. This is the only Cause that can withstand the tests of proving that this is the same evolving religion of God. The names of the Teachers change, but the spiritual lessons are the same. The books are added to, but the school is the same! Investigation. That's where even a Jew has choice! Why do you think I've been tearing my hair out to get answers out of you about all this?'

Hakim listened, but thought whoever had begun to teach Firuz had a lot further to go. 'You've become a fanatic. Bahá'u'lláh says, "Moderation in all things."'

Firuz beat his chest. 'Fanatics make me only appear fanatical!'

'Raving lunatic,' Hakim mumbled, as they both stared at the floor.

'Can I go now?' Firuz asked sedately.

Hakim still grumbled to himself, opening the door. 'Of all the . . . go.'

As Firuz stepped by, he stopped Hakim from shutting the door on him. 'You have to come too.'

They walked beside each other down the hallway. A nurse saw Hakim, welcoming him back, which brought him out of his thoughts. When Firuz turned to go up another hallway, Hakim went straight on. 'I'll deal with you later,' he said, without looking. There was no comment back from Firuz, which bothered him. He didn't have to be so hard on Firuz, he thought, then realized – the one you love most, you hurt most often with your own shortcomings.

Hakim knocked before being invited into the doctor's office. He prayed in his thoughts that God would protect that crazy Firuz, especially from souls like himself. Behind the desk sat Isfahani in his usual position of importance speaking with a well-dressed man, who arose from his chair to greet Hakim. He noticed another young man, standing at the rear, who smelled like a new Pasdar moving up in rank, with the same cheap after-shave Isfahani used to wear.

'Hakim Rahbari. How are you?'

'Hello, Doctor Dana. And how are you? You look very well.'

'Hakim. I would look better if I could stay. And it was a nice change here. I really regret leaving, but my wife longs to return home. If you could find me an assignment somewhere else,' he said, half-teasing.

'How about Azerbaijan, Doctor?' the young man interrupted, directly to Hakim.

Isfahani glared at his Assistant, which got Husayn to turn away and keep his mouth shut. Isfahani slowly swiveled back to the two. 'Well, Doctor Dana. Thank you for letting us meet in your office. And good-bye.'

Both doctors heard the cold cut-off.

'Yes, well. So it seems,' Doctor Dana said, trying to think what else he could say to Hakim before taking his leave. 'I just wanted to see what time had done to you, before we left. Take care, my friend. May God assist you always.'

'Thank you,' he said, grateful for his concern, watching him pay his last respects to the others, then go out without a further word. Isfahani had something he wanted to say to him alone, Hakim could well imagine, and hoped God had heard Doctor Dana's prayer.

'Sit down, Doctor,' Isfahani said in a mild tone.,

Hakim wanted it to be formal. 'Is this going to be long?'

'I hope not, Doctor,' he said, more shortly.

'Then I'll stand.' Hakim was certain that the other man had become Isfahani's assistant, he had the same thirsty ambition in his eyes as his Commander had had when he was an Assistant.

'May I introduce my Assistant, Husayn.'

Husayn nodded, 'I've heard a lot about you, Doctor.'

'And I thought you were young,' Hakim said to Isfahani.

'Sit down, old man, like the Commander instructed,' Husayn warned him.

Hakim's words were addressed to the Commander, not the Assistant. He wasn't looking for a challenge, but said firmly. 'I'll stand, son.'

Husayn took a step forward, pushing for a confrontation.

'That won't be necessary, Husayn,' Isfahani said, intervening. 'The doctor and I are old friends.'

'We could have been,' clarified Hakim, setting their relationship straight, 'but our goals in life are different.'

'You're playing brave again, Doctor,' Isfahani said, dropping his familiarity.

Hakim gave his nod.

Isfahani nodded back and went to his briefcase. He pulled out an envelope, pouring the cut-out cardboard rectangles and blank paper onto the desk. Hakim noticed a hand gun with extra clips in the briefcase on top of other papers. No one trusted anybody these days.

'I've had a man following you for some time now, Doctor. He swears before God that this is the letter you left at your hotel in Yazd at the front counter to be delivered for you. Where you visited the Rouhani family, who once lived in that city.'

Hakim came up and inspected the shapes and the address. He acted calm; there was nothing else to do. He put his glasses on. 'It's not my handwriting.'

Isfahani went on to another point, trying to unnerve him. 'Many people, Bahá'ís, visited your brother-in-law's shop while you were in Kashan.'

'Customers.'

'What sort of customers? Did you know an Ali Quli?'

Hakim felt that Isfahani was groping in the dark. He wasn't the calm self he usually was when he had something up his sleeve. 'I've known Ali Quli from my practice and have visited his home on occasion over the years.'

'He knows you too. We had a little chat with him about his current affairs, and he mentioned your name.'

'Yes?'

'Yes,' Isfahani said forcefully. 'Then there is the Rouhani

214

couple.' Isfahani swept the envelope off the table. 'Did you deliver this letter?'

Hakim did his best to answer his questions as truthfully as he could. 'I did deliver a letter on their behalf, as you mentioned.'

'Yes? Continue.'

Hakim paused, thinking. 'They wanted me to send a letter to Azerbaijan, as I was going to be going by a post box. If that is the envelope addressed to Azerbaijan by them, then that is the letter I asked the hotel clerk to deliver.'

Isfahani felt he was getting nowhere. The only thing he was aware of was Husayn breathing down his neck to take over in his own way, while laughing at him in his thoughts. Isfahani gathered up all the evidence. 'We are sending someone to find the addressee, as the couple have vanished, practically overnight.'

'They must have been planning this trip for a long time,' Hakim said, talking out his thoughts, wondering what would happen to all that they had left behind.

Husayn popped, 'There's no one in Azerbaijan by that name!'

Isfahani sat back in his chair and folded his arms. His assistant had said it all for him.

'Why are you so interested in finding this couple, Commander?'

'To tell them of their son's death. The one you treated.'

It was said coldly, not maliciously. Hakim knew, looking into Isfahani's stare, that he was out to get him again.

'Executing a hero demands evidence, Doctor.'

The door slowly opened behind Hakim. Isfahani and Husayn went for their guns immediately and aimed them at the door.

'Uncle Hakim?' Mitra whispered, as she stuck her head in to find him.

'Not now, Mitra,' he said, stepping before their aim, looking at her.

Isfahani lowered his weapon and put it back into his case. Husayn stayed in his readied position, looking over at his Commander in the expectation that some action would be taken. Isfahani couldn't see what action he was expected to take against a child. He was going to have to prove his authority and strength to Husayn, like the Ayatullah had to him. He despised that notion, but knew it would serve as a lesson to Husayn and to the doctor.

'Let the girl in,' he instructed Husayn.

Husayn went over and led her in by the hand, locking the door. Mitra came in willingly with her oversized children's book to her uncle's side. Hakim wanted to scream, remembering the set of similar conditions in which he had faced his trial of certitude. He didn't want to lose Mitra the same way. He loved her with the same devotion as he had loved his grandchild. He had no choice but to battle his fears.

Isfahani smiled at the little miss. 'We met yesterday, didn't we? You and your brother were waiting for your uncle to arrive. Do you remember?'

'Yes,' she answered coyly. 'You spoke with Saffa.'

Hakim never turned completely around to Isfahani, hoping this would pass soon.

'That's right,' Isfahani said, and came around the desk. 'What do you have there, little sister?'

'A book.'

'What's the book about?' he asked, resting against the front of the desk.

'Mulla Nasrud-din. Uncle Hakim tells the best stories about the Mulla.'

She gave her uncle the book, then sat herself on the wall couch, gazing up at him expectantly.

Hakim looked over at Isfahani.

'Please, Doctor.'

Hakim remembered taking the overdose of pills, vomiting in the hospital, Isfahani recounting his dream. Mitra had no idea of the danger she was exposed to. He didn't know how to get her out, yet remembered the prayer she used to say for him by heart: *'O God, guide me, protect me, illumine the lamp of my heart and make me a brilliant star. Thou art the Mighty and Powerful.'* He prayed for this as he took his seat beside Mitra and opened the book to a random page, without showing her where he was. 'I remember the Commander loves children – now that he's a father.'

Uncomfortable, Isfahani looked away.

Hakim glanced down at the page. He pretended to find what he was searching for, then closed the book on his finger, to find the reference again if he needed it. This was all done for Mitra's sake.

'One day, Mulla Nasrud-din was walking with his white donkey through the grand bazaar while visiting the great city of Isfahan, searching for a gift to buy for his wife, Fatimih.'

216

'What sort of a gift?' she asked, curiously.

'The most expensive gift money could buy! At least, what he could afford. In fact he had ridden his donkey, wearing his finest robes, all the way from his village to the great bazaar to find such a wonderful gift.'

Mitra's eyes were sparkling as she watched Hakim's facial expressions.

'He searched every shop to find the perfect present. Finally, he came to rest before the rugs of a wealthy carpet merchant. This was far enough, thought the Mulla. And his feet were tired anyway. He asked the shopkeeper, "How much is your most expensive carpet?"

'The shopkeeper looked at the inquiring Mulla, thinking he could make a fortune out of the apparently rich visitor. "It is very expensive," he said, warning him.

'"Is it more expensive than this prize of a donkey?" the Mulla asked, trying to determine just how expensive 'very expensive' was. The shop-keeper looked at the sad-looking mule, then laughed, "You will need much more than that." "How much more?" the Mulla demanded, showing him his small purse. "I must have the most expensive of your wares."

'The shopkeeper realized that this was not so rich a clergyman. His purse was light of coins. He went over to a most beautiful carpet and said, "This rug is worth more than a black-eyed damsel. As much as your wife!"

'"As much as my wife?" The Mulla stroked the length of his beard, thinking. "It's a difficult decision. But I must have the finest gift money can buy. You may have her tomorrow," he promised the shocked shopkeeper. "I will bring her myself!" With that, Mulla Nasrud-din left the bazaar, pleased with his good day of bargaining.'

Hakim glanced over at Isfahani and his Assistant, who were waiting for the outcome of the story too. Hakim closed the book on his lap and said to Mitra, 'He walked down the road to his village mosque and said to his mule, "You see, I was able to purchase the finest of gifts without even trading you away. I am not only a good mulla, but an excellent businessman. Mine is the reward of Paradise. Won't Fatimih be proud."'

Mitra giggled. 'That's a silly story.'

'Not to those like Mulla Nasrud-din,' he said, giving her back

217

her book.

'That story isn't in here.'

He fixed her scarf over her hair, then tapped her on the back, getting her to stand, and headed her towards the door to leave on her own.

Husayn blocked her way.

She stared innocently up at the man.

Hakim rose easily and faced Husayn. 'Let her pass,' he said calmly.

'He's trying to test your authority, Commander,' Husayn said, interpreting the story as a challenge.

Isfahani wasn't too sure how to proceed. He stood and walked around the desk back to his seat. If Husayn was right, then what was he supposed to do with a child, he thought. No, he was going to do nothing; he would wait to see what Husayn or the doctor would do.

Hakim didn't hear any instructions, which made it clear to him that Isfahani was stepping aside. He had done this before. Hakim gathered all his courage, then pierced Husayn with his gaze while speaking to both of them. 'If you wish to take her life, God is our witness. If you wish to test my strength to endure cruelty, God is my witness. If you wish to prove your authority, pray that God is your witness and not your judge.'

'I do not have to assert my authority, Doctor,' Isfahani said, leaning forward. 'You know my authority. There is no test here. This is not a court of justice.' Isfahani gestured to Husayn to let the girl out. 'I will have God both as your judge and my witness on that day.'

Husayn unlocked the door for her, letting Mitra go out on her own.

'That's all, Doctor.'

Husayn blocked Hakim's exit. 'I think the doctor was trying to insult you with that story, Commander.'

'Not an insult,' Hakim said directly to Husayn. 'The story just serves to point out what can happen to men who believe they can purchase vain imaginings for their loved ones by offering everything they hold dear, and who in the end betray the wives of their faiths and become the companions of asses.'

'We will see who the ass is,' Isfahani said bluntly.

Husayn spit. 'You're full of stories.'

'That's enough,' warned Isfahani. 'You've made your point, Doctor.'

Hakim glanced back. 'We'll see when we return to our wives, Commander.'

'Let him out, Assistant.'

Husayn did as instructed, then slammed the door behind Hakim. To Isfahani, he unleashed a hundred accusations against the doctor, telling him how dangerous and insolent Hakim was. Isfahani only half-listened to Husayn's raving. He was more interested in considering what Hakim had meant by the story, wondering what he himself had sold. In the back of his mind he couldn't help but feel that maybe there was some truth in what the doctor alluded to. He needed time to get away with his family, to relax, to re-establish his values. But he couldn't leave, with Husayn still so inexperienced and so power-hungry.

'I hope that the Commander will take into consideration all that I've said.'

Isfahani reached for the phone. 'I think it's time you were introduced to the prison system.'

'I am familiar with it already. The Ayatullah –'

Husayn shut up, listening to Isfahani make arrangements with the Khorramabad Prison Warden for his visit.

'He will be there in my stead. You will offer my Assistant the same courtesy, I hope, as you would if I was there. We would be pleased if you would attach him to your duties with the Mujtahid.'

Satisfied that Isfahani was doing this in his best interest, Husayn adopted a more submissive attitude when Isfahani spoke with him after the call.

'When you leave this place, you will be "representing me" – without any power of authority. You are to meet them in court and follow to completion the cases they are presenting. They expect some to face execution. Do not interfere. If there are any difficulties or if there is a need for my presence, you are to call me at my home. Understand?'

'Yes, Commander. Perfectly.'

Isfahani picked up the cardboard cut-outs, stared at them for a moment, then threw them into the trash bin.

'It is the hope of the Commander Rashti that you will replace me here. Let me not recommend otherwise.'

'No, Commander. I will be your finest example.'

Husayn knew that the Commander intended to stay for a while, and backed out through the doorway.

Hakim rinsed his face repeatedly in the washroom basin. He needed to refresh himself. When he came out into the hallway he caught a glimpse of Isfahani's assistant going out through the main entrance. He was glad to see that one leave, yet puzzled to find a few Pasdars still lingering around.

'Isfahani is still in the office,' said Firuz, coming up to Hakim with Mitra holding his hand.

She looked unscathed by the whole experience. He asked Firuz, frankly, 'Did you send her in there?'

'I thought it would break up the tension.'

'It didn't,' he said quietly.

They walked down the hall.

'Maryam found the address.'

'For Rouhani?' he asked without much thrill.

He gave Hakim the slip of paper with the necessary information. Firuz glanced down to Mitra, then up at Hakim. 'I just thought it was the only way – when I heard them yelling.'

Hakim patted Firuz on his shoulder, quieting him. 'Sometimes, to protect others, you yourself must withstand injustices. You have embraced the Bahá'í Faith – we all must withstand injustices, but a Bahá'í must learn to do this with radiant acquiescence. This proves our faith and our trust in God. All people have words, but a Bahá'í must prove himself by deeds. You see. Even an old man learns new tricks.'

Hakim was finding it difficult to express what he thought. 'It must have taken a lot of courage to send her in there. And a lot of faith . . . When you have time get hold of the Tablet of Bahá'u'lláh known as the "Words of Wisdom". One of its verses reveals what the source of power and courage is. Make an effort to memorize it. When you're ready to discuss it, we can talk more deeply about it together.'

'Yes, Hakim.'

'Good. Where's Saffa?'

'Over in that lab. Playing Doctor.'

Hakim led Mitra by her hand and went into the laboratory Firuz had pointed out. They stood at the back of the room watching Saffa. He looked the part of a young doctor, dressed in a white lab coat with the stethoscope in his ears. He was completely unaware that he was being watched as he continued to examine the suspended plastic skeleton at the rib cage, listening to the imaginary heart-beat.

'I think your patient's dead,' Hakim shouted, giving Saffa a start. He pulled the plugs out of his ears and spun around, seeing the two coming forward.

'Probably from lack of a proper diet,' Hakim diagnosed. 'Take your sister, Doctor. I'll take my stethoscope.'

'You can give it to me for Ayyám-i-Há tonight, if you like.'

Hakim stretched out his hand for the instrument. 'You're not my favorite charity.'

Saffa folded it up and handed it over. As he released it Hakim spotted the glint of a gold band on his finger. He thought it was something else Saffa had found lying around, and teased him. 'Are you married now too?'

'No. Some man gave it to me in the hallway yesterday.'

Hakim rolled Saffa's hand over.

'He said he knew I was your nephew and just gave it to me. It looks like the ring you once had.'

But I threw it away, Hakim told himself, trying to figure out how Saffa could have his Bahá'í ring, then realized who Mitra too had met yesterday. Isfahani.

'He must have been a Bahá'í,' Saffa guessed.

'He isn't,' he said instantly. It must have been Isfahani. But why he had kept it all this time and given it to Saffa was a mystery. Hakim really didn't understand that man. Maybe his Mulla Nasrud-din story proved, in some far-fetched way, how similar they were to each other. God knew.

'Put your ring away, Saffa. I have to go. Here.' Hakim handed the stethoscope back to him. 'Happy Ayyám-i-Há.'

'Doctor Irani!'

A nurse dashed into the back of the room. 'You're needed in emergency, Doctor. A bus accident.'

'Coming,' he said with a sigh. He saw the disappointment on their faces. 'Tomorrow we will celebrate, all right?'

They nodded.

He opened Mitra's book and pointed to a caricature, then looked up at Saffa and the skeleton. 'Ask your little nurse here to assist you. Her medical journal should say how to revive this malnourished patient.'

# CHAPTER 16

# The Promise Kept

There was no rush in Hakim's gait as he wandered through the city streets. He had given himself all afternoon to find the where-abouts of Zabih Rouhani and to pick out some gifts for Ayyám-i-Há. Work had forced him to miss the celebration with his family the night before and he had made certain that his duty was covered so he could get away.

A group of boys playing soccer in a field gave him the idea for Saffa's gift. And passing a shop filled with children's books made him think about a new treat for Mitra. He had to think what he could get his sister and the newlyweds too still. Giving gifts was customary at Naw-Ruz, a month after Ayyám-i-Há following the nineteen-day fast, but this year was special and Hakim wanted to remember it that way always.

There was a good chill in the air. His cap and coat kept his head and body warm, but his nose needed an occasional warming with a rub of his gloved hand.

A goat's neighing and a boy's laughter captured Hakim's atten-tion. He went up a street to find a young boy picking up his fallen hat off the snow beside him where he sat, obviously knocked down by the kid goat he was playing with. The boy was scolding the complaining kid as he stood back up, brushing off his trousers. Hakim lingered to watch the fun.

The boy slapped his palm against the kid's brow between his small horns, pushing him with all his might backwards to his hind legs, then lifted away his arm. The kid sprang forward, aiming at the boy's teasing hand. The boy pushed, and the kid bucked. It went on and on – the giggling and the neighing. It made Hakim chuckle, bringing back memories of his childhood, its carefree days and simplicity. He wouldn't mind being a child again, or even a goat, so long as he could return to happiness.

Hakim carried along up the street. Being a goat wasn't such a bad thought. At least that goat enjoyed hitting his head against walls, he thought to himself. His mind filled with notions of reincarnation. Some people entertained the fancy that reincarnation was a chance for purification, or said it was a punishment for man to return after death to this world as an animal. He could disprove that idea easily: here he was both man and mule in the same lifetime. There were others, though, who believed that man returned to this world again as another man. This too was absurd to Hakim. It denied returning to the presence of God, which all His Prophets and Manifestations had said was the true reality man would ultimately face. And Bahá'u'lláh too wrote clearly on this topic. One goes to the spiritual realms of God, perfect or imperfect, each at his appointed time, as a baby is born to this realm crippled or fit.

It was a profound concept to ponder. This realm was brought into being for us to nurture our spiritual virtues. He thought about the consequences of entering the next realm as a spiritual quadraplegic, which made him queasy. He had a better chance of fancying coming back to this world as a goat.

His stomach grumbled when he saw an elderly woman coming towards him with a bag of groceries in her arm. He wished he was Firuz, then he could offer to help the lady home, and accept her humble payment of feeding him a delicious meal. But he had to remember his task first, stomach later. He glanced around for a street sign, but none was in sight, so he removed his slip of paper to inquire.

'Good day, Doctor,' she said openly.

Hakim immediately glanced round to see how the woman had recognized his identity, only to discover he had been carrying his medical bag all the time. He really couldn't get away from work. 'How are you, Khanum?'

She stopped to tell him. 'Good, Doctor. For an old woman of my age, I cannot complain. Knock on wood.'

'Yes, yes. Khanum. I was wondering if you could assist me with a small problem I'm faced with.' He showed her the slip of paper, which she strained to read. 'I seem to have gone astray. Do you know where the Rouhani family live?'

'Rouhani,' she said, rolling the name on her tongue. She couldn't read. 'Do you know, Doctor, how many people are named "Rouhani".'

'They're not originally from here.'

'Is it a young family or an old family?'

'Young.'

'Zabih Rouhani?'

'Yes, that's the one.'

She muttered as she walked away. 'They live somewhere nearby. I don't know which house, but the wife and children shop where I shop.'

Hakim hurried to keep up with her. The woman's legs were in pretty fit shape.

Then she said, 'They live the next street up. But you won't find her home. And she won't be back for hours.' She turned and beckoned the doctor closer, stopping. She covered her mouth with a piece of her woolen scarf and whispered in his ear, looking both ways before confiding her secret.

Hakim stooped down, ready for the gossip.

'They're Bahá'í, you know.'

Hakim pulled his head back, staring at her in disbelief, at which she nodded emphatically.

'That's why they're not home. Her poor husband's in prison.'

Hakim stopped playing. 'Here?' he asked.

'The old prison. I saw her get on the bus this morning.'

'When was he arrested, Khanum?'

'Doctor, I do not follow the affairs of everyone in this city. But I believe the Revolutionary Court found him guilty of whatever they find one guilty of these days. It's terrible. No one is safe. I don't understand why everyone is trying to kill each other.'

'How true. Thank you, Khanum. I won't trouble you any longer. And I really couldn't stay for lunch.'

'It's all right, Doctor,' she said, going on her way, 'I can trust you.'

Hakim was glad she didn't hear so well, with him inviting himself for a meal. He put the slip of paper into his mouth and began to chew it. As far as he was concerned he had accomplished what he had set out to do. 'I'm going to call his parents. Tell them I found out where their son is, and Finish. Isfahani won't have to worry about me.' He kept chewing, filling in the future in his thoughts – 'Rouhani's parents would come, and Isfahani would interrogate them. And God knows what else.' He swallowed the lump. Either way he would end up in prison. It wasn't finished. But it wasn't going to interfere with his plans for the evening.

He was still going to buy gifts, and if on the way home time permitted, only then would he go by the prison gate and merely inquire if Zabih Rouhani was actually being detained there . . . Who was he fooling?

He found a public phone in the bazaar and told Asiyih he might be slightly late, as he was still in the middle of his shopping spree. He timed himself to be at the gate of the prison after visiting hours. Then they would definitely not let him in, nor could he enter with the stack of packages he had.

The sun set as he arrived. He spoke with a prison guard and waited for a superior to confirm Rouhani's presence.

'Why all the parcels, Doctor Irani?' the guard asked.

'I'm attending a family reunion this evening,' he said, then glanced at his watch. 'O my God. It is getting late, isn't it?'

Out of nowhere the sergeant returned. 'There is a Zabih Rouhani, Doctor.'

'Good,' he said lightly. 'Well, I'll come back tomorrow to speak with him. Thank you very much. Good-night.'

The sergeant was shaking his head. Hakim had a strange feeling and shook his head back. 'No? Sergeant, that "no" is going to ruin my evening, I fear.' He sighed. 'You don't have to tell me what that "no" means.'

'Our orders are not to let anyone in.'

It was the way that the sergeant said that, that made Hakim understand he was letting himself in for trouble. 'Good. Good. We all have to obey our orders. Where would the world be without obeying orders? You can't let me in. And I promised the man's parents that I would find him. And I did find him. I know where he is. Good! Finished. God is pleased with both of us.'

The sergeant heard the doctor out, then scratched his head and sniffed. 'Even if we could let you in, we couldn't let you enter with all those packages.'

Hakim's arguments to himself were hopeless. Anyway, he comforted his thoughts, Ayyám-i-Há did go on for four days this year. There was time tomorrow to buy more gifts and still celebrate. Everyone would understand.

'I'm sure,' he reluctantly began, 'that all of you have families to share these with.'

The gate came open and out filed the guards, emptying Hakim's arms, thanking him for his generosity. Hakim held back one gift, then decidedly placed it on top of the sergeant's bundle. The sergeant thanked him, but said, 'It's still my duty to get permission.'

Hakim knew the correct response. 'Of course, sergeant . . . I've been in and out before. No one will stop a medical doctor from slipping in and out to see a patient.'

He waited for the customary, ponderous decision, weighing heavily on the sergeant's shoulders.

The nod, and the gate opened.

Hakim opened his bag for inspection without being asked.

'Only for a short visit, Doctor,' the sergeant said. 'Have the guard on duty in solitary escort you out. No one will stop you, or ask questions.'

'Is that old man down there?' he asked, closing his bag up.

'Doctor, he'll be buried down there. Who wants the night shift on that block. One begins to smell like the place.'

Hakim was passed quickly through the compound down to solitary confinement. The old guard was there to greet him.

They went down the corridor to find the man he had come to see, peering into each of the now occupied cells.

'What makes you think he's down here, Doctor?'

'My luck with prisons so far.'

The old guard continued to call out the prisoner's name into each cell they passed. 'Zabih Rouhani? . . . Zabih Rouhani?'

There was no one answering his call. 'Every last one of them is filled,' he told him. 'This next lot is getting executed tomorrow at dawn for various offenses.'

'Do they know their fate?'

'I guess so.' He pointed to the cells at their sides. 'There are Bahá'ís in these cells,' he said factually. 'Every day they are brought out and returned to their cells, just to torment them. All you can accuse them of is chanting beautiful odes extolling the mysteries of God. What sounds . . . Zabih Rouhani?'

A muffled 'yes' came from a cell across from them, which the guard was quick to point out. He tried to unlock the newly-fitted bolt. Hakim pulled out his flashlight from his bag to let the guard have a better shot. The door came open.

'Don't be long, Doctor.'

'Zabih Rouhani?' Hakim asked, entering alone into the darkness.

'Yes,' came the quiet response.

Hakim put down his flashlight, illuminating the blackened ceiling as he had done before.

The prisoner stood up hesitantly, wary of the intruder.

'I've had to evade a score of followers to get here. Let alone convince the prison guards to let me through to see you.'

Hakim had remembered what the man looked like from seeing his photograph in his parents' home. Meeting him in prison showed how much he and his brother looked alike. There was only one major difference. This Rouhani's radiance and joy were non-existent.

Hakim put down his bag, which Zabih recognized as belonging to a doctor. 'Are you hurt anywhere?'

'No,' he answered defensively.

'Anywhere?'

'Nowhere.'

'Very good.' The direct approach was obviously not going to work. He diverted to the mild interrogation plan. 'So. Why are you in here?'

'Because of two stupid mistakes.'

'Yes?'

'One, because of my brother.' Zabih turned the conversation in a different direction. 'Why did they let a doctor in here so late – if you are a real doctor?'

'Special privileges. I'm a real doctor,' he said, bringing the topic back. 'What does your brother have to do with your imprisonment?'

Zabih didn't seem to care if he was talking to a doctor or not. He knew what his outcome would be. 'Some Revolutionary Guards were arresting – people – '

'Bahá'ís.'

Zabih studied Hakim's face more carefully. 'Yes. Bahá'ís . . . I accused one, in a moment of duress, of imprisoning my brother. I ran. Right into the rest of them. That was my second mistake.'

'You're lucky they didn't dismember you then and there.'

'If you're only a doctor, then how come you're asking so many questions and telling me so many answers?'

Hakim unbuttoned his coat. It was warm in there. 'I took care of your brother before they executed him.'

'Then they executed him,' he said in shock. He leaned against

227

the wall and slid to the ground in a squat. 'My parents lost their only son. Damn.'

Hakim felt his parental instincts rising. 'What does that mean?'

Zabih just stared at the ground.

'Look,' Hakim went on, 'your parents love you very much. Why do sons always think their parents don't love them?'

'If you'd really met my brother, Doctor, you'd understand. I'm supposed to be older and wiser, only I followed poorly in his footsteps, constantly tripping over my own clumsy feet. Aagh. It's hard to explain.'

The last thing Hakim wanted to hear was self-pity. He had enough of his own. He battled his desire to leave, reminding himself of his purpose. 'I promised your parents.'

Zabih looked straight up at him, not believing this was real. 'You've met my parents too?'

'Yes. That I would get you and your wife and family to them.'

That comment seemed to put a little life in the man. 'Are my parents here?'

'Zahedan. If all went well.'

Hakim slapped his palm against the cool plastered wall. They weren't ready yet to crumble. 'No one expected you to get yourself thrown into prison.'

'Oh, well,' he said, then attempted a laugh.

'This is impossible,' Hakim said to himself. 'O God.'

The prison became deadly quiet, only the sound of someone in another cell shuffling back and forth, another prisoner coughing, the distant clanging of closing metal gates.

Zabih looked over towards him. 'Did you ever wish you could live one moment over again to do differently?'

'One moment?' Hakim said, chuckling to himself. That's what he'd contemplated the whole afternoon. It was a serious question. He considered it more respectfully, thinking of the events throughout his life from childhood, school, marriage, his children, his imprisonment, to this moment. There was something he had in his thoughts. 'I wish I could have sacrificed my life, instead of everyone else's.'

Zabih was immersed in his own thoughts. 'For myself. I'd like to relive my moment in court. That would release me from this pit.'

Hakim was half-listening. 'What was that?'

'To have recanted . . . '

Hakim shook off his reflective mood. He stared at Zabih, not sure he had heard him correctly. 'What did you say?'

'Recant. In Islam, the Qur'án says if you are forced to renounce your faith, God knows what is in your heart and forgives your forced actions.'

'You are not a Muslim – you're a Bahá'í.'

'Bahá'u'lláh will know why I've merely given lip-service in recanting. In my heart I'll still be a Bahá'í.'

'There is no lip-service recanting in the heart. That is why it is against the law of God to recant in this age.'

'Look. Don't tell me what I can and can't do! I've got a wife and children to support. Who's going to look after them?'

Hakim loosened his tie. 'What if the Blessed Beauty withdrew His Covenant from mankind? What if God withdrew the dawn of His Most Great Manifestation, withheld His loving-kindness from this world for one second? What if no ear was willing to listen to His call, to champion His cry, to proclaim His Cause? If no one was willing to lay down his life as a sacrifice for the Best-Beloved of the world?'

'What if His followers were all executed?' Zabih rebuffed. 'Who would be left to teach His Cause then?'

'God, alone, would create a new race of men.'

Zabih looked away from him. He deserved to be told off, Hakim thought, glad that he had chastised him. He was getting sick of hearing people putting forth their own designs for God's. His thoughts boiled.

Zabih finally said, 'I don't profess to be a Manifestation of God. I'm just a human being. You wouldn't talk so bravely if you were in my position.'

Hakim held his anger back. There was real fear coming from Zabih. He couldn't force him to understand; he would have to tell him. 'I was, Zabih. And I failed.'

Hakim went to the back wall and leaned on it. He was still haunted by his past.

'No one cares, Doctor,' Zabih said, seeing his condition.

'I care.'

'Congratulations,' he said sarcastically.

Hakim ignored the slur. He massaged his hands, thinking aloud. 'It's so easy to fall down. To narrow your faith. You have to really blind yourself to reality and see only the pity of the injustices around you.'

Hakim didn't know if he was getting through to Zabih. He didn't want to leave him like this.

'Zabih, it's not easy for anyone these days. Nor was it any easier in the days of Bahá'u'lláh; for Himself, for His loved ones or His companions. It was painful for the Blessed Beauty. He lost so much outwardly, for merely unveiling that which God chose Him to pronounce. Persecution is a stage of reality and truth. This isn't my interpretation either, Zabih. If you can bear my quoting a meditation revealed by Bahá'u'lláh:

*I know not, O my God, whether I should speak forth the wonders of Thy praise among Thy servants, and lay bare before them the secrets of Thy mercy and the mysteries of Thy Cause, or keep them wrapped up within the receptacle of my heart. Though the lover be loth to share with any one the intimate conversations of his beloved, yet at whatever time Thine inescapable commandment to declare Thy Cause reacheth me, I will unhesitatingly obey it. I would proclaim Thee, undeterred by the darts of affliction that may rain down upon me from the clouds of Thy decree.*

*I swear by Thy might! Neither the hosts of the earth nor those of heaven can keep me back from revealing the things I am commanded to manifest. I have no will before Thy will, and can cherish no desire in the face of Thy desire. By Thy grace I am, at all times, ready to serve Thee and am rid of all attachment to any one except Thee.*

Hakim expected him to see the light, but instead heard:

'That was the Manifestation of God, not a servant.'

Hakim could have now explained so clearly why man was to stand up for certain principles, love this, overlook that. It was all to the benefit of mankind to do so. That's what it meant to surrender oneself to the will of God.

'God knows your condition, Zabih.'

'I know my condition. Everyone's against me.'

'Maybe it's because you're standing up. Rebelliousness can be positive if you apply yourself spiritually. Now if you'd let me quote.'

Zabih waved his arm uncaringly. He could do what he wished.

When Hakim cleared his voice to chant, Zabih sighed deeply. Hakim gave up. It was useless to inspire someone to death. He sat there.

Zabih said above a whisper, 'I just don't know what I believe. I just want my family to know that I love them.'

It was the same state of mind Hakim had been in when he was imprisoned. Zabih wasn't made of the same clay as his brother.

He turned from Hakim's gaze. A vicious gash had torn open the side of his scalp. Hakim could do nothing but stare at the injury.

'Doctor!' the old guard called through the passage.

Hakim rose slowly, going over to the cell door.

'Doctor? You've been in there for over an hour!'

'I'll be in here for quite some time. You'll have to take me out later!' Hakim shouted back.

'In a couple of hours, they'll be taking him out!' Hakim gripped the iron bars, looking out of the cell. That was an understatement.

A cold draft of fresh air blew against his face. He inhaled deeply. A voice in the back of his head told him that everything would work itself out. It was a positive thought. He couldn't forget the twisted look of the man beside him on the bus when he had told him he was happy to be back in Khorramabad. The thought made Hakim burst out laughing. He wiped the tear off his cheek, smiling to himself. 'Dear God,' he said softly. 'Do we now bandage his head, or do we bandage mine?'

He crossed his arms and looked over at Zabih. 'Do you know why I'm a good doctor?'

Zabih listened.

'Because I practice a lot!'

Zabih covered the side of his head with his hand, watching Hakim go over to his bag, reaching inside, talking to himself.

'White ointment – that'll have to do. Enough gauze . . . Paper? . . . good.'

Hakim placed the paper on the ground, then put on his spectacles. 'Come over here and sit in front of me.'

Zabih did as he was told. He began to trust this man, and lowered his hand for him to look at the wound. The light of the flashlight heated the throbbing area. And here was the gentle yet firm pressure of the doctor's hand as he felt the extent of the wound.

Hakim was pleased. It wasn't as serious as he had first thought. 'It will heal.'

He handed Zabih the flashlight, and made him aim its circle down on the center of the paper. 'There. Good.' Hakim took out his pen, pausing for thought, then said, 'You can really be happy anywhere if you know what the purpose of your being there is. Having goals. You can see the beginning in the end and the end in the beginning.' He snapped his fingers. 'I have to tell Firuz that.'

He caught Zabih's lost stare, which made him laugh and laugh. 'Never mind, never mind. Just the rambling thoughts of an old man. Just hold the light over the paper, son.'

Hakim put the date on the page. 'This is the best I can do for you,' he said, then looked back up at him. 'Will you do me a slight favor?'

Zabih gave his slight nod.

'Can you chant?'

'Yes,' he said, growing stronger.

Hakim felt the bond between their hearts. One of them had changed, maybe both. He liked to think it was Zabih, so that he would be able to go on without him. He put his hand on Zabih's shoulder. 'You can only sacrifice when you know you are in love.'

# CHAPTER 17

# The Touchstone of God

In the darkness of his bedroom, Firuz suddenly awoke. 'Tell me what?' He had slept poorly. It must have been a nightmare that now kept him from an easy night's rest. He was soaked in sweat and his heart pounded in his chest. He didn't know what was making him so restless, yet thought that an unsuspected noise might give his ears a clue. The place was calm. Maryam was asleep, undisturbed beside him. He pulled his blanket up to his chin. He breathed more easily. He couldn't recall to mind what images the dream had contained. He thought he had just eaten a bad meal or something; he eased his head back into his pillow, falling slowly back to sleep.

A faint knock rapped at the front door.

Firuz threw off his blankets. 'I knew it!' he said, marking his intuition.

Maryam woke, watching him bounce out of bed and wrap himself into his bathrobe. She straightened herself up, letting her hair fall across her face. 'Love, what is it?'

'I don't know.'

She tried to look outside through the curtain. There was a streak of magenta coloring the sky. Daybreak.

Firuz went out and switched on the outer light at the front door. 'Yes? Who is it?'

The muffled man's voice asked, 'Is Firuz Mostaqim there?'

There was no force in the voice. It didn't sound like an emergency, yet it made him wary. Any of a number of people could be out there and he couldn't see. He had to be cautious.

'Doctor Rahbari sent me,' the man said.

Maryam came out to the bedroom door, tying up her robe. She

233

stayed hidden in the shadows to listen from afar.

It took a moment for Firuz to recognize the name, which made him even more circumspect, but he unlatched the door and blocked his foot across its path to peer out. The cold air rushed into the room with a whistle. There was the figure of an older man in winter clothes and a cap and scarf. The man's glasses reflected the inside light on his rims.

Firuz noticed the medical bag in his grasp. He had been set up for a joke, he would never forget. Only one man had a bag like that beat-up old thing. He threw the door open, 'I don't think this is very amusing, Hakim.'

The man removed his cap, shaking his head.

Firuz felt his mistake in the pit of his stomach. 'You're not Hakim.'

'*Alláh'u'Abhá*,' he said.

Maryam heard the greeting and came up quickly to Firuz. 'He is Bahá'í.'

The man seemed sincerely so, but Firuz couldn't help feeling that what his eyes saw was not right. It was the clothes. 'What are you doing with the doctor's personal possessions?'

'Please,' said the man, imploring to be let inside.

Firuz let him enter, then backed against the door to begin the inquest. 'You are Bahá'í?'

'Yes.'

'Alone?'

'Yes.'

He turned to Maryam and said affectionately but firmly, 'Mouse, wait in the other room.'

Firuz could now see the man was a fraud. There was white grease slicked into his dark hair to make him appear old, but his face was twenty years younger than he was made up to be. The man put down the bag and removed his glasses and overcoat.

'This isn't just a social visit, is it, brother?' Firuz asked, completely unfriendly.

The man turned to put everything down in a neat roll on a chair back. 'The doctor lent me these to get here,' he explained.

'Who are you?'

'Zabih Rouhani.'

Firuz had heard the name, but didn't take the time to greet him.

234

It still didn't answer why he was dressed like that or anything. 'Where's the doctor?'

The man tried to control his shaking and shortness of breath. He reached inside the coat pocket and gave the letter to Firuz. 'This is for Asiyih Khanum. The doctor said you'd be able to get it to her.'

'I don't understand.' Firuz read Asiyih's name across the envelope. It was in Hakim's handwriting.

Zabih wiped the tears from his face. 'I, I must go. To my wife, my family . . . I – he. He told me to tell you to remember the days of Bahá'u'lláh, when He was imprisoned wrongly in the Black Pit, with the other believers. And how when the executioner came to call out their names, others stood up in their place and said they were the ones whom the guard called to martyrdom.'

'What are you talking about? Where is he?'

Maryam ran out to tell him she understood, only to trip over her robe. 'Firuz!'

He rushed to her side. 'All right?'

'I'm sorry I wasn't strong enough,' Zabih said to himself, then pulled the door open and ran out before Firuz could stop him.

'Wait!'

Maryam held him in her arms. 'The doctor's in prison.'

'What?' He sensed that she was telling him a truth he didn't want to hear. He hurried into the bedroom and dressed quickly. 'I'm going to the hotel, then to the prison.'

'I'll go to the hotel,' she said, throwing on a coat, and a scarf over her hair.

He handed her the keys and the envelope and ran out. 'Take the car.'

Maryam ran outside after him, locking up, then got into the hospital car. The engine turned over without any problems in the cold. The streets were clear of traffic to the hotel.

She woke the hotel manager to find out which room Asiyih was in, in too much of a panic to think straight for herself. When she found the door she knocked repeatedly, calling out for Asiyih.

Saffa was the one to answer.

'Saffa? I need to speak with your mother!'

Saffa was quick to let her in, recognizing Maryam's voice. He switched the light on.

235

Asiyih came up to the flushed girl. 'Maryam Khanum. What is it?'

Maryam revealed the letter, which Asiyih took, looking at her to see what this meant.

Maryam tried to slow down with a deep breath. 'We'd better sit, Khanum. Please.'

They went to the edge of the bed.

Saffa watched as his mother tore open the envelope and read its contents at a whisper. She strained to read further, as the tears streamed down her face. Then she wailed, putting her face in the letter. *'Ya Bahá'u'l-Abhá. Ya Bahá'u'l-Abhá.'*

Maryam embraced Asiyih, stifling her cries.

From beneath the blankets, Mitra sat up. She was crying too. 'Mama? Mama?'

Asiyih controlled herself. She looked over at Mitra. 'Nothing, dear. Go back to sleep.' She looked at Saffa.

'Uncle Hakim?' he asked gently. She didn't have to tell him, her eyes told him. He went over and sat on her other side.

She put her face in his shoulder and wept. 'He's all right. He's all right. He's all right. My God. He's all right.'

'Is Uncle Hakim coming for Ayyám-i-Há?' Mitra asked.

Saffa closed his eyes. 'Not this year, Mitra. Uncle Hakim is very busy, he's a doctor, you know . . .'


The magenta line of dawn became more golden with the sunrise, as the light angled into the prison's inner courtyard. The Warden and the middle-aged Mujtahid stood in the frosty cold, waiting for the last prisoner to be brought out for execution, waiting also for Isfahani's assistant, Husayn, to make his way across to them.

'Well?' inquired the Mujtahid impatiently.

Husayn had telephoned Isfahani at their request to find out what time the Commander would be arriving, though he thought he was handling his duties quite well without him. He was making a good impression on the Mujtahid, they had many acquaintances in common, which would be fortunate for Husayn when he became a Commander. It had taken him a little longer to get back outside. Seeing the Mujtahid bothered by this fact didn't bother Husayn: he had learned some interesting gossip from the prison guards while away.

'Commander Isfahani is attending to some other affairs just now, and begs your pardon. He will be with us presently.'

'Are you happy, Assistant?' the Mujtahid asked, seeing the pert smirk across Husayn's face.

'Yes, Mujtahid. Very.' He was going to enjoy telling them what he had discovered. 'Guards here have informed me that the doctor whom Commander Isfahani has longed to convict of anti-Islamic activities has finally sealed his fate.'

The Warden wanted to get on with the last execution. It was too cold for him. 'You're obsessed with capturing this fictitious doctor, brother,' he said, deflating the hearsay.

Husayn thought the Warden would be quite surprised by his information. 'Doctor Irani, Warden, is not a fictitious character.'

The disclosure made the Warden burst out with a snicker. 'Doctor Irani?' He treated it as a joke. 'Not only have you chosen to slander the finest doctor in the entire province, but a recognized national Islamic hero as well. May my life be a sacrifice to his services. I'd greatly enjoy your trying to prove our beloved doctor is a spy.'

The ridicule infuriated Husayn. He spoke out rashly. 'I have proof that he entered this prison last night and conversed with this last convicted criminal we are executing.'

'Preposterous,' the Warden said, then signaled his men to bring out the last prisoner.

'I don't underestimate the doctor's influence, Warden. The guards as well as their Warden are only capable of seeing Doctor Irani's medical abilities. Commander Isfahani and I are aware of his other "services". That is why I am here.'

'You flatter yourself.'

The Mujtahid cleared his throat to signal his entry into the debate to finish it off. 'If what the Assistant says is the finding of Commander Isfahani, then this Doctor Irani should be brought before the Revolutionary Court. Shouldn't he, Warden?'

'If Commander Isfahani discovers this fact then I will be beside the Commander in the fulfillment of his duties.'

The Warden made certain that Husayn understood where his loyalties lay, with his superior. Then the Mujtahid voiced similar sentiments, reminding Husayn of his subservient position. He said nothing further about the matter and directed his gaze across the courtyard to see the last prisoner brought before the firing squad.

The Warden and Mujtahid left him out of their conversation. Husayn watched the prison guards step away from the prisoner in front of the firing wall. He focused on the hat the prisoner was wearing. Then he realized it wasn't a hat but a gauze bandage wrapped around the prisoner's head. Only a doctor could have done that. This was the proof Husayn needed for the eyes of the Mujtahid and Warden. He was about to point it out when he thought of a better plan, and asked the Mujtahid, 'I wonder if I might not be allowed to have a few words with this heretic before he is executed?'

'For what reason?' the Mujtahid inquired.

'This prisoner did know Doctor Irani. And any last information might assist the Commander's inquiry.'

The Mujtahid glanced at the Warden. 'Very well, Assistant. Make it fast. We have other appointments to attend to without having to drag this out.'

Husayn strutted over to the prisoner, ready to challenge him with his keen skills of interrogation. He walked right up to him, eye to eye. But his questions left him as he recognized the face.

Hakim stared back at him without fear, watching the young jackal begin to circle around him, debating his next action.

'Doctor, Doctor, Doctor. Truly I am guided by Gabriel to this hidden treasure.'

Husayn looked across the courtyard at the Mujtahid and Warden, thinking how dumbfounded they would be at his discovery, how even his Commander would be shocked.

There were only two options open to Hakim; either this man was going to expose him or not. It was that simple and Hakim was not going to dwell on it. He had said his prayers to God to stand in this position and he was going to stand tall and wait for God's command.

'Then again, Doctor. If I expose you, everyone else will take the credit for uncovering your true identity. Who would believe it was my work against the word of a Warden and Mujtahid seeking glory?' Husayn looked back at Hakim's profile and spoke into his ear. 'Then again, Doctor. If I let you be shot, no one will ever know who you were. I mean, to all concerned, you are Zabih

Rouhani. I could make everyone look like fools.'

A fiendish smile broadened across his face. 'I could pretend to do some investigating after your disappearance. Seek the support of the Mujtahid, then make the Warden look like . . .' He put his arms behind his back, and shouted to the squad commander, 'Carry on.' Then went back to the Mujtahid's side.

'Well, Assistant?' he asked.

'The prisoner had nothing to say. It makes it clear that Doctor Irani was here.'

'You will have to prove that,' the Mujtahid said.

'Yes, Mujtahid. I will.'

The Warden gave the squad commander his nod; the guard saluted back and went over to the prisoner.

Hakim looked down at the black scarf he was offered. 'No thank you, my friend. I want to see where I'm going.'

The squad commander put away the blindfold and swallowed hard, shaken by the prisoner's attitude. 'You can offer your last prayers now,' he said, and turned to leave him to himself.

'What do I say?' he asked himself, then glanced at the Assistant with the Warden and clergyman. If he said he wasn't frightened at that moment, he would be lying. He wasn't frightened by the Assistant or his threats; he was scared that he would fail again before the test of God.

He sighed. 'Oh, Hakim.' Then dropped to his knees and placed his palms upward on his thighs, offering his supplication. 'Isn't this another proof to your worthless soul that creation moves by God's decree? How could it be my wish to live, or to die, unless it is the good-pleasure of God?'

He searched for a last prayer to offer and softly began to chant. He faced due west to the point of adoration, Akka, which caused a stir of questions amongst the nearby guards, who wondered why he wasn't facing Mecca. He was a follower of Bahá'u'lláh.

Hakim opened his eyes, then prostrated himself, kissing the blood-stained soil, and uttered in a whisper, 'Thank you.'

He stood up, facing the ready squadron. As he rose, he saw Isfahani and a few of his Pasdars arrive. They stopped halfway between him and the Mujtahid and the others.

One of the firing squad said to a companion, 'The last one offered us sweets.'

239

The squad commander heard the comment and called his men to attention, then stared at the prisoner. Hakim nodded, then smiled. He was ready for the command.

The squad commander turned away. He had to think. He put his men at ease and wandered over to the prisoner, standing behind him. He was aware that all the officials were watching his actions. He pulled out his revolver and turned towards the prisoner, firing instantly the single fatal shot into the back of the prisoner's head.

The body fell to the ground.

The squad commander looked over at the officials, then holstered his gun. Without ceremony, he dismissed his men, leaving the prison guards to clear.

As the guards dragged the body out past Isfahani, another guard approached the Commander with an envelope and indicated that it was from the executed soul. Isfahani read his name on the envelope. His throat tightened. 'It's not possible.'

The Mujtahid led the others over. 'The work of Allah is done. May God have mercy on their misguided souls. Ah, good-morning, Commander. I am beginning to believe this Assistant of yours will one day have your job if you are not careful.' He said no more when he saw the fire burning in Isfahani's eyes. 'What is the trouble, Commander?'

Isfahani slowly peered over at Husayn. 'Who was that last prisoner, brother?'

'Rouhani,' he answered immediately, reassuring him.

'And who bandaged his head, Warden?'

'I don't know, Commander,' he said, thinking it over. 'He wasn't bandaged yesterday.'

'Husayn?'

'Yes, Commander?'

He gave the envelope to Husayn. 'Do you know this handwriting?'

Husayn took his time to study it. He had to compose his answer to avoid suspicion. 'No, Commander. Though I did see the prison guard hand this to you. Rouhani's will, I imagine.'

Their eyes met in a cold stare. Isfahani knew he was withholding what they both knew. 'In the handwriting of Doctor Irani, Husayn?'

The Mujtahid broke in. 'How is that possible?'

'Are you insinuating that my men killed the doctor?' the shocked Warden asked. 'That's impossible!'

Husayn looked across the yard. His plan had failed. He shrugged his shoulders, then laughed. 'What does it matter, one Bahá'í or the next –'

With the back of his hand Isfahani slapped Husayn hard across his face. Husayn rose, prepared to strike back.

Isfahani's men moved up beside their Commander, who tore the envelope from Husayn's hand. 'It was a human life!' he bellowed.

'I've never seen you like this, Commander Isfahani.' The Mujtahid stepped in between them.

'Eliminating enemies of Islam, I could tolerate. Stupidity and arrogance, never. On anyone's part.'

'It is your duty to protect Islam from the heretical factions in Iran, Commander. Vipers, manifestations of Satan.'

Isfahani advanced forward towards the Mujtahid. And the Mujtahid stepped back. 'I'm beginning to realize who the vipers are.'

'I'll report this incident to the Ayatullah –'

' – Get out of my sight before I handle this my way. And take this ass of an Assistant with you.'

Isfahani motioned to his Pasdars to hustle them out of his presence. The Warden was making countless excuses, and pleas of innocence, disassociating himself from the others. Isfahani ignored him and walked away alone. He unsealed the letter and read it as he walked towards the firing squad wall.

As he passed the wall he stopped. He crumpled the letter in his fist, then let it fall to the ground, staring aimlessly, till his chin fell to his chest. His eyes stared at the reddened soil and patches of snow around him. He reached down. The blood was still warm to the touch. Emotionlessly, he wiped it off on the breast of his coat, then turned away, heading out of the confines.

Firuz was finally permitted access to the cell where Zabih Rouhani had been incarcerated. It didn't matter to him that he was 'too late', he had to see the cell.

'You see,' said the guard who opened the cell, agitated by

having to come down there to prove his point, 'it's empty.'

Firuz took the guard's flashlight and searched from corner to corner. There was absolutely nothing there.

'Give up, medic. It's empty. Now let's go.'

Firuz dropped the light to his side. He guessed what consequences 'empty' meant. He smacked his head against the wall.

'OUT!' the guard ordered.

The old guard came down to the ruckus, asking another of the guards, 'Who's that?'

'Doctor Irani's colleague.'

Firuz was followed out of the cell by the pushy guard.

'Is your name Firuz Mostaqim?' the old guard asked, coming up to him.

'Yes,' he sighed.

The guard began to search his clothes. 'I saw Doctor Irani last night. He came just to bandage that prisoner. Now where is that? Ah!'

The old guard gave him an envelope. It had the markings of the hospital on its sealed flap. 'The prisoner gave me this for you. He seemed to be sure you were coming. You came fast, too.'

Firuz ripped it open.

'They took him a little while ago. Was he a special case or something?'

Firuz disregarded the question. He went over beneath a corridor light, unfolding the letter to read:

My beloved friend,
    Alláh'u'Abhá!
It was my fervent prayer that the Blessed Beauty, His Holiness Bahá'u'lláh, would allow you to come by this letter. I have left my will and testament with Asiyih Khanum, and in it I have made a small provision for you and your wife, of what little I have, so that you will finish your education and continue your work as a qualified Doctor of Medicine.

*The source of courage and power is the promotion of the Word of God, and steadfastness in His love.*

Zabih Rouhani needed time to develop his courage. I think you might understand this, as you became a Bahá'í through your own choice of investigation. It is a little different when your family is there to guide you through your life. With a little time, he will be able on his own to investigate the reality of this Cause, not because of family, but because of the validity of the Messenger and His Message.

In these last few moments, I have been thinking about the imprisonments and banishments of Bahá'u'lláh. I believe His greatest sufferings came not from the trials of incarceration, or the attacks against His Personage, but rather from the misdeeds of His supposedly sincere loved ones.

What more can I write? One day people will read about the reality of what the Bahá'ís endured throughout Iran, not just stories that people tell, but true accounts of real people and places. And those fair-minded souls who investigate this Most Great Cause will fall upon the dust imploring God to accept their services for the blood spilt by His loved ones. Until that day, the Bahá'ís throughout the world will have to continue to summon all mankind to the Call of His Cause, not only by their tongues, professions and pens, but by their humble deeds of sacrifice that will illumine the heavens through this darkness. And God will inspire us all with 'whatsoever he desireth'. Dawn nears.

*O Son of Justice! Whither can a lover go but to the land of his beloved? and what seeker findeth rest away from his heart's desire? To the true lover reunion is life and separation is death. His breast is void of patience and his heart hath no peace. A myriad lives he would forsake to hasten to the abode of his beloved.* – Bahá'u'lláh

Remember this undeserving soul in your prayers.

Hakim

The prison guard added, 'The prisoner was a Bahá'í, you know.'

Firuz turned from him, crying. 'My Beloved God. You insane, intoxicated, drunken, BAHÁ'Í.'

He ran out past the guard post till his legs stopped outside the prison gate. He stared aimlessly into the gutter, hearing the gates closing in succession in the echo of his mind.

Paces from him, Isfahani stood in the same fashion. There was nothing they could say to each other. What was there to say? They still had to go on. There was a funeral to prepare and a Bahá'í festival to celebrate. There was a funeral to attend and a career to

243

re-examine. The path of God was straight, but pathways were many.

And without a word they stepped out into the blackened snow of the street and headed off in different directions.

*The pen groaneth and the ink sheddeth tears, and the river of the heart moveth in waves of blood. 'Nothing can befall us but what God hath destined for us.' Peace be upon him who followeth the Right Path!*

The Seven Valleys